MANAGEMENT, WORK AND ORGANISATIONS

Series editors: **Gibson Burrell,** The Management Centre, University of Leicester
Mick Marchington, Manchester Business School
Paul Thompson, Department of Human Resource Management,
University of Strathclyde

This series of new textbooks covers the areas of human resource management, employee relations, organisational behaviour and related business and management fields. Each text has been specially commissioned to be written by leading experts in a clear and accessible way. The books contain serious and challenging material, take an analytical rather than prescriptive approach and are particularly suitable for use by students with no prior specialist knowledge.

  This series is relevant for many business and management courses, including MBA and post-experience courses, specialist masters and postgraduate diplomas, professional courses and final-year undergraduate courses. These texts have become essential reading at business and management schools worldwide.

Published

Stephen Bach and Ian Kessler
The Modernisation of the Public Services and Employee Relations

Emma Bell
Reading Management and Organization in Film

Paul Blyton and Peter Turnbull
The Dynamics of Employee Relations (3rd edn)

Sharon C. Bolton and Maeve Houlihan (eds)
Searching for the Human in Human Resource Management

Sharon C. Bolton
Emotional Management in the Workplace

Peter Boxall and John Purcell
Strategy and Human Resource Management (3rd edn)

J. Martin Corbett
Critical Cases in Organisational Behaviour

Susan Corby, Steve Palmer and Esmond Lindop
Rethinking Reward

Ian Greener
Public Management

Keith Grint
Leadership

Irena Grugulis
Skills, Training and Human Resource Development

Geraldine Healy, Gill Kirton and Mike Noon (eds)
Equality, Inequalities and Diversity

Damian Hodgson and Svetlana Cicmil (eds)
Making Projects Critical

Marek Korczynski
Human Resource Management in Service Work

Karen Legge
Human Resource Management: anniversary edition

Patricia Lewis and Ruth Simpson (eds)
Gendering Emotions in Organizations

Patricia Lewis and Ruth Simpson (eds)
Voice, Visibility and the Gendering of Organizations

Pullen et al. (eds)
Exploring Identity

Jill Rubery and Damian Grimshaw
The Organisation of Employment

Hugh Scullion and Margaret Linehan (eds)
International Human Resource Management

Colin C. Williams
Rethinking the Future of Work

Diana Winstanley and Jean Woodall (eds)
Ethical Issues in Contemporary Human Resource Management

For more information on titles in the Series please go to www.palgrave.com/business/mcp

The Modernisation of the Public Services and Employee Relations

Targeted Change

Stephen Bach
and
Ian Kessler

palgrave
macmillan

First published 2012 by
PALGRAVE MACMILLAN

Palgrave Macmillan in the UK is an imprint of Macmillan Publishers Limited, registered in England, company number 785998, of Houndmills, Basingstoke, Hampshire RG21 6XS.

Palgrave Macmillan in the US is a division of St Martin's Press LLC, 175 Fifth Avenue, New York, NY 10010.

Palgrave Macmillan is the global academic imprint of the above companies and has companies and representatives throughout the world.

Palgrave® and Macmillan® are registered trademarks in the United States, the United Kingdom, Europe and other countries.

ISBN: 978–0–230–23050–7

This book is printed on paper suitable for recycling and made from fully managed and sustained forest sources. Logging, pulping and manufacturing processes are expected to conform to the environmental regulations of the country of origin.

A catalogue record for this book is available from the British Library.

A catalog record for this book is available from the Library of Congress.

10 9 8 7 6 5 4 3 2 1
21 20 19 18 17 16 15 14 13 12

Printed and bound in Great Britain by
CPI Antony Rowe, Chippenham and Eastbourne

Contents

List of tables

List of figures

Foreword

This book is based upon our long-standing research interest in employee relations in the public services. This interest can be traced back to our studies at Warwick University where we both completed Master's dissertations on aspects of industrial relations in the sector, and went on to develop this work into doctoral theses. At the time, there was a sharp scholarly focus on industrial relations in the private sector, particularly manufacturing, reflecting the structure of the British economy in the 1950s, 1960s and 1970s, the locus of union strength and industrial conflict. This private sector focus has, in part, continued, the turn towards strategic human resource management, exploring the relationship between workforce management and corporate performance. At the same time, however, employee relations in the public services has emerged as a more dynamic space for the regulation of the employment relationship, as traditional state bureaucracies have been re-organised, and as the sector has been subject to a relentless process of reform, becoming central to political debates and policy formation. Indeed, over the past 30 years, and in the context of economic re-structuring, it is the public service sector which has emerged as the key site for dynamic forms of employee relations, and the major source of union membership and industrial strife.

During this period, and in various research projects, we have sought to map, understand and critically evaluate changes in the nature of employee relations in the public services and their consequences for key actors: workers, managers, policy makers and service users. We were involved with John Purcell and Jackie Coyle-Shapiro in an Economic and Social Research Council (ESRC) project exploring human resources management in the public service during the Conservative government of the 1980s and early 1990s. In more recent years, and particularly working with Paul Heron and Rebecca Givan, we have carried out research, again supported by ESRC, as well as by Skills for Care, the Society of Local Authority Chief Executives, the National Institute for Health Research (SDO programme), the Leverhulme Trust, the Scottish Government and the Migration Advisory Committee on different aspects of workforce management in the public services: new roles, new ways of working, new employee relations policies and practices, trade union responses to modernisation; the impact of public–private partnerships; and the consequences of nurse migration for the NHS workforce.

This research work has been informed by the traditions, habits and analytical principles nurtured during our time at Warwick: exploring through detailed case studies how and with what consequences stakeholders, with often conflicting interests, have regulated the employment relationship. During this research work, we have spoken to and relied on the co-operation of many policy makers, management and union practitioners, and employees. We would like to thank all of those who have provided this support. We would also like to thank co-researchers in our previous work and colleagues whom we have worked with outside the UK. In particular, Lorenzo Bordogna has frequently challenged us to move beyond a UK-centric view of new public management reforms and been a thoughtful and supportive colleague, while recently, colleagues at the Utrecht School of Governance, in particular Paul Boselie and Peter Leisink, have been keen to explore with us the relationship between employee relations and public management.

In producing this book, we have again relied on support from various people. We would like to thank Stephanie Tailby, who was heavily involved in the early stages of our work and who made a valuable contribution to our deliberations on the structure and nature of the book. Stephen would like to thank colleagues in the Human Resource Management and Public Services Groups in the Department of Management at King's who have proved stimulating and supportive colleagues as this project progressed. Stephen also owes a great debt of gratitude to his family – Caroline, Alexandra and Richard – for the huge amount of support they have provided and their tolerance of the anti-social working hours such a project inevitably entails. He has also valued greatly, his brother, Jonathan's insights into the complexities of school management under New Labour. Ian would like to express thanks to his parents for all their care and support over the years. He is also grateful for the help provided by Val Upton, Roger Undy, Marc Thompson and other colleagues in the industrial relations group at the Säid Business School and at the Future of Work group at Green Templeton College.

Finally we would like to extend a special thanks to David Winchester who at Warwick originally stimulated our interest in employee relations in the public services and provided encouragement and help in the early stages of our careers. He has remained a colleague and close friend over the years, and continues to act as a valued source of guidance, support and cricket updates.

1

Introduction

On 25 February 2000, Victoria Climbé died in the Intensive Care Unit of St. Mary's Hospital Paddington (London). She died as a result of months of appalling ill-treatment at the hands of two individuals who were supposed to be caring for her. On 12 January 2001 at the Central Court, Marie-Therese Kouao and Carl John Manning were convicted of her murder.

These were the opening words of a report into the death of eight-year-old Victoria Climbé, presented to the New Labour government in Britain on 28th January 2003 by Lord Laming (2003: 2). Sadly, the significance of Victoria's story lies not in her murder by those whom she knew and trusted: over the last decade, an average of one child a week has died at the hands of someone close to them (Laming 2009: 12). It resides in the litany of public service failure exposed by Laming as contributing to Victoria's death. During her life, Victoria Climbé was known to and engaged with an array of public services: primary and secondary healthcare, education and children's social care, and the police and ambulance services. She was let down by them all.

For the New Labour government, the report was a confirmation and a stimulus. It confirmed the weight they had placed on the reform of the public services. The party assumed office in May 1997 promising to 'Save the NHS', with one of its five specific pledges being to reduce hospital waiting times, and another being to reduce class sizes in primary schools (Labour Party 1996). Constrained by its commitment to the preceding Conservative government's spending plans during its first two years, reform of the public services assumed even greater importance as a platform for New Labour's 2001 election success. As Tony Blair stressed in launching the Labour manifesto for that election: 'We cannot renew our schools, hospitals and public services without investment. But money alone is not enough. That is why we

1

are committed to fundamental reform of our key public services' (quoted in Parker 2001). At the same time, the Laming report was a stimulus to further, more intense and concerted action, revealing the profound ongoing problems with public service delivery. Indeed, in the wake of this report, the government launched its Every Child Matters initiative, seeking major changes in the provision of children's services.

In reviewing the causes of the Climbé tragedy, as set out by Laming, it is difficult not to be struck by how many of them related to the mismanagement of staff and to flaws in professional practice. Laming did not use the term, but the tragedy was rooted in poor *employee relations*: in the range of public service agencies involved, there were recruitment and retention problems, alongside and partly related to low staff morale; worker capabilities and capacity were revealed as underdeveloped, reflecting weaknesses in employee training, communication and knowledge; patterns of work organisation were inappropriate, inexperienced temporary workers being employed in the most vital of functions.

In general, the Victoria Climbé case highlights the importance of employee relations policy and practice in the public services. Invariably public services workers are dealing with the most vulnerable members of the community: the young, the elderly, the sick, the disabled, the displaced and the marginal. Those researching strategic human resource management in private sector organisations preoccupy themselves with the link between staff management and corporate performance, defined in terms of profit or turnover or rate of return on investment or shareholder value (Richardson and Thompson 1999). In the public services the connection between employee relations policies and practices, worker attitudes and behaviours, and organisational outcomes clearly assumes a very different form. Getting people management 'right' in the public services clearly matters in quite profound ways. More specifically, and in public policy terms, the Climbé case reveals the crucial link between the reforms of public services and the management of the public services workforce. Most public services revolve around the direct interaction between employee and service user. The performance of these employees will determine the efficiency and the effectiveness of service delivery; any attempt to change forms of delivery will depend on the management of these staff.

This book explores the relationship between New Labour's public services modernisation programme as it relates to central government, health, and local government, including education and social care, and the management of the sector's workforce. In doing so, the book seeks to achieve a number of objectives. First, it contributes to debates on the performance of the New Labour government. Any such assessment of New Labour's performance must place its success in managing the public services workforce at its core. While commentators reviewing the New Labour period in office have often assessed effectiveness in terms of public services reform, especially in health and education (Bevir 2005; Shaw 2007; Casey 2009; Toynbee and Walker 2010), few have considered New Labour's management of the public services workforce as a significant influence on the implementation of this change programme. Second, the book seeks to develop our understanding of the relationship between public services reform and employee relations, particularly under the New Labour government: how and with what consequences was the modernisation of public services connected to staff management? Third, and closely related, the book attempts to re-orient two fields of study – public management and employee relations – which in combination have much to offer in advancing our understanding of this relationship, but which have rarely engaged with one another to this effect.

Public services reform

Over the last 25 years or so, public service reform has been a high priority issue amongst policy makers in most OECD countries (Eliassen and Sitter 2008). A growing demand for public services in the context of demographic shifts and increasing user expectations has often combined with constraints on governments in supplying these services given changing economic conditions and the need to control public expenditure. This combination of factors has encouraged policy makers to address fundamental questions on the boundaries of public service provision, and on the mechanisms by which such services are delivered. Tackling these issues has not been straightforward as the public services contain multiple stakeholders with diverse objectives: service users, professionals, other workers and their representatives, general managers, elected national and local policy-makers. These stakeholders frequently have differing ideas about what constitutes efficient and effective public services and the appropriate policies to achieve these goals.

An integral component of public service reform has been attempts to alter the management of the workforce. This is most clearly illustrated by the preoccupation of governments in many countries with seeking reductions in the size of the public service workforce in pursuit of a smaller state. There has been some cutting back of public service employment, but this has not always been on the scale claimed by some policy makers and commentators. For example, in Britain, after a significant decline during the 1980s, public sector employment as a proportion of total employment increased to around

20 per cent of the workforce, approximately 6 million employees, by 2010 (see Table 1.1).

These figures disguise changes in workforce structure and conceal what Light (1999) refers to as the 'shadow state'. This term is designed to highlight the fact that many workers providing public services financed by the government are actually employed by the private and third sectors. In Britain this amounts to a diverse £79 billion industry (Julius 2008), including cleaning and catering staff employed by private contractors in schools and hospitals, as well as social workers, residential home care employees and housing officers employed in the independent sector to provide services commissioned by local government. The resilience of public service workforce numbers might also be related to the nature of public service provision. Despite technological advances in delivery, many public services continue to take the form of unmediated interaction between the employee and various types of service user, for instance, the patient, pupil or prisoner. Any reduction in the number of public service employees, therefore, has an unusually direct and demonstrable impact on the scale and quality of services, often with broader social, economic and political consequences. Until recently, this has encouraged policy makers to seek efficiency and effectiveness in the management of staff less through crude workforce reductions, particular amongst front-line workers, and more through new approaches to work organisation, rewards, employee engagement and patterns of working (Bach and Kessler 2007).

Table 1.1   UK Public Sector employment (selected years); Seasonally adjusted Headcount (Thousands)

	Central government (incl. NHS)	Local government	Total general government	Total public corporations	Total public sector	*of which:* civil service
1991	2,306	3,072	5,378	600	5,978	589
1993	2,274	2,788	5,062	531	5,593	598
1995	2,156	2,758	4,914	454	5,368	552
1997	2,079	2,728	4,807	368	5,175	513
1999	2,115	2,735	4,850	352	5,202	504
2001	2,232	2,771	5,003	373	5,376	522
2003	2,434	2,832	5,266	373	5,639	560
2005	2,564	2,923	5,487	367	5,854	570
2007	2,505	2,941	5,446	339	5,785	539
2009	2,594	2,926	5,520	571	6,091	533
2010	2,572	2,885	5,457	557	6,014	515

Source: Hicks and Lindsay 2005; ONS 2008; 2010.

In this politically charged context, British governments over the last quarter of a century have tried to implement their own model of public service reform and rarely expressed themselves satisfied with the results (Cabinet Office 2006). The post-1945 social and political consensus on a strong public sector underpinning the welfare state was shattered as a succession of Conservative governments throughout the 1980s and early 1990s sought to 'roll back the frontiers of the state'. After 1997, and with the election of a New Labour government, reform was framed as the 'modernisation' of public services. As Newman has noted, 'The election of a Labour government in 1997 signalled a shift in the political terrain. Both the emerging policy agenda and the programme of institutional reform were underpinned by a discourse of modernisation' (2001: 79).

For around a decade New Labour's modernisation agenda was founded upon unprecedented levels of investment in services, with a concomitant increase in the public service workforce. This agenda, however, also led to major changes in the structure and composition of the workforce as well as to shifts in the relations between employers and their workforce as the government sought the maximum return from its investment in the sector. Successive New Labour governments emphasised the importance of highly motivated front-line staff to achieve the goal of developing world-class public services (Cabinet Office 2008a), but work experience of modernisation was often mixed, with concerns about morale, reservations about the process and outcomes of modernisation, and uncertainty about the extent of staff and user engagement (Department of Health 2008a; Lawson 2007; Wind-Cowie and Olliff Cooper 2009). This halting progress slowed down after 2008 when the global economic crisis precipitated a sharp deterioration in public finances and ushered in a period of retrenchment. In Britain, as elsewhere, this retrenchment has contributed to workforce reductions in the sector, along with changes in service provision, in the search for economies and efficiencies.

This book seeks to explore the extent to which changes in the management and organisation of the public services under New Labour influenced employee relations in the sector. More specifically, it examines the ways in which the implementation of a modernisation agenda was related to the employment relationship and how this affected workers and other key stakeholders. We focus on the core public services, those provided by local government (including social services and education), the NHS and the civil service. In this chapter we sketch out the detailed aims of the book, the key debates we engage with, and our analytical framework, and conclude by outlining the overall structure of the book.

The public management perspective

Several literatures from different disciplines and with distinct theoretical perspectives shed light on the consequences of modernisation for the management of the employment relationship. In isolation, however, they provide only an incomplete understanding of developments. The two most obvious and relevant such literatures are those which relate to public management and employee relations.

There has been much debate on the origins of public management as a field of study, in particular whether and how it might be distinguished from the subject matter of public administration. Some have adopted a broad definition. Lynne (2005: 28), for example, suggests an inclusive approach: public management is seen as synonymous with public administration, 'encompassing the organisational structures, managerial practices and institutionalised values by which officials enact the will of sovereign authority, whether that authority is prince, parliament or civil society.' Others have drawn a slightly sharper distinction, suggesting that public administration was tied to a specific model of service delivery founded on the principles of an ideal type Weberian bureaucracy (Christensen et al. 2007) which provided little managerial discretion. Notwithstanding these differences, public management scholars have often distinguished three models of public service delivery based on hierarchy, markets and networks. While there has been much debate on the relationship between these models and their precise form, they have informed debate in this literature over the years. The models founded on hierarchy and markets are considered in this section, while networks, closely related to the New Labour modernisation agenda, are considered in the next chapter.

Bureaucracy, hierarchy and administration

The classic bureaucratic model was characterised by a rational system based on explicit rules and a system of hierarchical authority underpinned by functional specialisation. Discretion was strictly regulated and set out in written procedures lending themselves more to administration than to proactive, autonomous managerial action on the part of the public official. This model was adapted to the particular circumstances of many public services in which professions had a dominant role in shaping patterns of service delivery. Mintzberg (1979) coined the phrase *professional bureaucracy* to indicate that public service organisations combined professional dominance with elements of bureaucratic structures.

For many the paradigm shift in public policy and commentary, which sought more 'dynamic' and 'flexible' forms of public service in the later 1970s and early 1980s, represented the emergence of public management. Indeed public management was typically presented as assuming a particular form, New Public Management (NPM). As Hood (2005: 14) has noted:

> The public management movement of the 1980s and 1990s was a reaction against those in public law and public administration who put the focus on constitutional and institutional design of the machinery of government. It stressed production engineering and managerial leadership, rather than rule bound bureaucracy as the essence of executive government.

Markets, contracts and incentives

The emergence of the NPM can be related to a number of developments. In the late 1960s criticism of how bureaucracies functioned was sharpened by public choice critics who questioned the motives of those who led public bureaucracies and emphasised 'producer capture'. Downs (1967) argued that in the absence of the profit motive and other incentives to enhance performance, politicians had little information or scope to monitor and control the behaviour of state administrators. This vacuum led to bureau-maximising behaviour in which state administrators pursued their own goals to increase their status and remuneration with little regard for efficiency or user satisfaction (Niskanen 1971). Related criticism pointed to the disdain for management in the public sector. It was argued that the civil service was dominated by officials interested in policy formulation rather than implementation (Ibbs 1988) and in health and education, the dominant professions assigned a low priority to efficiency (Griffiths 1983). The proposed solution was to shrink the state and make remaining public services more responsive to users by embracing private sector solutions in a shift from hierarchy to market.

In the late 1970s, such criticism found politically fertile ground in the election of neo-liberal governments in Britain and the United States with the election of the Thatcher and Reagan governments, committed to the marketisation of public service delivery based upon an antipathy to state professional bureaucracies. The pursuit of such an agenda amongst governments of other party political complexions, such as the Labour government in New Zealand, was, however, a testament to the broader search for solutions in delivering public services given emerging economic and fiscal pressures at the time. Thus deep-seated public expenditure and financial problems in the wake of the 1970s oil crisis were forcing a search across the developed economies for new and more efficient models of public service provision.

The complex provenance of the NPM – part theoretical, part ideological and part 'solution' to crisis – helps explain the different ways in which this term has been viewed and used. At times NPM has become entangled in policy and managerial prescription. However, as a research stream there have been attempts to unpack the notion of NPM. It has been seen to comprise a number of elements: attempting to implant private sector style initiatives into the public services; focusing on competition amongst service providers based on contractual relations; stronger managerial authority; and enhancing forms of centralised performance management (Hood 1991; Newman 2001; Power 2001). This unpacking has enabled the main contours of reform to be classified and the experience of different sectors and countries to be compared (Boston et al. 1996; Ferlie et al. 1996; Osborne and Gaebler 1992; Pollitt and Bouckaert 2004).

In Britain this research literature focused on the policy outcomes associated with attempts to implement a particular form of NPM. The first such consequence was a shift in authority from the professions to general managers as part of a switch in focus from inputs to outputs. Managers were increasingly viewed as the custodians of public service organisations by emphasising their unique competencies and stressing their accountability for individual and organisational performance. This involved the establishment of a cadre of managers with more direct operational control, but still subject to centralised forms of audit (Power 2001). Rather than adhering to administrative requirements demanded by central government, there would be separate agencies focusing on the achievement of their priorities, so enhancing the outcome for service users. To achieve these goals more elaborate systems of performance management were required, accompanied by devolved pay systems that rewarded desired behaviour.

The second was a new interest in the disaggregation and the fragmentation of the public sector with the proliferation of semi-autonomous agencies focused on delivery. The search for coherence in this more fragmented public sector encouraged NPM to stress a shift from management by hierarchy to management by contract. However this in turn led to significant transaction costs as nominally independent units duplicated HR and other functions, in the process weakening central capacity and institutional learning. The break-up of a unified civil service made 'joined-up' government more difficult, inhibiting the movement within and between departments possible within a unified civil service (Kessler et al. 2006). Rhodes (1997; 2007) pointed to the hollowing out of the state from above (by ceding competencies to the European Union), from below (by outsourcing) and sideways (from the spread of executive agencies).

The third consequence was the use of incentives and targets to regulate managerial and workforce behaviour. An approach based on such incentives and targets assumed that public service employees performed effectively only when rewarded with financial incentives, backed up by tight performance monitoring. This also signalled a degree of scepticism about the existence of a public service ethos founded on motives which extended beyond extrinsic rewards to a desire to do public good. The NPM approach assumed that public sector workers were inclined to act as selfish 'knaves' rather than as altruistic 'knights', preoccupied with their own producer interests rather than with the interests of the users they served (Le Grand 2003).

In general, there were shortcomings with the managerial, contract-orientated model of reform, which employee relations specialists have been aware of for many years. This has been highlighted in research on outsourcing that analyses the difficulties of specifying and monitoring contract outcomes in outsourced services (Bach 1989; Grimshaw et al. 2002). Such a critique reflects a profound difference in the focus and approach to the study of public services reform in the employee relations literature.

The employee relations perspective

The employee relations literature has been less preoccupied with the overall contours of the public service reform agenda, more specifically concentrating on the employment relationship: the interplay between those party to this relationship, the processes and institutions shaping it and outcomes for the various stakeholders. Within employee relations the focus has not exclusively or even principally been on employer behaviour. The role of other parties – the state and trade unions – has been much more to the fore (Thomson and Beaumont 1978; Aaron et al. 1988; Beaumont 1992). Detailed studies of managerial and worker behaviour analysed the formal and informal rules which governed the workplace, with sensitivity to influences from beyond the workplace (Kochan 1974; Batstone et al. 1984).

In general, attention has been focused on the interaction between these parties as they seek to regulate and control the employment relationship in pursuit of their various, often conflicting, interests. Gospel (1992) has suggested that this interaction takes place in three overlapping but analytically distinct domains which relate to industrial relations, work relations and employment relations or human resource management. *Industrial relations* refers to the system of labour-management engagement and the choices confronting the employer on the nature and extent of employee voice and involvement. This has been mainly concentrated on the collective side of the employment relationship: relations between employers and trade unions, typically enacted through collective bargaining. *Employment Relations* focuses on the management of the individual employee, concentrating on recruitment, reward, working patterns, equalities and performance appraisal. Employers might focus on policies that accentuate an investment orientation in staff or gravitate towards approaches which focus on cost minimisation. *Work relations* relates to employee tasks and responsibilities, and how they are structured and organised within a particular production or service process. This includes looking at the shape and nature of work roles, as well as at how work routines are designed to control employee attitudes and behaviours.

This typology has considerable value to the study of employee relations in the public services. As a mapping device, it allows for an evaluation of the changing shape and nature of the public service employee relations agenda over the years. Thus, until 1997 industrial relations and to some extent employment relations were the main domains of interest amongst policy makers and researchers. This is not to deny the importance of work relations, which during the period of NPM became a key sphere of debate amongst scholars, but it is to suggest that for researchers and policy makers these were the principal areas of concern.

The domains of activity distinguished by the typology also facilitate analysis: they can be related more or less directly to a number of different themes which have underpinned the study of public service employee relations over the years. Three such themes can be indentified:

• The model employer
• Work experience
• Legitimate institutions and actors.

Each of these is considered in turn and related to Gospel's three domains of employee relations.

The 'model employer' narrative

The 'model employer' approach was founded on the principle that as a major employer, the government would seek to manage its employees along 'best practice' lines. There has been scope to debate the form assumed by 'best practice'. It might, for example, involve adopting those 'leading edge' approaches found outside the public services, say in the private sector. Alternatively it might be reflected in the state assuming the role of an exemplar. In this case the government presents a vision of 'best practice' linked to public policy goals and values, treating its employees accordingly and with a view to encouraging the adoption of such practices across the whole economy. For much of the twentieth century, the model employer approach explicitly assumed the latter form and was associated with particular industrial relations practices rooted in collective institutions (Beaumont 1992). The Whitley Reports, 1916, sparked a sustained public policy commitment to trade union membership as the main vehicle for industrial citizenship, and to collective bargaining as the preferred means for determining pay and conditions of employment. The government felt obliged to follow these prescriptions in relation to its own staff as a means of setting an example, and as a consequence encouraged union membership in the public services, supported the development of consultative mechanisms at different levels in the sector, and established national joint councils for bargaining purposes.

It was a set of institutional arrangements which supported a bureaucratic approach to public service provision, but in so doing reflected and contributed to a narrow and limited employee relations agenda. Collective bargaining was mainly restricted to pay and terms of conditions of employment, work organisation and the management of individual employee performance being regulated by clear, often unilaterally determined, procedures and codes. The national joint determination of these substantive conditions of employment ensured transparency and standardisation, but provided little scope for dynamic forms of industrial relations at local or workplace levels. This was reflected in much of the industrial relations research literature in the immediate post-war decades, limited to fairly prosaic descriptions of this national bargaining machinery (Levinson 1972). This is not to deny the periodic pressure placed on this machinery: the 'downside' of the model employer approach was that governments in the 1960s and 1970s applied income policies with particular vigour to public service employees, provoking cyclical rounds of industrial conflict (Winchester 1983). However such conflicts were still played out at the national level, and did not question the ongoing viability of the national machinery or the public policy commitment to union membership and recognition in the sector.

These collective industrial relations institutions were severely challenged by Conservative governments from 1979 onwards. The model employer commitment to trade union membership and collective bargaining was reversed by the Thatcher government as an integral part of attempts to 'recapture' public services from the 'producer', in the interest of the 'customer'. The government de-recognition of trade unions at GCHQ in 1984 was a symbolic act designed to signal this change of government orientation. It was accompanied by a challenge to national systems of pay bargaining and representation. These were viewed as incompatible with market-style reforms, leading to the devolution of collective bargaining to individual employers. This process enabled and encouraged employers to link pay determination to local labour and product market conditions. This shift in policy was exemplified by the abolition of national pay bargaining in the civil service in the mid-1990s, new and fragmented bargaining units being established for individual civil service executive agencies (Kessler et al. 2006). These attempts to undermine the collective, national institutions in the public services encouraged a continued research focus on the industrial relations domain. There was much debate, for example, on whether the fragmentation and devolution of pay bargaining provided scope for the development of a more dynamic form of workplace industrial relations and the opportunity for a renewal of union activism in the sector (Fairbrother 2000; Kessler and Heron 2001).

Whilst the model employer narrative has mainly been rooted in the industrial relations domain, 'best practice' issues have also arisen in the employment relations domain. Here they have been typically related to the adoption of private sector practices, the public sector not so much driving as following 'leading edge' developments in other parts of the economy. This was the case in the 1980s and early 1990s when Conservative governments sought to draw upon the private sector's enthusiasm for individualised HR practices, particularly individual performance related pay (IPRP). IPRP was widely used in the civil service, the government mandating departments and agencies to introduce such schemes, (Marsden and Richardson 1994), although in the NHS and local authorities, where the government's influence was less direct, the take-up was much lower (Kessler 2003).

Work experience narrative

Over the years the nature and quality of the employees' work experience in the public services has remained a key narrative, often revolving around the balance between enrichment and degradation. It is a narrative rooted in both the work relations and employment relations domains, partly depending upon the perceived source of degradation or enrichment.

The employment relations domain has been seen as providing elements of both enrichment and degradation. For example, during the period of state bureaucracy in Britain, the transparency and 'fairness' of employment relations practices provided the basis for the enrichment of working life. These practices ensured open competition on recruitment, a high degree of job security, career opportunities founded upon internal job ladders, and guaranteed pay increases based on service and comparability with the private sector (Bach and Della Rocca 2000). Even during this period, however, there was a darker side to public service employment. Certainly not all groups were covered by these welfare-oriented and supportive practices. For instance in the 1960s concerns about low pay and productivity amongst public services manual workers encouraged the establishment of incentive bonus schemes to boost pay and performance (NBPI 1969). In addition, a pattern of occupational segregation developed in the public services. This was not only reflected in the concentration of women in low-paying public services jobs, particularly in health, education and social care, but in the development of work roles which were not paid at their 'true worth' relative to male occupational roles (Winchester 1983).

The research literature from the work relations domain presents a similarly mixed picture. It suggests that at any given time work organisation had a similar potential both to enrich and degrade, although equally striking was a shift in the nature of work experience over the years, under different service delivery regimes. Public services work has traditionally been presented as generating considerable intrinsic reward. Often working with the most vulnerable and deprived members of the community, public servants have an opportunity to make a difference to lives and communities. Working within state bureaucracies, public professionals, in particular, had the necessary authority, discretion and resources to make this difference and reap the associated intrinsic rewards (Ackroyd et al. 1989). The succeeding period of Conservative government, however, presented significant challenges to the standing of the professional. As implied above, the NPM principles informing government policy positioned the professions as part of the 'problem' rather than the 'solution', greater control over their power being essential to the re-capture of the services on behalf of the 'customer'.

There has been considerable debate over the consequences of this assault on the professions. A number of researchers have drawn upon labour process theory to highlight the degradation of professional work under this regime, pointing to the de-skilling associated with tightening performance management systems and increasingly centralised, managerial control over aspects of work organisation (Karger 1986; Ozga 1995; Harris 1998). Ironside and Seifert (1995) pointed to the introduction of the National Curriculum in primary and secondary education to highlight the loss of teacher discretion in schools. Moreover, this was a period of under-investment and weakening workforce capacity in the public services, contributing to workplace pressures. However, others have stressed the resilience of public service professionals, noting the embedded nature of professional authority, and the adaptive capabilities of the professional, not least reflected in the emergence of new, potentially enriching hybrid professional roles such as the clinical director in the NHS (Kirkpatrick et al. 2004).

The institutional infrastructure narrative

A final narrative informing much of the employee relations literature has focused on the institutional infrastructure underpinning and supporting the regulation of the employment relationship. Mainstream research has traditionally focused on an infrastructure mainly comprising Dunlop's (1958) three key actors – the employer, the state and the unions – interacting within formal bargaining machinery to agree formal substantive and procedural rules on pay and other terms and conditions of employment. There has been some acknowledgement that this infrastructure assumes a distinctive form within the public services. For many years the state was the main employer of public services workers, whether in the form of central government, as in the case of civil servants and healthcare workers, or local government employing a diverse range of council workers including teachers, social workers, refuse workers, street cleaners and various administrative groups.

As an employer the state brings to the management of the employment relationship an inevitable degree of political contingency (Ferner 1988). Central and local governments comprise politicians with their ideologically driven agendas sensitive to electoral impact and need. This infuses employee relations in the public services with an uncertain, cyclical, values-based dynamic not found in the private sector (Kessler and Dopson 2008). There are frequent illustrations of the inherent political sensitivity of managing public employees. The most dramatic was the 'Winter of Discontent' in 1978–79, the industrial relations dispute involving local authority workers, seen by many as contributing to the defeat of the Callaghan Labour government in 1979. More generally, instances of public service 'failure', often linked to shortcomings in the management of the public services, have had sharp and significant political consequences, signalling government (in)competence or a lack of commitment to the sector.

The political contingency informing interaction between the main actors in public service employee relations has encouraged transparency and accountability in the management of the employment relationship. For example, following the Priestly Commission report in the mid-1950s, civil service pay and conditions were determined on the basis of comparability with the private sector, a process which continued under the auspices of the Pay Research Unit until 1981 and provided legitimacy for pay increases funded by the tax payer (White 1996). This political contingency also highlights the importance of clearly distinguishing different employer side actors, the employer-side politician, accountable to the electorate, and the general or specialist manager reporting with varying degrees of directness to the politician. The employee relations research literature has, however, been less sensitive to actors beyond the government, employers, workers and their representatives, who might have an equally legitimate role in regulating the public services employment relationship (Kessler and Bach 2011).

The work domain, with its focus on the organisation and management of work, and the employment relations domain with its interest in the individual employee, might be seen to provide a site for the engagement of a broader range of actors and structures in the regulation of employment. As already implied, in the past state bureaucracies provided little scope for joint discussion on those substantive issues related to work and individual employee performance. However, in circumstances where work organisation and the management of individual employee performance become more open to change, other groups emerge as legitimate actors in employee relations and new sites provide space for the regulation of the employment relationship. In terms of actors, scholars in organisational studies have devoted considerable attention to the customer or user as a key influence on work and employment, particularly in interactive services (Korczynski 2001). Given that public service organisation is in the main founded upon the delivery of interactive services, it is surprising that so little attention has been given to the service user as actor in employee relations.

As for new sites, the employee relations literature has given limited consideration to spaces other than those dealing with the enactment of national collective bargaining. Certainly, attention has been drawn to institutions beyond those facilitating collective bargaining, for instance pay review bodies (White 2004). However, there has been little attempt to consider institutions other than those concerned with pay and conditions of employment. Once more, a focus on the work relations domain provides an opportunity to consider other potentially influential institutions. Under Conservative government, those quasi-state organisations with a responsibility for auditing the performance management regime came to play an important role in work organisation, while longer-standing regulatory bodies, particularly covering healthcare professionals, have continued to shape and control the allocation of tasks and responsibilities.

An analytical framework

Integrated

The comparison between the public management and employee relations perspectives highlights some overlapping areas of interest. The public management literature has explored some broad areas of human resource management (Beattie and Waterhouse 2009), with a focus on select groups of employees, in particular, the professions. The employee relations literature, with varying degrees of explicitness, has sought to relate the management of the employment relationship to the prevailing policy agenda as it relates to the organisation of the public services and the model of service delivery (Kessler and Purcell 1996; Gill-McLure and Seifert 2008). It is equally apparent, however, that there are some important differences between the two perspectives. First, public management scholarship has focused on the upstream consequences of public service delivery mechanisms, concentrating on the organisational and management context and on the nature of employer policy. In contrast, employee relations have been less inclined to adhere to a managerially defined agenda, being attuned to the perspectives of all stakeholders, especially the workforce and its trade unions.

Second, the public management literature has critically evaluated the transfer of management practices prevailing in the private sector to the public sector, but with a challenge to the assumption that public and private sector management are fundamentally different (Boyne 2002). Employee relations research acknowledges the growing influence of private sector employment practices on the public management agenda, but remains unconvinced that a process of convergence between public and private sector employment practices is occurring (Bach et al. 2009). Recognition of the distinctive features of state employment makes employment relations scholars cautious about the transfer of employment practices (Bordogna 2008), with workplace behaviour being anchored or 'embedded' in broader features of the economic and political context.

This book seeks to provide an integrated account of changes in the management of the employment relationship in the public services which combines analytical insights from public management literature and draws on the workplace traditions of employee relations. This requires the development of an analytical framework, as set out in Figure 1.1 below, which connects upstream changes in the organisation and management of the public services to downstream developments in employee relations.

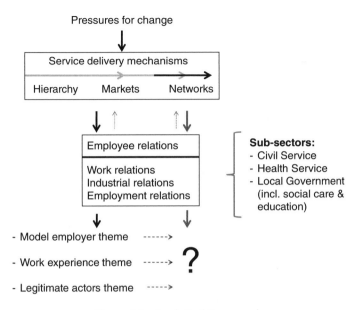

Figure 1.1 Analytical Framework

Sector wide

This framework also needs to display some sensitivity to the different parts of the public services sector. At various times the public management and employee relations literatures have explored general patterns across the public services, showing limited appreciation of sub-sector differences. On other occasions the distinctive features of specific parts of the sector have been examined, but this has precluded comparisons between sub-sectors. The public services comprise sub-sectors which, while all providing publicly funded services, are underpinned by different institutional arrangements. The main sub-sectors typically distinguished are the civil service, the National Health Service, and local government, including education and social care. They might be seen to vary in terms of their governance structures, their sources of funding, the services provided, their workforce composition, and their employee relations and broad, service regulatory frameworks. We argue that these differences matter, possibly impacting on the development of employee relations under different public service delivery models. Given their importance we briefly set out the key features of the institutional infrastructures in these three sub-sectors, particularly how they evolved up to the election of the New Labour government in 1997.

Civil service

The government has more direct control over the management of the civil service than over other public services with revenues allocated by parliament, and each department headed by a minister who is accountable to parliament. The civil service comprises a much smaller sector of employment than local government or the NHS. During the 1979–97 Conservative period of government, privatisation and sub-contracting contributed to a decline of around 25 per cent. When New Labour took office in 1997, there were just over half a million civil servants in post (see Table 1.1). A large proportion of civil servants are employed by executive agencies, focused on service delivery, rather than employed directly by Whitehall departments that have a stronger policy orientation. The largest ten executive agencies, such as Jobcentre Plus, the National Offender Management Service (formerly HM Prison Service) and the UK Border Agency, employ over 40 per cent of all civil servants working as benefit case workers, prison officers, immigration officers and tax planners, and procurement officers for the military (Institute for Government 2009). In contrast to the other sub-sectors, employment is not concentrated amongst a small number of professions, but instead administrative and clerical roles predominate with an increasing proportion of civil servants located outside of Whitehall.

Interest in civil service reform has a long pedigree. In 1968, the Fulton Report identified a lack of skilled managers, poor personnel management and an over reliance on generalists. Despite incremental reforms, the 1979 Conservative government entered office convinced that the civil service's monopoly position had produced a bloated organisation and it set in train a reduction in civil service staffing. The most radical change stemmed from *The Next Steps* Report (Ibbs 1988). It argued that the civil service was too big and too diverse to manage as a single entity; too little attention had been given to management and service delivery in comparison with policy making. The solution was to devolve the executive activities of government, as distinct from its policy advice, into separate agencies with each agency required to meet performance targets set by government. By 1997, 76 per cent of all civil servants worked in 138 executive agencies and their progress in achieving 1,244 performance targets was evaluated (Cabinet Office 1998).

The National Health Service

The NHS is part of central government. It is financed from general taxation with the overwhelming majority of health services directly provided by it. The NHS comprises primary healthcare, delivering a range of community services including general practice, district nursing and health visiting;

secondary healthcare, mainly revolving around acute hospitals; and tertiary care, dispensing more specialist service, in a small number of hospitals. For most of its history a strategic, intermediate tier has been an essential feature of the NHS structure. Over the years, this tier has been located at different levels, but it has continued to undertake various planning and co-ordinating activities, not least in relation to workforce training and development. The NHS has long been the largest employer in the country, employing over a million workers. It is a highly professionalised workforce; as Table 1.2 indicates, in 1997 it employed almost 90,000 doctors and over 300,000 nurses.

The combination of state financing and provision has made the NHS susceptible to high levels of centralised control with major implications for staff and patients. The Thatcher and Major governments demonstrated tenacity in implementing NPM reforms, rarely matched in other parts of the public services. This approach can be partly attributed to central government's responsibility for overall policy and management, public concern about waiting times for treatment and central government anxieties about the health service's insatiable demand for resources. From the mid-1980s a more corporate-style management structure was introduced with the appointment of general managers who were accountable to central government and over time these roles evolved into chief executive positions. At the start of

Table 1.2 Selected groups of general government workers in the UK public sector workforce 1997–2009 (Headcount)

	1997	2009	% change 1997–2009
National Health Service	1,190,000	1,578,000	+33%
Of which:			
Doctors (England)	*89,619*	*140,897*	*+57%*
Nurses (England)	*318,856*	*417,164*	*+31%*
Education	1,131,000	1,410,000	+25%
Of which:			
Teachers (England)	*400,300*	*442,700*	*+11%*
Teaching assistants (England)	*60,600*	*183,700*	*+203%*
Police	230,000	294,000	+28%
Public administration	1,139,000	1,207,000	+6%
Of which:			
Civil service	*516,000*	*527,000*	*+2%*
Other Public Sector	708,000	738,000	+4%
HM Forces	220,000	197,000	−10%
Other health and social work	436,000	374,000	−14%
Construction	124,000	54,000	−56%
All general government	**4,835,000**	**5,494,000**	**+14%**

Source: cited in IFS 2011:167 http://www.ifs.org.uk/budgets/gb2011/11chap7.pdf

the 1990s, an internal market was established to separate out the purchasing of healthcare, undertaken by Primary Care Trusts, from its provision by more than 400 individual NHS trusts, including acute, mental health and ambulance trusts. The government rationale was that by encouraging competition for contracts, in the form of patients treated, efficiency would be boosted. In practice the 'market' was managed by central government, discouraging managers from radically changing pay and working practices (West 1997; Bach 2004).

Local government

In contrast to the civil service and the NHS, local authorities have the capacity to raise taxes, and are governed by councillors subject to periodic election. The model of political accountability through local elections focused on local priorities has been in retreat for more than two decades. Successive governments have implemented new public management style reforms and local government has become increasingly dependent on central government finance and subject to intensive central government scrutiny. Local authorities have to work alongside a plethora of other agencies which have been allocated powers in areas such as housing and transport which were previously their sole responsibility. Despite these changes, local government remains the largest component of public sector employment and has responsibility for a wide range of local services including schools, social services, environmental and leisure services. The largest single occupational group is teachers in England (see Table 1.2). Social care is a major employer, and although local authorities employ a shrinking proportion of social care staff, there are still around 50,000 social workers in England (http://www.lga.gov.uk/lga/aio/15142112).

Local government has frequently been portrayed as the poor relation of public services and has not attracted the same level of investment in service provision or the workforce as the NHS. The most important Conservative government initiative related to the policy of compulsory competitive tendering (CCT) which required a wide range of council services to be subject to competition and resulted in job losses, extensive alterations to terms and conditions of employment, and radical re-structuring of management and organisation (Colling 1999). Services less directly affected by CCT were not immune from management changes.

The landmark 1988 Education Reform Act introduced the Local Management of Schools (LMS) which delegated responsibility for financial and staff management to governing bodies. Schools were encouraged to opt out of local authority control and attempts were made to foster competition between schools for pupils with league tables compiled to guide parental choice (Ironside and Seifert 1995). At the same time central government intervened to an unprecedented degree in shaping the working lives of teachers: a national curriculum was established and a more punitive system of inspection was introduced by the establishment of the Office of Standards in Education (Ofsted). Head teachers welcomed their enhanced role, but schools are relatively small employers and their willingness to act independently in a context of limited competition for pupils discouraged radical shifts in pay and conditions during much of the 1980s and 1990s (Bach and Winchester 2003).

New Labour modernisation

Our primary focus is on New Labour's modernisation of the public services and its impact on the management of the employment relationship in the civil service, the NHS and local government. Our analytical framework encourages a detailed consideration of New Labour modernisation and how this connects to the employee relations agenda in the public services. In general the public management literature has suggested an important shift in the principles and mechanisms underpinning public service in the 1990s. This shift has been conceptualised in different ways and views on its timing have varied. At the very least, however, it has been seen as a decisive modification of the NPM model. Newman (2001) explicitly presents modernisation as the successor model to NPM and aligns this shift with the emergence of the New Labour government in 1997. Others have characterised the new model of public management more in terms of governance (Bouvaird and Löffler 2009), focusing on the range of organisations increasingly involved in the delivery of public services. Such an approach places much greater emphasis on the need for governments to develop systems which manage and regulate these organisations, presented by Osborne and Gaebler (1992) as 'steering not rowing'.

In following Newman (2001) and taking the modernisation of the public services as a New Labour project, we remain sensitive to its potential tensions and contradictions between principle and practice. We also remain wary of assuming too decisive a shift from NPM. Chapter 2 examines these issues, in particular, the nature of the New Labour modernisation project in the public services. It considers the novelty of this reform project, whether and how it linked to past models of public service provision and the tensions which might be inherent within it. It then considers how this project relates to the management of the employment relationship: the extent, for example, to which potential contradictions within the model of modernisation might feed through to employee relations. The chapter argues that, in the context of various political and economic pressures, New Labour adopted a hybrid or layered model of public service provision (Thelen 2004), combining features of new public management and network governance. This model was closely related to an employee relations agenda, taken forward with some coherence and determination by the government. But the hybrid model was also founded on certain contradictions, which translated into tensions within the employee relations system.

Focused: terrain and substance

The succeeding chapters (as set out in Figure 1.2) explore in detail the downstream consequences of New Labour modernisation, based upon a layered model of public services delivery, for employee relations within the domains distinguished: work relations, employment relations and industrial relations, with a particular emphasis on how the three main narratives related to the model employer, to work experience and to institutional infrastructure have developed within them. It was noted that each of these narratives intersected with the three domains in a variety of ways. However, while the different narratives are not exclusive to a given domain, there are strong associations.

The employment relations domain overlaps quite significantly with the work experience narrative, and the extent to which employment relations practices flowing from modernised services have enriched or degraded the public servants' working life. As noted at the outset, New Labour's much vaunted attempt to create a highly motivated workforce through 'soft' human resources practices might be seen to sit alongside the harsh reality of a new, tighter and constraining performance management regime. Similarly, in its attempt to improve the work experience of women, steps have been taken under New Labour to progress the equal-pay agenda and provide for more flexible, family-friendly forms of employment. However, occupational segregation remains pervasive within the public services, with not only women but those from ethnic minority groups and an increasing swathe of migrant workers in the sector, still concentrated in low-paid roles at the margins of the labour market. Chapters 3 and 4 explore these employment relations issues; the former focusing on pay and performance and the latter on flexibility, diversity and equal opportunities in the modernised public services.

The work relations domain is closely aligned with the institutional infrastructure narrative, with a particular focus on the service user as employee

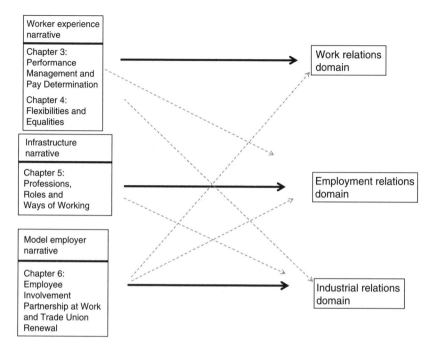

Figure 1.2 Book Outline

relations actor, and on institutions dealing with issues other than those related to pay and conditions. The development of personalised and user-centred services will be seen as central to New Labour modernisation, generating attempts to re-organise public service work and encouraging a public policy rhetoric on the need to empower and engage the service user. Moreover, New Labour was distinctive in seeking to develop institutions which supported and furthered workforce capacity in the context of its broader public service reform agenda. Chapter 5 on work relations explores the re-structuring of the public service workforce. More specifically it considers the extent to which the rhetoric of user empowerment and workforce development has been reflected in practice and in ways which have elevated the user as a new actor in the employee relations system and established new institutions as essential to the management of the public services workforce.

The industrial relations domain closely maps onto the 'model employer' narrative given its traditional basis in collective institutions. The challenges faced by these institutions under Conservative governments in the 1980s and early 1990s raise questions about the status and possible renewal of the model employer approach. New Labour espoused a partnership approach with public service trade unions and showed some signs of seeking to use collectively bargained agreements to pursue its public service reform agenda. However, New Labour displayed considerable ambiguity in its relations with trade unions and encouraged other forms of direct staff involvement. Chapter 6 explores patterns of direct and indirect involvement, the consequences of union-management partnership and trade union responses to the modernisation agenda.

Chapter 7 returns to the themes of the previous chapters and draws out the main points of our analysis. More specifically, it identifies key developments in the three domains to help assess and understand patterns of change in employee relations during the New Labour period. As a means of exploring the sustainability of these developments, and as a way of looking to the future, this chapter also explores the Conservative-led coalition's plans for public service reform and the emerging impact on employee relations in the sector.

In summary, our attempt to explore the management of the employment relationship in the public services under the New Labour modernisation agenda comprises a number of elements. First it relates upstream public policy developments on modernisation to their downstream employee relations consequences. Second it explores how three narratives related to the model employer, to work experience and to institutional infrastructure have been enacted within the domains traditionally seen as characterising the study of the employment relationship: employment relations, work relations and industrial relations.

In general these narratives map themselves onto particular domains. The model employer narrative relates principally to the industrial relations domain, raising such questions as what form has the model employer approach assumed under modernisation? How have collective arrangements and institutions fared? To what extent have unions been engaged as partners? The work experience narrative is closely associated with the employment relations domain encouraging an interest in such questions as has employment relations practice under modernisation degraded or enriched the working lives' of public servants? The institutional infrastructure narrative heavily overlaps with the work relations domain generating such questions as has the service user been empowered as an actor in work relations or has this remained public policy rhetoric? Have new institutions been developed to support New Labour's attempt to build workforce capacity in the public services, and, if so, how effective have they been?

2

Upstream decisions and employee relations under New Labour

The legacy of NPM

New Labour came into office in 1997 on an electoral landslide with a mandate to invest in and reform public services. A sustained period of Conservative government had been marked by attempts to embed new public management reforms (NPM). As noted in Chapter 1, NPM has a chameleon like quality and its appearance and emphasis have been adapted to fit the prevailing political and economic circumstances. NPM has a neo-liberal ideological dimension with a belief in the superiority of market principles but it also has been interpreted in a more technical sense as a toolkit of management practices which can be adopted or discarded as necessary (Pollitt et al. 2007). A distinctive feature of New Labour's approach to public service modernisation was the presentation of its reforms as essentially technical 'common sense' managerial changes that were ostensibly stripped of the neo-liberal ideological imprint of its Conservative predecessors. In substantive terms, there has been much debate on the form assumed by New Labour's preferred model of public service delivery, views differing on the degree of continuity with the preceding government's template.

Successive Conservative governments introduced a wide-ranging programme of reform which incorporated the main components of the NPM toolkit. Large parts of the public sector were privatised, the remaining public services were re-structured into semi-autonomous 'enterprises' with less predictable income streams, with an increasing variety of services also subject to outsourcing. These reforms were accompanied by the development of a

25

more assertive tier of senior managers with greater discretion to reform work organisation and pay. The changes reflected scepticism about the existence of a public sector ethos and the value of the model employer tradition. Trade unions were excluded from national policy-making and often faced severe difficulties in safeguarding their members' terms and conditions of employment (Bach and Winchester 2003).

Despite 18 years of Conservative government, on leaving office the public sector revolution was incomplete. The government had been unable to convert their ideological hostility into a coherent programme of public sector reform, while significant variations between sub-sectors remained in the scope and impact of NPM reforms. The government managed to implement its market-style reforms, but in diluted forms that only partially challenged the control of key professions over the organisation of work (Kirkpatrick et al. 2005). Although senior management became more prominent, reflected in increased pay, status, and budgetary authority, their operational autonomy remained constrained. Managers were subject to prescriptive central government policies on which they were monitored closely and they confronted the resistance of highly organised professional groups. Central government increased its regulation and control of the public sector because it was only by strengthening the role of the state that Mrs. Thatcher could impose her vision of a market society (Jenkins 2007). Distrust of Conservative government policies and a buoyant economy led to severe staff shortages emerging amongst many professional groups by the mid-1990s (Bach and Winchester 2003).

The Labour government embraced the core components of this Thatcherite legacy, reflecting its journey towards New Labour in the 1990s. As former Prime Minister Tony Blair commented in his memoirs: 'Britain needed the industrial and economic reforms of the Thatcher period' (Blair 2010: 99). New Labour therefore accepted the values and assumptions of neo-liberalism (Smith and Morton 2006), but attempted to implement them in a more consensual manner. As Gamble (2009) points out, although the term signifies moving away from Keynesian demand management policies that underpinned the welfare state and assigning primacy to developing market relations, there has never been one form of neo-liberalism. Gamble distinguishes between a laisser-faire market-fundamentalist strand and a social market strand. Although both variants may be compatible with an active state, market fundamentalists view the role of the state as minimalist and limited to removing impediments to the functioning of markets, but the social market variant envisages a more active role for the state. A variety of interventions that embed market principles are compatible with this form of neo-liberalism. The regulation of outsourced workers' wages, for example, by protecting workers may encourage increased labour supply and reduce opposition to privatisation, fostering private sector involvement (Bach and Givan 2010).

The Labour government placed the improvement of public services at the centre of its agenda. Its unprecedented 1997 electoral victory indicated that it had a mandate to invest in public services, as unease about commercialisation, staff shortages and lengthening waiting lists created anxiety about Conservative commitment towards cherished institutions, notably the NHS. The Labour government was initially cautious, which stemmed from its commitment to retain the spending plans of the previous government for its first two years in office. This was justified partly by the need to reduce the substantial budget deficit it inherited, and partly to sustain its 'business friendly' credentials. This strategy was effective if judged in these terms, but led to a tight squeeze on expenditure (Mullard 2001), limiting the scope for radical reform.

After 2000, public service expenditure grew rapidly, especially in high-profile services such as health and education. Total managed public expenditure increased from 36 per cent of GDP in 1999/00 to over 43 per cent in 2008/9 (Harker and Oppenheim 2010). In the NHS an annual, real growth rate of 4 per cent was increased to 7 per cent per annum, with the result that by 2010/11 it was 9.5 of GDP close to the EU average (Toynbee and Walker 2010: 51). In primary education spending per pupil increased by a third in real terms between 1997/8 and 2007/8 (Ibid: 18), with capital investment in schools eight time higher in 2008 than in 1997 (Ibid: 30). The Labour government required a return on this investment: the public services had to be modernised. However, the precise character and consequences of this reform agenda remained contested by commentators.

For critics, the neo-liberal bias of public service modernisation was self evident with the creation of opportunities for private firms to take over the management of public services (Leys 2001; Mooney and Law 2007). New Labour represented a continuation and indeed an intensification of the previous Conservative government's embrace of new public management. According to Pollock (2004: vii) the NHS 'has been progressively dismantled and privatised' and Ball (2007) largely concurred; privatisation and commercialisation have been the dominant trends in education. Overall, these accounts have been generally pessimistic about the consequences for the workforce, emphasising the loss of autonomy and work intensification brought about by commercialisation and systems of performance management as well as the reduced scope for the expression of employee voice. This perspective was reflected in book titles such as 'New Labour/Hard labour?' (Mooney and Law 2007) and 'New Labour's Attack on Public Services' (Whitfield 2006).

In contrast to these perspectives, it has been argued that although New Labour shared many of the values associated with Conservative policies, they forged their own approach to public service reform. Osborne (2010) identifies a distinctive agenda which he terms new public governance, one of several labels, identifying a shift to network governance. It signalled an emphasis on collaboration between a wider range of actors within networks to produce more coherent 'joined-up' solutions. In shifting away from a reliance on market mechanisms and contractual incentives, Osborne (2010) contends that governance has replaced new public management reforms. This implied a change in the management of the workforce. Top-down styles of leadership gave way to more inclusive and distributed forms of leadership which encouraged increased employee involvement but at the same time posed significant challenges to traditional ways of working and existing systems of employment relations. New Labour was viewed as being in the vanguard of these governance reforms (Eliassen and Sitter 2008).

This chapter explores the character and substance of New Labour's public services modernisation agenda: in essence, the government's upstream approach to public service delivery. It evaluates the balance between new public management and network governance sought by the government in its model of service provision: To what extent did New Labour's modernisation agenda represent old wine in new bottles, embracing NPM reforms bequeathed by Conservative governments? Is there any basis for the claims that New Labour shifted towards forms of network governance? Is it more useful to recognise that public service reforms invariably have a layered quality in which institutions evolve unevenly as existing actors shape and refashion reform measures (Thelen 2004)? Finally, the chapter outlines the main organisational changes instituted by New Labour in the various sub-sectors: the civil service, the NHS and local government. This provides the basis for considering developments in workforce management in the succeeding chapters.

Network governance

New Labour's reform agenda was informed by a network governance model of public service delivery (Bevir 2005), a response to some of the perceived failings of the new public management. However, in pursuing a range of objectives, New Labour also retained, and in certain instances further developed, key elements underpinning the Conservative government's approach to reform. As a consequence, New Labour modernisation acquired a layered or hybrid quality rather than conforming to a pure network governance model, creating a range of tensions which impacted on general public policy and more specifically on the management of the public services workforce.

The term governance has played an increasingly prominent role in debates about change in the management of public services, but there is some ambiguity in how the term has been used and its relationship to new public management reforms. Notwithstanding this ambiguity, differing definitions of governance share an assumption that public service policy and delivery is no longer the exclusive concern of government. Governance signals the involvement of a wider range of actors, collaborating within networks, to develop user-centred solutions to the challenges faced by public services (Rhodes 1997; Osborne 2010). It represents both a shift from a preoccupation with top-down hierarchical solutions imposed by government and a move away from market-based solutions geared towards contract fulfilment and competitive incentives.

Two aspects of this turn towards governance can be identified in the public management literature (Osborne 2010). First, a central theme of the governance literature is that its various components represent a policy response to the limitations of NPM reforms, addressing the fragmentation of public services and the distrust of the workforce. Second, a closely related theme focuses on how this fragmentation might be addressed, retaining some balance between the engagement of a wide and diverse range of service delivery partners, while ensuring that they act in a co-ordinated and collaborative way. Each aspect is considered in turn.

The limitations of new public management

New public management reforms had their ideological roots in New Right public choice theory with its application of neo-classical economics to the public domain. Niskanen (1971) argued that public bureaucracies were no different from firms and organisation members were seeking to maximise their own utility. Taking account of the informational advantages possessed by bureaucrats, this invariably led to the growth of public services. Civil servants were motivated to maximise the size of their budgets because this was a tangible sign of their status and political influence. Principal-agent theory addressed similar problems in identifying that the interests of principals (politicians) could differ from those of the agents (bureaucrats) in the management of public services. The challenge was to design incentives and control systems which ensured that the interests of principals and agents were aligned. It was a short step from these theoretical assumptions to the establishment of competitive mechanisms to guide agent behaviour, including the disaggregation of organisations into competing enterprises, the establishment of financial and other incentives to ensure agents behaved in the interests of their principals, and the generation of performance data to control and monitor behaviour.

NPM reforms, however, built on these assumptions ran into a number of difficulties. A major concern was the implications for the workforce of the emergent contract culture. As Le Grand (1997) noted NPM reforms implied that policy makers no longer viewed the public service workforce as altruistic knights, but rather as self-interested knaves that encouraged the use of low-trust policies based on contractual relations. This perspective resonated with Fox's (1974) analysis of employment contracts. He contrasted high-trust relations based on status and the continuing honouring of mutual obligations, with low-trust relationships based on contracts. In low-trust relationships, the presumption amongst managers was that employees pursued their own interests, which led to a battery of control structures – tight supervision, formal rules and clearly defined performance obligations. The upshot was that the workforce, often professionals used to high levels of discretion, perceived these measures as signalling a lack of trust in them. Tighter managerial control was resented, reinforcing a low-trust dynamic and making it harder to achieve results. Moreover, by encouraging the workforce to respond to the priorities established within contracts, NPM reforms frequently altered behaviour and directed staff to achieving narrow performance requirements. The development of a competitive ethos discouraged co-operation and had detrimental consequences as collective, system-wide needs were neglected.

A further limitation of NPM reforms concerned the consequences of the fragmentation and disaggregation of public services into more autonomous units. NPM reforms were premised on each enterprise, such as a civil service agency or trust hospital focusing on delivering their own services, 'sticking to the knitting' in the phrase popularised by Peters and Waterman (1982). The drawback was that these single-purpose organisations, formed part of a wider public service landscape that frequently needed to co-operate to achieve complex government objectives. By encouraging the establishment of separate silos, judged against narrow financial criteria, the fragmentation of public services led to co-ordination problems and a short-term perspective.

Actors and institutions: co-ordination and collaboration

An important aspect of governance is the extent to which a broader set of policy instruments and actors are involved in shaping policy and management.

NPM reforms were centred on the role of more assertive managers in responding to incentives and legislative requirements, concentrating on the internal workings of organisations (Hughes 2010: 96). NPM encouraged organisational re-structuring and outsourcing, but these 'make or buy' decisions were managed on an arms-length basis and were intended to strengthen the focus on the remaining core activities. By contrast governance involves closer relationships between various actors that alter the nature of the interaction between them. Eliasser and Sitter (2008: 107) highlight the blurring of the boundaries between the public, private and voluntary or third sectors. The spread of public–private partnerships involving interdependent relationships in the management of schools and hospitals rather than arms-length contracting is seen as indicative of this shift towards network governance. Similarly public–public partnerships are encouraged via the development of joint commissioning and joint service provision, developing seamless services for recipients of health and social care. It is an approach which also opens the possibility for new actors more proactively to engage as partners in the delivery of public services. The service user, in particular, emerges as a key stakeholder in this respect, although giving meaningful effect to their involvement is by no means unproblematic, with the risk that it assumes a tokenistic form.

Network governance acknowledges that the pursuit of closer relationships in the delivery of public services requires more co-ordinated approaches to policy development and implementation. This involves a recognition that so called 'wicked' problems cannot be resolved by a single organisation but need joined-up thinking and collaboration across networks between interdependent actors. This necessitates the development of new institutions, not locked into existing practices and ways of thinking, with authority to resolve complex problems within parameters set by central government. These institutions might acquire a traditional standard setting role, while also encouraging the spread of best practice and promoting cross boundary working.

Attempts to improve co-ordination might also involve the development of a stronger centre within government, as a response to the hollowing out of the state. Hollowing out refers to a number of changes in government, including the privatisation of services, fragmentation of service delivery, the shift of functions from central and local government to outside agencies, and the loss of authority arising from the development of European Union institutions. This process hampers the ability of politicians to steer and new governance mechanisms evolve to remedy the fragmentation of policy and delivery (Rhodes 1997; 2007). The co-ordination imperative within the network governance model provides a rationale for the creation of new, central units, designed to monitor and facilitate more integrative approaches (Barber 2008: 30; Christensen and Laegrid 2007).

At the same time, this emphasis on the role of the centre in managing co-ordination opens-up the possibility of a more directive and controlling approach by government. Certainly, the governance literature suggests that the monitoring of performance by the centre needs to be flexible and appropriate to the diverse circumstances of each organisation, but it also implies a light-touch regulation with successful performance engendering increased autonomy (Eliassen and Sitter 2008: 110). However, intrinsic to the network governance model of public services is a need to balance stakeholder engagement and collaboration with the co-ordination needed to demonstrate and publicise the achievement of broader public policy goals. Where the state adopts a strong centralising performance management regime to achieve this balance, some of the assumptions underpinning the new public management model begin to inform network governance, changing its character and generating contradictions and dilemmas.

There are strong grounds for suggesting that this was the balance struck by New Labour, a balance which established a hybrid model of public services delivery. The emphasis within network governance on stakeholder involvement and collaboration was combined with a target-driven approach to ensure co-ordination and the achievement of national standards. The next section explores this hybrid model in greater detail, assessing its implications for public policy and its wider effects on employee relations across and within different parts of the service sector.

New Labour's agenda

The Third Way

New Labour's 'Third Way' not only framed their approach to public services reform but also assigned a high priority to modernised public services (Giddens 2000). As the term 'Third Way' suggests it implied a synthesis of market and hierarchy principles with the network governance model addressing their respective weaknesses. Moreover, such a model provided the basis for a more positive centre-left modernisation project designed to protect and develop a more inclusive and integrated form of public service provision. It was an approach, however, which generated a number of policy dilemmas and choices. These were addressed by New Labour in a manner which led to the emergence of a modified form of network governance for the delivery of public services.

For Newman (2001) New Labour and the Third Way combined a political narrative that sought to distinguish itself from both its predecessor Conservative government and Old Labour. Tony Blair (2010: 212) summarised this change:

> our mantra was 'investment and reform together' – emphasising rhetorically the difference in the public services between New Labour and Old Labour (investment without reform) and New Labour and the Thatcherite Tories (reform without investment).

This narrative was rooted in a Third Way approach which accepted a neo-liberal interpretation of change (Giddens 2000). Emphasis was placed, in particular, on the importance of citizen expectations and globalisation, influences which fed through to New Labour's approach to public services reform. The Third Way suggested that society had become more individualistic with active, knowledgeable citizens who demanded higher service standards. It was a perspective which not only encouraged New Labour to pursue service quality, but a particular form of service quality, one linked to individual user choice, voice and control, and increasingly articulated in the form of personalised public services. Le Grand (2003; 2007) described this as involving an agenda that shifted away from service users as 'pawns', who accepted without question the judgment of public service professionals, to active users who expressed their preferences. These choices were backed up by resources, to drive forward service improvement and innovation. It was an approach which also addressed New Labour's more immediate concern to maintain political support for the welfare state amongst more affluent voters. Indeed, an articulate middle class constituency was viewed as important in expressing 'voice' to ensure public services achieved high service standards (Stevens 2004: 37).

Improvement in public services, however, was not an end in itself. It was essential to enhancing the competitiveness of the British economy in response to globalisation. This required maximising employment, necessitating vigorous welfare policies that reduced benefits for those not actively seeking work. The importance of globalisation was a core assumption of New Labour policy which was viewed as a benign force in creating wealth and opportunity, but to capture its benefits required an *interventionist* state rather than a *big* state that modernised public services and equipped citizens for a more uncertain and competitive world (Giddens 2000: 164). The weight placed upon the interventionist state might be seen to sit somewhat uneasily alongside individualised, user-centred services, a tension New Labour sought to resolve by inducing a sense of reciprocity. The individual citizen had a right to services sensitive to personal needs and circumstances, but in return this citizen had an obligation to take advantage of these services in a responsible way, so contributing to the development of an economy 'fit for purpose' in the context of global competition.

This commitment to an interventionist state also informed the Third Way approach to the regulation of public service provision. In accordance with the reliance placed by network governance on engagement with a broad array of actors, the Third Way encouraged a variety of private and third sector providers to compete for public funding to meet user needs. Indeed, public service organisations were re-instituted as legitimate providers, as New Labour adopted a less ideological, more pragmatic approach to service provision than the preceding Conservative government. However, in line with a social market approach, New Labour was prepared to retain qualified market principles in determining the allocation of public services activities. Equally striking, it continued to regulate this market through the commissioning process and a comprehensive system of centrally determined performance targets.

The active state as a regulator of markets and of public service provision was crucial in a number of respects. It supported the quality agenda- users needed performance data to make informed decisions. It also addressed a wider range of overlapping stakeholders – tax payers, the electorate and (global) corporate interests – signalling the achievement of value for money from the investment made in public services. Nonetheless this reliance on targets, with their assumptions of economic rationality on the part of stakeholders and rooted in contracts and incentives (Jordan 2010) ensured the continued influence of new public management principles and practices, alongside provider diversity and partnership engagement of the network governance model. The next section explores how this hybrid model was taken forward in New Labour's general approach to the modernisation of the public services, with the succeeding section setting out how this hybrid model manifest itself in the different parts of the public services: the civil service, the NHS and local government. This provides the basis for the following, substantive chapters which explore how these developments relate to our three employee relations domains.

Modernising government: general approach

Modernisation rather than the Third Way was the label used by New Labour to describe their public services agenda, exemplified by the 1999 *Modernising Government* White Paper (Cabinet Office 1999). While focusing mainly on central government and to a lesser extent local government, it was an important document in setting out New Labour's general direction of travel in the reform of the public services. More specifically, it revealed a degree of strategic intent in New Labour's approach to reform. Over the period of New Labour government there were significant changes in the direction and emphasis of the public service reform programme, but in retrospect many of the themes, aspirations and values outlined in *Modernising Government* continued to shape the government's approach. It highlighted that from the outset the government was sensitive to the relationship between upstream decisions on public services reform and downstream employee relations issues. This was reflected in the commitments presented in *Modernising Government,* which not only continued to drive reform for much of the New Labour period, but also included specific workforce goals. Thus, the White Paper set out five commitments, to: stronger and longer-term policy making; responsive service delivery that met the needs of citizens rather than the convenience of service providers; quality public services, using choice and competition to stimulate innovation as appropriate; information age government; and public services which valued rather than denigrated the public service workforce.

The importance of partnership working and establishing joined-up government was emphasised, defined as improved co-ordination 'between Whitehall, the devolved administrations, local government and the voluntary and private sectors' (Cabinet Office 1999: 16). *Modernising Government* advocated one-stop shops, making more effective use of information technology, to provide a single gateway to a range of services. The implication was that staff would require different skills to deal with a wider range of queries, be willing to shift work location and work more flexible hours to meet raised public expectations about service quality and convenience.

To ensure high-quality services, policy making and implementation required improvement and co-ordination because 'Too often the work of Departments, their agencies and other bodies had been fragmented and the focus of scrutiny had been on their individual achievements rather than on their contribution to the government's overall strategic purpose' (Cabinet Office 1999: 16). The response was to strengthen cross-cutting policy making by the establishment of specific units (e.g. the social exclusion unit), programmes and 'tsars' to ensure that policy making transcended the perspective of a single department. This approach was accompanied by strengthening the focus on delivery with more direct accountability of senior civil servants for performance. Public service agreements (PSAs) were introduced that set out expected standards and identified a number of cross-cutting targets that could only be achieved by joint working between departments. Monitoring was to be achieved by a strengthened centre, notably the Delivery Unit, and the use of inspection with intervention in inverse proportion to success.

Finally, *Modernising Government* signalled that the government was seeking a new relationship with its workforce recognising that it needed to be a good employer to encourage staff to engage with reform and be part of the solution. This was translated into measures to be a family-friendly employer, involving staff more fully to improve service delivery, encouraging training and working in partnership with trade unions. This support was, however, far from unconditional and in return for releasing staff from structures and systems that inhibited initiative, and dealing with long-standing problems of low pay and gender inequality, the expectation was that the workforce would embrace modernisation. This required a much sharper emphasis on individual and team performance with rewards and career progression linked to results rather than primarily seniority or qualifications. Bringing in more external appointments, the increased use of short-term contracts, and secondments were intended to foster culture change and challenge existing working practices.

In a similar manner to other areas of policy, the creation of new institutions was used as a basis to stimulate change, notably the establishment of a National College of School Leadership for aspiring head teachers that would promote a specific model of leadership. Although not discussed in detail, there were also indications that local managerial discretion had to be set within coherent national frameworks to limit the spread of a multitude of enterprise-specific terms and conditions of employment. This was primarily to limit legal challenges relating to gender inequality, but it was also recognised that a degree of re-regulation was required to protect staff and limit resistance to outsourcing and other forms of re-structuring.

While *Modernising Government* identified many of the ideas that would animate New Labour policy, it was a relatively cautious document. The former Head of the Prime Minister's Delivery Unit argued that it was: 'platitudinous and lacked real bite' (Barber 2008: 45). This reflected its preoccupation with the limitations of Conservative government reforms rather than providing a comprehensive blueprint for change. The emphasis on standards and investment continued throughout the Labour government's period in office but some themes were very sketchy. The emphasis on user choice, structural change via the creation of more autonomous providers, and competition for service provision became much more prominent themes after 2001. This initial timidity reflected high levels of anxiety amongst senior figures in New Labour about the likelihood of gaining a second term in office, an overly rational belief in the effectiveness of centralised targets to bring about reform, and an initially benign view of the workforce and the civil service which rapidly turned into frustration about the pace of change (Blair 2010; Mandelson 2010). Blair commented (2010: 214/288 and 313/314):

> 'Bureaucracies are run by people. People have interests. And whereas the market compels change, there is no similar compulsion in the public sector...I had worked out the crucial failure of the first term: the mistaken view that raising standards and performance could be separated from structural reform....I was now clear that public service reform needed major structural change, including a much closer relationship with the private sector'.

This evolution was reflected in subsequent policy documents. By 2002, three additional reform principles were prominent. First, devolution and a shift towards more diverse service provision not only externally but *within* the public services reflected in the development of specialist schools, the emergence of academy schools and NHS foundation trusts. Second, flexibility with more emphasis on financial incentives and rewards for front-line staff to encourage change. Third, choice interpreted in terms of scope for users to select from amongst a wider range of providers (Office of Public Services Reform 2002). By 2008, these shifts in emphasis had been consolidated into an account of reform which started with standards and investment, added incentives and encouragement to new providers from around 2001 and built on these reforms by encouraging greater empowerment of citizens and personalisation of services, in conjunction with a 'new professionalism' (Cabinet Office 2008a). This later term represented an admission that too many top-down targets had been disempowering for staff, and acknowledged the contribution of a range of staff, extending beyond the traditional professions. It also signalled that rewards should be linked more closely to outcomes, taking account of user perspectives.

Modernising government: sub-sector developments

Inevitably these reform principles had to be tailored to the specific needs of each sub-sector – the civil service, the National Health Service (NHS) and local government – and often the process of reform differed within sub-sectors. This variation not only reflected, the diversity of sectors such as local government, containing education and social care services, but even within service areas, the emphasis on diversity and personalisation led to a complex picture of change emerging.

Civil service

The Labour government, whilst accepting that agency status had been ben-
eficial (Cabinet Office 1998), recognised the need to strengthen steering.
New Labour therefore combined elements of NPM with measures to join-up
government and foster collaboration. This would create challenges in trying to reconcile reforms that simultaneously encouraged competition and
co-operation; managerial autonomy and tighter centralised control. NPM
reforms and a continuation of Conservative government emphasis on efficiency and private sector expertise were exemplified by two main developments. First, there was an increased reliance on outside appointments,
especially from the private sector, to jobs in the senior civil service (SCS).
Since 2005, more than half of all entrants to the 'Top 200' group of senior
civil servants have come from outside the civil service, the majority being
from the private sector. This has been justified by the need to plug shortages
of specialist skills such as human resources, finance or information technology, but it has created resentment as salaries are on average 20 per cent
more than internal appointments and this has been combined with concerns
about outsiders' performance and their commitment to a public service ethos
(Public Administration Select Committee 2010).

Second, there has been a continuing emphasis on privatisation (e.g.
National Air Traffic Services), outsourcing and efficiency savings. In 2004,
the government accepted the recommendations made by the industrialist,
Sir Peter Gershon, who reviewed efficiency across the civil service. The government, without prior notification to its social partners, announced that
between April 2004–2008, there would be gross reductions of 70,600 posts
after some re-allocation of staff to the front line. The largest decrease (30,000)
was planned in the Department for Work and Pensions (Gershon 2004: 31).
This emphasis on centrally directed change was championed by the Treasury
which controlled public expenditure, established performance agreements
with spending departments and increased its own spending role, reinforcing
its already powerful position within government (Rawnsley 2010: 68–70).

Despite strong elements of continuity, there have been important depar-
tures from NPM reforms to strengthen policy development and coherence.
The creation of the Department for Work and Pensions brought together separate social security and employment services and was designed to integrate
active labour market policies, encouraging individuals into employment at
the same time as dealing with their benefits. The focus on the holistic needs
of a client group also underpinned the creation in 2007 of the Department
for Children, Schools and Families (Department for Children, Schools and

Families), a children focused rather than exclusively education orientated department. These so called 'machinery of government' changes altered ways of working, including work locations, and brought together differing employment relations traditions and priorities.

The National Health Service

The Labour government's approach to the NHS involved a succession of partially implemented and contradictory structural reforms (Paton 2006), but underpinning these changes has been a shifting emphasis between a mixture of investment, targets and contestability to enhance patient choice (Stevens 2004). Lawson's judgment is less equivocal 'New Labour adopted an aggressive form of new public management which sees the government primarily as a service commissioner and people as consumers' (Lawson 2007: 8). There has certainly been a strong emphasis on centrally directed performance management. National targets were established for waiting times and to reduce mortality from cancer and heart disease, contributing to large reductions in waiting time and improved clinical outcomes (King's Fund 2010). At the same time some targets focused on encouraging investment rather than boosting efficiency. Workforce targets to increase staffing numbers were set and exceeded, using international recruitment strategies (Bach 2007), indicating that targets had differing functions.

From around 2001–2002, there was a renewed emphasis on encouraging market competition and boosting consumer choice. This involved creating more diverse and expanded healthcare provision and fostering contestability between these providers. For hospitals, opportunities were created to gain foundation status which provided some additional operational freedoms and the veneer of increased patient involvement in trust governance. Foundation trusts rekindled trade union fears about a move away from national pay and conditions, which had surfaced in the 1990s, and reinforced concerns that foundation status would be a transitional stage towards privatisation (Pollock 2004). The latter point seemed to be vindicated by the government's commissioning of additional hospital and community capacity from private companies, often using the controversial private finance initiative. The Independent Sector Treatment Centre (ISTC) programme had a high profile and the accountability, staffing and training practices of ISTCs attracted censure (House of Commons Health Committee 2006; Givan and Bach 2007). A revamped hospital payment system – 'payment by results' – enabled any approved provider to compete for patient income.

This endorsement of market incentives and support for enhanced managerial autonomy via foundation status, however, did not preclude the adoption of policies more akin to forms of network governance with the encouragement of partnership working and the empowerment of new actors, especially patients. A separate strand of health policy was trying to redesign health services starting with the clinical needs of the patient, rather than the existing pattern of service provision. National service frameworks, set out how the treatment of cancer, diabetes and other conditions would improve, using agreed patient pathways to map out the patient journey. For cancer and other treatments, it was expected that different providers would work in partnership within local health economies to generate the best outcomes for patients. An obvious difficulty, however, was reconciling the competitive ethos fostered by market incentives with the collaboration and trust required to create effective networks, especially as the Department of Health was inclined to view co-operation as collusive 'anti-competitive' behaviour (Paton 2007: 322). Partnership working between health and social care organisations was also promoted and Primary Care Trusts (PCTs) were encouraged to shift services into community settings, but an array of competing initiatives and the continuing dominance of acute NHS trusts with few incentives to shift work to the community, alienated local authorities and limited the effectiveness of joint working (Evans and Forbes 2009).

The empowerment of patients, with all patients offered a choice of hospital for non-urgent treatment, was intended to challenge professional power, drive up service standards and bring about shifts in service provision. There was considerable ambiguity about the government's stance towards service users, sometimes being viewed as passive consumers at other times as engaged citizens (Clarke et al 2007). In some case patients were cast as experts by experience and became co-producers of services with professionals, challenging and re-shaping existing working practices (see Chapter 5). In the majority of situations, however, service users remained 'pawns' (Le Grand 2003) and had minimal influence over service provision.

In summary, an expanded cadre of powerful, if insecure, managers had to respond to the visible hand of central government targets and rather opaque market incentives. They also had to take account of developments beyond their own trust with an emphasis on empowering local networks of professionals and users. Undoubtedly, unprecedented investment in new hospital infrastructure and staff and measures to make the NHS an employer of choice helped to address staff shortages. Overall, however, the main trajectory has been a tension between intensified NPM reforms and inchoate forms of network governance, creating considerable uncertainty for staff about the direction and consistency of government policy.

Local government

The Labour government attached a very high priority to raising school standards as part of its drive to enhance national competitiveness and reduce social exclusion. Its education policies had some similarities to its NHS agenda with an emphasis on more autonomous and diverse providers, enhanced performance management and attempts to foster competition for pupils and more personalisation. This involved in the words of the Prime Minister's spokesman moving away from 'bog-standard' comprehensives to develop more diverse provision, including from the private sector. This trend was exemplified by the establishment of academy schools from 2000 that were no longer under the control of local authorities and had increased discretion to alter national terms and conditions of employment. Central government targets focused on pupil test results in conjunction with national literacy and numeracy strategies to raise standards. Reforms were also introduced to ease teacher workloads and 'remodel' the workforce (Bach et al. 2006).

What united these school reforms was a commitment to delivery and the introduction of measures that penetrated workplace practice and challenged professional traditions to a far greater extent than in the past (Ball 2003). The government also encouraged pupil choice by increasing school capacity, often using the private finance initiative, and encouraged differentiation between schools accompanied by a strong emphasis on league tables, closing 'failing' schools and dismissing poor 'leaders' (DfES 2004; Gunter and Forrester 2009). The emphasis on joined-up government was also evident with the remit of schools being extended via the Every Child Matters (DfES 2003) reforms with additional social support being available at schools and greater attention directed at the personal needs of each child. Schools and their staff had to strike a complex balance: between competing with other schools for pupils and collaborating to foster better community outcomes; and between a focus on narrow examination results and a wider orientation to social inclusion and child protection that was receptive to other professional input and priorities, such as from social workers.

More broadly, the Labour government's policy of 'best value' for local government services eased the prescriptive nature of CCT, and was intended to focus on service quality rather than cost minimisation. Ministers' belief that local government was still underperforming led to the service-specific best value regime being replaced by Comprehensive Performance Assessment (CPA). It focused on an authority-wide evaluation, policed by the Audit

Commission, and provided a judgment ranging from 'weak' to 'excellent'; reinforcing the pressure on senior managers and their staff (Entwistle et al. 2005). The emphasis on joined-up government has been pursued vigorously with central government requiring multiple forms of partnership working. Local Area Agreements (LAAs) comprised three year agreements which brought together plans for local services, provided opportunities to pool resources, and identified the contribution of a variety of stakeholders. Laffin (2008) however, raises important issues about the consequences of partnership working when it is mandated by central government and when the various partners have very different incentives to participate. Undoubtedly it raises challenges for the workforce, more familiar with working in functional services within traditional hierarchies.

There were also important reforms of social care which over the last two decades had witnessed a significant shift towards private and third sector provision, accompanied by increased performance management and enhanced regulation (Newman et al. 2008). What marks out reforms in social care were initiatives to dissolve the boundaries between separate healthcare and social services organisations as part of attempts to develop more user-centred services. This involved a combination of joint commissioning, joint appointments and integrated teams of health and social services professionals, backed up by efforts to develop core competencies and career pathways across the sectors. In contrast to health and education policy, individual choice was accompanied by the allocation of financial resources to individuals, enabling users to have more direct influence over their own support, via the growth of direct payments and personal budgets. Social workers had a distinctive professional identity that had often made them more receptive to shifts in occupational practice that enhanced user autonomy compared to more traditional professions (Lymbery 2001). Social workers, however, like other local government workers confronted more intensive forms of audit and scrutiny that have a continuing impact on their working lives.

Overall, local government is different from the NHS and the civil service because it is distinguished more by its system of finance, geographical orientation and local political accountability rather than being identified with one dominant service. Indeed the two major areas of service provision, education and social care, have relatively little in common beyond their inclusion within local government. Although local government has been subject to NPM and network governance reforms a distinctive challenge has been to reconcile the differing needs of distinctive services, subject to specific policy agendas. This has also been in a context in which most local government services have rarely attracted the investment of more politically sensitive services such as health.

Discussion

This chapter was designed to address a number of issues, crucial in framing a more detailed analysis of developments in public services employee relations under the New Labour government. It sought to unpack the nature of New Labour's public services modernisation project, principally with a view to exploring the relationship between reform and the management of the public services workforce. It then began to examine these linkages, in particular, focusing on the form they assumed in different parts of the public services: the civil service, the NHS and local government, including education and social care. This provided an opportunity not only to present background information on the institutional features of the respective sub-sectors, but to raise the possibility that the consequences of modernisation on employees were mediated by these features.

The attempt to characterise New Labour's public services modernisation centred on how far the Labour government's reform agenda marked a departure from NPM policies and a shift towards forms of network governance. It noted two dominant perspectives. The first viewed modernisation as 'old wine in new bottles', effectively the intensification of NPM reforms using altered language. With modernisation's deep roots in a neo-liberalism, these commentators (Leys 2001; Mooney and Law 2007) provide a more explicit ideological interpretation of policies which other commentators (e.g. Barber 2008) view more neutrally as sensible technical reforms, ensuring the adoption of 'what works'.

The second perspective discerned more of a break with NPM policy, reflecting a shift in emphasis towards network governance and collaboration rather than the predominance of market mechanisms and competition. Governance perspectives tended to concentrate on the implications for citizen engagement with public services, the interaction between different actors within networks, and the organisational complexities of managing in networks (Newman and Clarke 2009). These reforms could appear less tangible than an agenda of managerialism and marketisation, but they derived from debates which suggested that network governance was usurping NPM as the dominant architecture of modernisation (Eliassen and Sitter 2008: 104). In contrast to an emphasis on traditional bureaucracy dominated by welfare professionals or attempts to galvanise change by market mechanisms, governance writers emphasised the key role of networks in co-ordinating and delivering change. In this altered context the role of the state became less about the direct provision of services and more concerned with establishing a policy and budgetary framework to encourage effective partnership working between a variety of local actors, the regulation and licensing of providers, and the collection and dissemination of performance information to monitor and inform communities about outcomes.

These two perspectives are not necessarily mutually exclusive. The chapter's analysis suggests that New Labour combined features of the NPM and network governance approaches to create a layered or hybrid model of public services delivery: not so much 'old' or 'new' wine as a distinctive cocktail of the two. With varying degrees of explicitness, New Labour reacted against some of the perceived limitations of the NPM, in particular, the fragmentation and parochialism of public service provision and the power imbalance between the general manager and the professional. In the process, it appeared to embrace elements of network governance (Bevir 2005). New Labour adopted: a catholic approach to service provision, seeking providers from the private, public and independent sectors; wider stakeholder involvement in service delivery, not least in the form of greater service user engagement, and a more interventionist role in facilitating and co-ordinating partnership as well as supporting collaborative service activities.

At the same time, however, New Labour was seen to retain key features of the new public management. Despite attempts to present these in pragmatic, ideologically neutral terms, they were underpinned by certain neo-liberal principles and values. Fierce debate amongst commentators, policy makers and academics has revolved around this neo-liberal dimension. The nature of New Labour's neo-liberalism has been explored, with a case for it being viewed more as a social rather than as a fundamentalist market approach. The rationale for this neo-liberalism has also been heavily scrutinised. There has been discussion about how tightly New Labour was locked into a market approach to public service reform given the economy's institutional infrastructure; some have suggested that this rendered the public sector particularly exposed to global pressures, others countering that the government still had considerable room for manoeuvre (Hay 1999; Garrett 2000; Coates 2001). Others have been more inclined to explore the developments within the context of the left wing project in Britain, arguing about whether New Labour's brand of neo-liberalism represented the pursuit of traditional socialist values in a 'modern setting' or a betrayal of the party's 'soul' (Shaw 2007).

More prosaically, and in substantive terms, these residual NPM features were apparent in a number of tangible policy developments. Retaining a commitment to service quality defined in terms of consumer choice, voice and control, New Labour not only relied on (regulated) markets to give effect to this agenda, but also deepened and strengthened the Conservative government's target-driven performance management regime. The light-touch interventionist state of the network governance model flipped over into an intrusive, controlling state, in part as means of supporting this consumerist agenda, but also as an attempt to demonstrate value for money to various stakeholders in the context of historically high levels of investment on the public services. Combined with aspects of network governance, this targeted change, rooted in contracts and incentives, created contradictions and dilemmas both for the public services reform project and for the management of the workforce.

The tensions between a public services reform project based upon a hybrid model of network governance and employee relations were particularly acute under New Labour, a consequence of the government's sensitivity to the close relationship between modernisation and the management of the sector's workforce. From the outset New Labour acknowledged that in a labour intensive sector founded upon the delivery of interactive services, the success of its reform agenda depended on a re-shaping of employee relations: a 'modern' approach to public service delivery required the 'modern' management of the public services workforce. This prompted a move away from the hostility of the previous Conservative government, which viewed the public services worker, and particularly the professional, as having captured service provision to the detriment of the customer, to a more nuanced position. It was a position which regarded the workforce in instrumental terms, creating a 'doubled edge' employee relations' agenda. Cutting across the employee relations domains – employment, work and industrial relations- was an agenda which combined the 'soft' with the 'hard': the 'soft' to ensure workforce capacity- employee recruitment, retention, motivation and capability, the 'hard' to ensure that this capacity was mobilised to deliver a service which promoted user choice, voice and control.

The chapter began to explore the ways in which this balance between the 'soft' and the 'hard' had been achieved over time and in different sub-sectors. For example, the emphasis on the co-design and co-production of service became much more prominent during the last term of Labour government compared to the earlier phases, when developing centralised standards and ensuring delivery against targets was the highest priority. Moreover, it was clear that variation between sub-sectors in terms of institutional infrastructure– for instance, governance mechanisms, sources and forms of funding- had affected the pattern of change in employee relations. It was equally apparent, however, that in all parts of the public services a 'soft', supportive and developmental employee relations agenda was taken forward under the shadow of a hard, more assertive and confrontational one, underpinned by a comprehensive and target-driven performance management regime.

We now turn to a more detailed consideration of the relationship between New Labour's upstream hybrid model of public service and the downstream domains of employee relations.

3

Employment relations: performance management and pay determination

As in most sectors of the economy, pay and the management of employee performance are core features of employee relations in the public services. However, as a labour-intensive sector, providing interactive services, they assume particular significance in the public services. This is reflected in the public sector paybill, in excess of £180 billion in 2009 representing 30 per cent of all government expenditure. The general government paybill (i.e. excluding public corporations) increased from £111 billion (in 2009 prices) in 1998 to £160 billion in 2006, and subsequently increased more slowly to reach £168 billion in 2009 (Bozio and Disney 2011: 166). These data need careful interpretation, but a combination of increased employment (see Chapter 1) and strong wage growth indicates that New Labour invested very significantly in the public sector workforce. Despite this growth, the Treasury, as custodian of public expenditure emphasised the need to control the public sector paybill and reiterated the importance of affordability and achieving the government's inflation target as key criteria in establishing public sector pay, whilst recognising that pay levels needed to be sufficient to recruit and retain staff. In addition to this market function of pay – signalling to potential employees the level of rewards they can expect – pay also has a managerial function which enables employers to use it as an incentive or sanction to motivate staff and alter their behaviour. During the 1980s and 1990s Conservative governments attempted to decentralise collective bargaining and link public sector pay more closely to local labour market conditions and the success of the individual 'enterprise'. Although some attention was focused on the managerial function of pay, especially in terms of promoting individual performance-related pay (PRP), these governments sought to address the market function of pay and to reform pay bargaining, attempts which, outside of the civil service, largely failed (Bach and Winchester 1994).

Successive Labour government's focused on both market and managerial functions of pay and attempted to create a system of incentives and rewards which encouraged high levels of performance, advanced new ways of working and addressed gender and other forms of pay inequality. In contrast to a narrow focus on PRP, the Labour government used a much wider set of strategies to enhance performance, emphasising the value of total rewards. This included pensions, the promotion of non-pay benefits and measures to encourage career advancement and upskilling. At the same time, New Labour reinforced and deepened forms of new public management, exemplified by the establishment of individual and organisational targets, strict monitoring of these standards and the publication of organisational results using star ratings and league tables, accompanied by central intervention to remedy poor performance. These reforms were combined with attempts to transcend the fragmentation of NPM measures by placing much more emphasis on coherent national pay frameworks and the use of targets which mandated collaboration and partnership working.

This chapter considers first the Labour government's use of targets and performance appraisal to strengthen individual and organisational performance. It then examines the main components of the government's approach towards reward management and the way in which these were implemented, before examining the main reforms of pay determination in the civil service, local government and the NHS.

Performance management

The extent to which performance management would be an integral feature of public service modernisation was evident from the 1997 Labour Party manifesto. It outlined five pledges which included reducing NHS waiting lists by 100,000 patients, cutting class-sizes in primary schools to 30 or under and it signalled zero tolerance for public service underperformance (Labour Party 1997). The broad principles of how these pledges were to be translated into policy was unveiled in *Modernising Government* (Cabinet Office 1999). In a clear rejection of its Conservative predecessors' distrust of government and emphasis on shrinking the state, its vision statement stated baldly that 'Government matters' (p. 9) but argued that public services had to be recast to meet the expectations of citizens.

Performance management figured strongly but was framed as part of an integrated HR agenda in which the government 'would value public service, not denigrate it' (p. 55), working in partnership with public service trade unions. Change was required because 'incentives to modernise have been weak' (p. 35) and 'performance management is not effective enough' (p. 59). To achieve these aims, civil servants would be selected and trained in the required core competencies and appraised on these attributes. Pay reform placed a similar emphasis on designing incentives to enhance performance. These themes were reiterated in subsequent statements and the government rejected a traditional public sector interpretation of 'fair pay', associated with comparability, a rate for the job and progression based on seniority. Instead it favoured a performance-orientated approach drawing on NPM precepts: 'part of what makes people feel valued at work is the sense that they are being treated fairly – rewarded for their individual contribution and performance' (Office of Public Service Reform 2002: 21). For the Labour government there was also a desire to control more directly the behaviour of professionals to ensure their actions fulfilled user expectations (Gash et al. 2008).

In this context, it is not surprising that an emphasis on performance management and the spread of the 'target culture' has been viewed as a defining feature of New Labour's modernisation agenda (Bevan and Hood 2006). This emphasis, however, is not confined to the UK, reflecting an international trend. Formal performance management has become a widespread feature of public service governance, facilitated by improved communication technologies and raised citizen expectations about accessing performance data (OECD 2008). The most prominent and widely debated component of this performance management agenda has been the development of targets and the consequences for the workforce. Less attention has been directed at a related dimension of this reform agenda, namely the spread of individual performance appraisal.

Part of the prominence of performance management was derived from Third Way assumptions that ideological differences between left and right had lost their potency (Giddens 2000: 39–43) and the implication that governments were supported and evaluated on the basis of results not sentiment. Consequently the Prime Minister viewed his role as akin to a chief executive of a large company in which project management was key. As Tony Blair (2010: 18) explained: 'the skills are actually quite analogous to those of the private sector. This is true of civil servants. It is also true of politicians.' Ironically, considering the emphasis within new public management on the separation of political 'steering' from managerial 'rowing', this approach implied greater interdependence; policy becoming increasingly managerial and focused on delivery and at the same time management became increasingly political, focused on achieving electoral commitments.

Frustration, however with perceived civil service inertia (Blair 2010: 205) led to the establishment of the Prime Minister's Delivery Unit in 2001, whose Director worked directly for the Prime Minister and was located in Downing Street. It focused on the implementation of a small number of key targets in health, education, the Home Office and Transport, and 'was performing for the Prime Minister the internal performance management function of a large company' (Barber 2007: 60). This task was facilitated by the use of auditing and inspection regimes, especially the publication of performance data, which enabled the government to use organisations such as the Audit Commission to put pressure on councils to follow government policy and adhere to best practice (Kelly 2006). These forms of indirect steering mechanisms proliferated with the establishment of organisations such as The Local Government Association's Improvement and Development Agency and the NHS Modernisation Agency which benchmarked performance and encouraged innovation. Martin (2010: 54) suggested that inspection was associated with changes in leadership and management and with some improvements in service outcomes.

What is missing from a narrow focus on organisational improvement is a recognition of the unintended consequences of inspection and the limitations of existing government data. This was apparent in primary and secondary education where in a survey of 157 head teachers, 61 per cent of respondents stated that league table data were 'not very useful', increasing to 75 per cent for secondary heads only. In contrast almost 90 per cent of head teachers considered their own internal data such as predicted grades very useful in managing performance (National Audit Office [NAO] 2006a: 26–27). Head teachers also were concerned about the detrimental effect of a poor Office for Standards in Education (Ofsted) outcome in terms of staff morale (75 per cent of head teachers) and on recruitment and retention (51 per cent) (NAO 2006a: 29). Moreover an increased vulnerability to dismissal because of poor results and a perceived excessive personal accountability was regarded as a major barrier to recruitment of head teachers, contributing to continuous difficulties in filling headship positions (Smithers and Robinson 2007). Around one-third of head teacher posts in primary schools and a quarter in secondary schools remained unfilled after an advertisement was placed in 2009–2010 (Howson and Sprigade 2010). The Labour government was clearly aware of the ambivalent attitude towards inspection because it offered the removal of inspection, or at least reduced frequency of inspection, as a reward for high-performing schools and hospitals.

Targets and terror?

Targets did not originate with the Labour government but were formalised and made an integral component of public service modernisation. At the apex of the system was the system of Public Service Agreements (PSA) targets. These were developed every three years as part of the comprehensive spending review and identified cross-departmental targets, with individual departments leading on specific targets. Over time the number of PSAs was reduced to 30 but with a larger number of performance indicators to ascertain delivery. These targets were the basis of an evolving performance regime, intended to encourage collaboration and partnership working at local level. In local government, local area agreements (LAAs) comprised up to 51 targets negotiated with central government and agreed locally through partnership forums which included health, voluntary and private sector partners.

The use of targets has proved contentious exemplified by Bevan and Hood's (2006) phrase 'targets and terror' to characterise the performance regime. Targets, however, had the benefit of signalling an accountable form of commitment amongst politicians to achieving results, while creating transparency about progress and value for money. The political risks were highlighted by David Blunkett: their 'head was on the block' if a target was not achieved (Barber 2007: 32). There was also considerable evidence that targets were effective, despite the temptation to manipulate data, when they focused on relatively straight forward quantifiable outcomes. In the NHS, targets were credited with large reductions in waiting times for NHS treatment (Wanless et al. 2007), a finding reinforced by comparisons with the record in Scotland which did not use a target regime (Propper et al. 2007). They also stimulated change that had not been forthcoming prior to the target regime and enabled resources to be channelled to formerly neglected areas of public service, such as mental health, because of the increased visibility which targets established (Levenson et al. 2008).

Concerns were raised, however, about the distortions and perverse incentives introduced by targets (Flanagan 2008; Marley 2008). Chapman (2007: 122) noted that targets encouraged staff to face the wrong way, concentrating on satisfying the requirements of central government, rather than meeting the needs of service users. This difficulty was exacerbated because the workforce often felt insufficiently involved in establishing targets and felt disengaged from a process which focused on standardised outcomes, irrespective of the local context (Bach 2004). A second concern was that lack of staff involvement encouraged 'gaming' because of the financial and managerial consequences that stemmed from failure. NHS staff re-designated corridors as 'pre-admission units' to circumvent waiting time targets for accident and emergency care treatment (Public Administration Select Committee 2003). In many cases there were significant discrepancies between officially reported levels of performance and the lower levels of service experienced by patients (Bevan and Hood 2006: 528–529). Finally, staff resented the workload involved in collecting data to document compliance. The Audit Commission (2002: 22) pinpointed targets and the paperwork associated with them as the most important reason why public sector workers left their jobs, cited by half of former public sector workers.

Towards the end of its period in office the government acknowledged the validity of these criticisms, and noted that 'persisting with too many top-down targets can be counterproductive; we know services must value professionals if we are to foster innovation and excellence' (Cabinet Office 2008a: 11). Criticisms of targets confirmed Tony Blair's view that standards or targets were an essential first phase of reform, but genuine modernisation of public service required devolution and more contestability to bring about performance enhancement. In other words it was structures, such as the establishment of academy schools, rather than standards which were the key to performance improvement (Barber 2007: 82; Blair 2010: 578).

Performance appraisal

It was also recognised that achieving targets required a link between organisational and individual objectives, encouraging the growth of individual performance appraisal, often linked to contribution. By 2004 public sector workplaces were more likely to conduct performance appraisals than in the private sector, and amongst non-managerial employees 88 per cent of employees were subject to performance appraisal compared to 81 per cent in the private sector. Even more significant was the growth of coverage within the public sector which increased (amongst non-managerial staff) from 68 per cent (1990) to 79 per cent (1998) to 81 per cent (2004) (Bach et al. 2009: 325). Whilst these were clearly long-run trends, New Labour applied performance appraisal more systematically and provided a link with rewards to embed systems of performance management (Cutler and Waine 2001).

In the NHS, the *Agenda for Change* reforms introduced appraisal for all non-medical staff in the form of the Knowledge and Skills Framework (KSF) development review, intended to identify the competencies needed to undertake the role effectively. In schools, revised performance management regulations introduced from 2007 formalised the process, ensuring tighter alignment with performance, but also enabling teachers to progress faster through the main pay scale on the basis of 'excellent performance'. Individual performance appraisal and the objectives set for each teacher stemmed from a school's improvement plan, self-evaluation and planning frameworks (Rewards and Incentives Group [RIG] 2009). Crucial was appraisal's focus on effective teaching and evaluation by achievement of targets (based on predicted pupil grades), a process underpinned by regular line management observation of lessons and grading using Ofsted categories. This provided head teachers with more scope to initiate capability proceedings: 'more "business-like" head teachers meant that more [capability] cases were being escalated at an earlier stage' (Morrell et al. 2010: 5).

These developments, however, cannot simplistically be equated with a strengthening of new public management arrangements. The presence of new actors and institutions, for example RIG, suggested the emergence of standards governance networks. For example, pupils became involved indirectly in performance management arrangements with their feedback integral to recruitment and selection of teachers in many schools. In addition each school had a School Improvement Partner – often a head teacher from another school – which contributed to performance management arrangements. More broadly, the spread of 'mystery shoppers', evaluating the performance of public service staff, indicated a broadening of stakeholders' involvement in evaluating individual staff performance (see Lambley and Chamberlain 2009).

Moreover, the increased use of performance appraisal did not always result in effective management of performance. In the civil service it was acknowledged that performance management required strengthening: survey data from senior civil servants indicated that in 2006 only 33 per cent were satisfied with performance management in their organisation, and only 19 per cent believed that performance management was dealt with effectively (Normington 2008: 22). Guidance to permanent secretaries lamented the poor state of performance management:

> Too many managers are still setting poor quality objectives or worse still, not agreeing objectives formally with their staff until very late in the reporting year. As a result, there is poor linkage to departmental goals and reduced accountability for the delivery of results (Cabinet Office 2007: 7).

In the NHS, the coverage of performance appraisal was uneven with less than two-thirds of NHS staff (61 per cent) reporting that they had received an appraisal or performance development review during 2007, only a slight improvement on 2006 (58 per cent) (Healthcare Commission 2007). In addition, senior hospital medical staff expressed doubts about the impact of performance appraisal, viewing it as creating the impression of accountability which did not alter professional practice (McGivern and Ferlie 2007).

Overall, there was a more prominent role for systems of performance management prompted by the need for increased transparency, with more data available on organisational and individual performance, the increased use of targets and the spread of performance appraisal, sometimes linked to rewards. Some uncertainties remained about the effective management of performance, but this stemmed less from the absence of systems and data, more from a degree of managerial wariness about the process and its outcomes. Performance management systems were seen as problematic in addressing issues of poor performance. This stemmed in part from complex procedures, shifting political agendas creating ambiguity about priorities, and a lack of clarity about who was responsible for managing performance and what constituted poor performance.

Reward management

Modernising Government identified the overall aim of pay reform as ensuring that 'pay encourages more of the best people to join and stay' (p. 58). This goal was to be achieved in a number of ways. First, reforming outdated systems which were inflexible, challenging the idea that 'fair pay' meant everyone received the same pay increase or that pay and conditions had to be set nationally. Second, recruiting and retaining staff by increased pay awards and revising pay scales enabling more staff to remain in front-line roles. Third, making better use of non-pay incentives such as training and work–life balance initiatives. Fourth, rewarding results and performance on an individual or team basis and challenging systems which gave automatic pay increases to poor performers (Cabinet Office 1999: 58–59). Pay reform was envisaged as a means to address gender inequality, strengthen the link with performance, and encourage more flexibility in workplace roles (Perkins and White 2010).

This task was not straightforward because the Labour government inherited an uneven pattern of reform in which decentralised pay determination accompanied managerial reform. Workplace employment relations survey data indicated a sharp increase from 36 per cent in 1990 to 59 per cent in 1998 in the proportion of employee relations managers who were responsible for pay and conditions. Formal responsibility for pay and conditions, however, did not always translate into local managerial authority over decision making for workplace pay and conditions. Overall, in 2004, 92 per cent of local public sector managers had to follow policy on pay rates set elsewhere in the organisation (Bach et al. 2009). In the civil service where the government had most direct control, delegated pay determination resulted in extensive pay bargaining decentralisation with pay determined at the level of the agency or department. In the NHS, however, local pay determination had failed. Managerial reluctance to antagonise the workforce in a context of forceful union opposition, alongside limited managerial skills and severe financial constraints stymied local pay (Bach and Winchester 1994). By contrast in local government the 1997 single-status agreement seemed to signal a different approach to pay reform which was viewed as a model for subsequent pay reform in the NHS and the universities. The Labour government's predilection for centralised control resulted in less fervent support for pay decentralisation with local flexibility fostered within more integrated national reward systems.

Reforming outdated pay systems

The government identified its NHS pay proposals *Agenda for Change* and the single-status agreement in local government as exemplifying its commitment to simplifying pay and conditions, providing increased flexibility to employers and paying fairly and equitably for work done (Cabinet Office 1999: 58). It was the emphasis on equity which proved to have a decisive influence over pay reform and took precedence over establishing local managerial flexibility. A tension emerged between strengthening local managerial autonomy with discretion to respond to shortages and reward individual performance and the need to limit managerial discretion to preclude discriminatory practice and ensure fairness. The uneven moves towards pay decentralisation under Conservative governments had exposed the extent to which public sector pay systems did not comply with equal pay legislation. Key issues included: the use of length of service as a criteria for pay differentials (which can discriminate indirectly against women taking career breaks); access to bonus payments (which can exclude some groups); comparability between jobs on separate pay structures within the same service or organisation; and the use of job evaluation to ensure that pay systems were equal value proof (Income Data Services 2000).

Although previous governments had faced litigation, the length of time involved in bringing cases, reflected in the notorious 14-year *Enderby* case in the NHS, and the cost of gender-proofing public sector pay systems discouraged government action. The emergence of more litigation amongst low-paid women such as home helps and cleaners, disadvantaged by the absence of bonus schemes available to (male) gardeners and refuse collectors, resulted in equal pay compensation which could be backdated for six years (Corby 2007). The Labour government implemented reforms of pay systems which became strongly influenced by the need to address pay inequality. This was evident in the increased use of analytical job evaluation to underpin pay structures, the harmonisation of employment conditions between manual and non-manual workers, and the use of narrow pay bands. In 1990, 27 per cent of public sector workplaces with more than 25 employees had job evaluation schemes and this increased to 44 per cent by 2004 (Kersley et al. 2006: 247).

The implementation of reformed pay systems had not been straightforward with the eventual cost in local government alone in compensation and adjustments to the paybill after job evaluation and re-grading estimated at £4 billion (Local Government Association 2010: 25). Local authorities had difficulties financing this increase in paybill which led to slow progress and continuing vulnerability to equal pay claims. A potent element in the equal pay arena was the emergence of no fee–no win lawyers, taking cases for individuals and winning much larger settlements than the proposed deals between trade unions and employers. In 2006, 1600 women at two Cumbrian hospitals won an equal pay claim totalling £300 million, having rejected an initial offer of £1.5 million brokered between the trust and trade unions. Redressing pay inequality was crucial to remedying the gender pay gap, but it had other, unintended consequences. Whereas no win–no fee lawyers only had regard to the immediate financial interests of their client, trade unions had to consider the interests of the whole workforce and the affordability of any settlement for the employer. This process, however, carried considerable risks for trade unions which were subject to legal challenges for not pursuing vigorously enough the interests of affected members (Hall 2008). Trade unions therefore were obliged to seek maximum redress and local employers were also wary of their legal liabilities. The upshot was that the process of collective bargaining, particularly in local government, was curtailed creating frustration amongst employers and trade unions (Perkins and White 2010). Moreover, for managers, limiting the use of local bonus schemes for occupations such as refuse collectors represented a loss of local managerial discretion.

Other aspects of the Labour government's pay reforms reinforced the emphasis on national pay frameworks with some scope for local flexibility. There was very little explicit reference within policy documents to the role of pay review bodies (PRBs). It was therefore striking that their role expanded with limited consideration of the implications for pay modernisation, especially the extent to which they were compatible with more local flexibility. White (2000: 71) describes PRBs as institutions 'halfway between fully-fledged collective bargaining and unilateral imposition by government' because they collect evidence from interested parties and make recommendations on national pay increases and related matters to government. The pay review body system makes recommendations affecting around 2,250,000 workers with an aggregate paybill of approximately £80 billion (http://www.ome.uk.com/About_Us.aspx).

Separate pay review bodies exist for each professional group, including doctors and dentists, nurses, senior civil servants and judges, teachers and the armed forces. In 2001, a pay review body for the prison service was established; the first review body ever created by a Labour government and the review body for nurses was extended to cover all NHS staff (except doctors, dentists and top managers) and renamed the NHS Pay Review Body (NHSPRB). The extension of the pay review system marked an important departure from previous Labour government's ambivalent attitude towards independent pay review, which in the past was based on trade union concerns about the loss of formal bargaining rights. The Labour government's support for independent pay review indicated a broader shift in values and a more tepid attitude towards collective bargaining than its predecessors.

The expansion of the PRB system had certain other attractions for the Labour government. First, there were suggestions that it might discourage industrial action, generating less conflictual relations. As an official review concluded: 'the history of the pay review body system as a whole shows that it is associated with improved industrial relations where previously they were poor' (Booth 2007: ix). This proved an important consideration because labour disputes were concentrated in the public sector (Hale 2010) and New Labour was very conscious that the 'winter of discontent' in 1978–1979 severely damaged the Labour Party's electoral prospects for many years. The establishment of the prison service review body was therefore accompanied by a voluntary agreement precluding strike action, reinforcing a pattern of trading off industrial action in return for the granting of independent pay review.

Second, independent review distanced ministers from direct pay negotiations with trade unions and accommodated politically sensitive groups such as the armed forces which do not have a right to strike, whilst enabling government to exert a very powerful influence over their deliberations. The terms of reference or remit of each review body is set by government and they co-ordinate evidence to the review bodies. The remit process was expanded and after 1997 the Labour government instructed the review bodies to have regard for affordability, whilst stressing its inflation target and other priorities, such as promoting greater regional variation in pay settlements (Incomes

Data Services 2006). Government also retained ultimate control over the cost of review body recommendations with its discretion to accept, stage or reject the recommendations of each PRB. The Labour government intervened actively to encourage the pay review bodies to moderate pay growth. For example, it staged pay awards in 2007 which reduced the value of awards from 2.5 per cent to 1.9 percent. There were, however, risks, with considerable political capital expended on not accepting review body recommendations, and the credibility of *independent* pay review jeopardised if overly susceptible to Treasury control.

Recruiting and retaining staff

Modernising Government stated that public sector pay should be 'fair', providing few indications about how government would address recruitment and retention, but three main components of government policy can be identified. First, the Labour government boosted earnings of public service workers. Second, it sought to encourage staff to stay in front-line roles. Third, it attempted to make more use of non-pay incentives, discussed in detail in Chapter 4. The government couched increased pay in the language of modernisation and the reform of working practices, but its inheritance of labour shortages, unreformed pay systems and low morale indicated the need for intervention. In the past, public sector pay had been characterised by periods of relative decline in comparison to the private sector, followed by periods of catch-up when labour shortages prompted industrial action and/or government reviews which led to a boost in earnings. Relative decline in public sector pay during the 1990s suggested that the public sector was ripe for a period of catch-up (Bozio and Johnson 2008).

Despite New Labour's implied concern to address public sector pay, there is some debate about relative wage movements over this period, and a considerable challenge to be faced in analysing public sector earnings, particularly establishing meaningful comparisons with the private sector. More specifically making meaningful comparisons is complicated by differences in occupational composition of the sectors: higher levels of skilled workers in the public sector, especially the employment of more professional workers, renders crude comparisons of average wages problematic. Moreover other factors need to be taken into account not least deferred pay, the value to be attached to pensions, and other benefits (Bozio and Disney 2011). Even disaggregated data by occupation based on job titles can be misleading as the public sector employs more specialist roles which require high levels of skill. For example, the job of a local government housing officer carries more responsibility than a similarly named job in the independent or private sector. The composition of the workforce in both sectors has altered in recent years with the outsourcing of many lower-paid public service jobs to the private sector, exerting an upward influence on average wages in the public sector. In general the wage structure of the public services is more compressed than the private sector with fewer minimum wage jobs and fewer very high-paid jobs. Consequently whereas the private sector resembles more of a pyramid pay structure, the public services are more akin to a diamond shape distribution (IDS 2010).

Taking account of these caveats, the level of investment in public services especially in the period after 2000 contributed to a period of catch-up for public sector workers in relation to the private sector, as the growth of earnings indicated, with cost per head increasing by about 2 per cent per annum (Figure 3.1). However, this general trend masks important variation in earnings growth by sub-sector and occupation.

As Figure 3.2 reveals earnings growth was most marked amongst those occupational groups benefiting from public expenditure increases and particularly where this included investment in reformed pay systems. This was reflected in the NHS Agenda for Change reforms implemented during 2005–2006, including registered nurses, comprising around 35 per cent of the NHS workforce and accounting for 40 per cent of the NHS paybill (NAO 2009). It has been estimated that between 2003–2004 and 2007–2008 earnings for

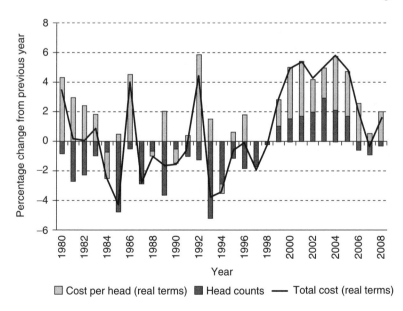

Figure 3.1 Public Services Labour Costs 1980–2008
Source: ONS Blue book 2009 cited in IFS green budget 2010 IFS: page 215

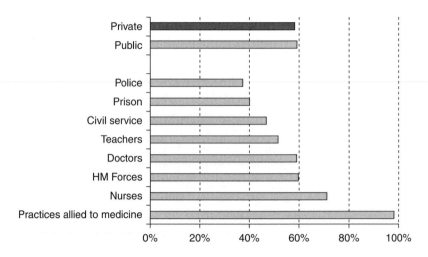

Figure 3.2 Average Increase in Nominal Earnings, 1997–2009

Note: 'Practices allied to Medicine' refers to occupations such as medical radiographers and physiotherapists

Source: Labour Force Survey data cited in IFS green budget 2010: 224

[details at: http://www.ifs.org.uk/budgets/gb2010/10chap9.pdf

staff on Agenda for Change terms and conditions increased by 5.8 per cent a year on average. Registered nurses received a lower but still noteworthy increase of 4.2 per cent because of the legacy of clinical re-grading (NAO 2009: 21). Moreover these pay uplifts were not confined to professional staff with assimilation to new grades boosting the pay of low-paid workers such as cleaners and healthcare assistants by between 7 and 20 per cent (Grimshaw 2008: 186). Indeed it was non-professional staff who gained the largest increase in earnings although these pay increases were premised on the acceptance of changes in working conditions which would boost productivity, translate into improved patient care and address recruitment and retention problems (Department of Health 1999a).

Pay modernisation was also extended to general practitioners (family doctors) and the most senior, consultant medical staff during 2003–2004. The pay increases achieved by these groups under new contracts were even more striking although the government achieved the unusual feat of antagonising the medical profession to an unprecedented degree at the same time. In 2005–2006, the average pay of consultants was £109,974, an increase of 27 per cent in three years (NAO 2007) whilst for GPs, pre-tax take home pay in England increased by 58 per cent from £72,011 in 2002–2003 to £113,614 in 2005–2006 (NAO 2008).

More incremental changes in pay systems boosted the earnings of many public sector workers. These changes were less straightforward and assumed a variety of forms. A range of techniques was used to deal with labour supply issues. Recruitment and retention pay premia, worth up to 30 per cent for a specific post in the NHS, were used to fill hard-to-fill posts on a short- or long-term basis. Within local government, market supplements were used by almost two-thirds of local authorities with over half using them to recruit and retain children's social workers, compared to around a quarter which used supplements for planning officers, another prominent shortage occupation (Local Government Association 2010: 31). Supplements were not always used as intended. In the NHS senior manager salaries were increased to make their remuneration more attractive, relative to NHS managers employed by Foundation trusts who were not subject to the same pay framework (Review Body of Senior Salaries 2010: 47). Teachers in shortage subjects, such as maths or science, often negotiated supplements or higher-base salaries. More generally, and supplementing pay responses to labour market pressure, the use of annual incremental progression ensured any initial higher-base salary was maintained on an ongoing basis. This progression was sometimes along extended pay scales: the addition of spinal points at the top of a grade or the removal of points at the bottom as well as assimilation to new pay scales with additional increments boosted pay for all staff.

Another form of earnings growth arose from changes in the composition of the workforce with an increase in the proportion of higher-paid jobs, especially at managerial levels. For example, despite relative stability in the civil service workforce, between 2000–2009 there was a 37 per cent increase in the number of senior civil servants (Review Body on Senior Salaries 2010: 9), while it has been suggested that the NHS also saw a rapid growth in managerial staff. However, it was the most senior top one per cent of earners, for example those in Foundation trusts less subject to Treasury control over earnings, who pulled away from other groups, even highly paid senior managers, in public sector organisations (Hutton 2010).

Finally, the implementation of performance-related pay schemes was used to boost earnings. The highest profile case was teachers. The government proposed that once teachers had reached the top of the main pay scale, they could apply to cross a 'performance threshold' and, if successful, receive an immediate £2,000 pay increase by moving on to a new upper scale with a maximum salary 25 per cent above the top of the main scale. The opposition of teachers' unions to these proposals focused on the inclusion of 'pupil progress' as one of the eight standards to be assessed and the complexity of the assessment process was also criticised. Despite the widespread reservations of teachers, almost 200,000 (80 per cent of those who were eligible) applied to cross the threshold by the middle of 2000. A few months later, 97 per cent of the teachers who had applied were told that they had met the performance standards and, in the Spring of 2001, received the threshold payment of £2,000 and progressed to the upper pay scale. Not surprisingly advocates of individual performance-related pay dismissed the scheme as a tick-box exercise which has 'failed to generate systemic change' (Wolf 2010: 64), but arguably it was a convenient way for the government to legitimise pay increases needed to address legacy problems of labour supply and low morale.

Maintaining staff on the front line

In addition to increases in pay, the second main component of recruitment and retention strategies addressed *Modernising Government*'s concern that existing pay structures did not encourage staff to remain in front-line roles. Staff frequently had to shift into managerial roles to boost their salary, jobs which were not always attractive to professionals, exacerbating recruitment and retention problems. By reforming existing pay structures and establishing single pay spines to cover all staff in a sector (i.e. NHS, local government), the government created increased scope for career and pay progression whilst enabling staff to remain in front-line roles and concentrate on service delivery. In the NHS, the Careers Framework removed separate occupational silos and identified nine job levels, intended to accommodate workforce innovation. It was envisaged that some levels such as assistant practitioner (level 4) and advanced practitioners (level 7) would expand as new roles evolved. Nursing was in the forefront of these developments with the establishment of clinical specialist/ advanced practitioner roles intended to focus on improving front-line nursing (see Chapter 5). Within medicine, Associate Specialist grades used to be termed 'non-career' grades because they did not lead to consultant posts, but these grades were reformed in 2008, establishing the grade of 'specialty doctor' with improved salary and career prospects (NHS Employers 2008). In schools, a similar process of reforming pay systems to encourage a more differentiated workforce and more scope for career advancement, laterally as well as vertically, has occurred. The main pay scale for teachers was shortened and when teachers reached the top of the main pay scale they had the option to apply to become an Advanced Skills Teacher, demonstrating specialist knowledge in a subject, to apply for Excellent Teacher status or to pursue a more traditional career by becoming a member of the leadership group.

The reform of pay structures may have been a necessary step to encourage workforce reform. However there were unintended consequences, these reforms arguably going too far in encouraging individuals to remain within their professions, so weakening the take-up of traditional managerial roles.

In nursing, nurse specialist roles were viewed as more autonomous and satisfying with less stress enabling the greater use of specialist knowledge compared to demanding ward manager roles (Doherty 2009; RCN 2009; Wise 2007). Within teaching, similar reservations were expressed about the extent to which the expansion of the leadership group and more diverse career paths had narrowed pay differentials and contributed to the reluctance of teachers to put themselves forward for headship roles (Smithers and Robinson 2007). Despite the development of new roles and ways of working (see Chapter 5) considerable doubts remained about the extent to which pay reforms contributed to new ways of working. These concerns have been expressed forcibly in the NHS: 'It is alarming but perhaps not surprising, therefore, that in the context of the sharp expansion in staff numbers and pay levels, workforce reform (which ultimately aims to increase productivity) has received relatively little attention.' (Health Committee 2007: 28). This intemperate language may have been designed to make a political impact, but other evidence highlights the continuing barriers to alter ways of working and sustain new roles within the NHS (Bach et al. forthcoming).

Finally, the government emphasised the importance of making better use of non-pay incentives to indicate that public services were model employers. Public service employers developed a wide range of policies to remove discriminatory practice and enhance work–life balance (Chapter 4). However, following significant increases in public sector pay, a much less favourable public sector expenditure context emerged in the third term of Labour government after 2007. This encouraged a re-orientation of rewards policy and a shift towards a total reward approach. The role of pay was downgraded as the main cause of recruitment and retention problems and an emphasis placed on other aspects of the reward package in a period of pay restraint. The Cabinet Office devised a total rewards framework and toolkit underpinned by the assumption that pay was only one component of the rewards package and which aimed to ensure a better understanding of the total reward package; an improved link between reward strategies and organisational performance; and the use of rewards to improve employee engagement and encourage skills development.

The take-up of the total reward concept was limited, with only 10 per cent of local authorities implementing such an approach by 2010 (Local Government Association 2010: 38). Usually employers adopted total reward principles because they confronted recruitment and retention difficulties and had some discretion to address these challenges. Kent County Council was an indicative case. The authority's benefits programme, outsourced and made accessible via the web, provided staff with opportunities to purchase salary-sacrifice benefits (e.g. childcare vouchers), buy or sell annual leave and access other benefits as part of their compensation (IRS 2008). More common was the government's emphasis on the value of the total remuneration package for those working in the public services, not least the worth of public sector pensions, especially for staff covered by defined benefit pension schemes. Public sector pensions were more generous than private sector provision, a difference which was deepening (Bozio and Disney 2011). In the private sector, pension schemes were in flux with a number of final salary schemes closed to new entrants, employee contributions increased and a shift towards career average earnings occurring.

Contribution-based pay

The final dimension of the modernisation of pay determination was an emphasis on aligning rewards to performance. Conservative government's favoured individual performance-related pay which provoked strong trade union opposition and limited support from managers who mainly used it to increase work effort (Kessler 2000; Marsden 2004). The Labour administration adopted a broader approach to rewards with the intention to move away from pay progression based on annual increments towards some form of performance-based progression. The aim was to reduce the cost of incremental progression, remove a plethora of costly allowances and enhance managerial control. Across the sector the language was softened to make reform more acceptable to the workforce, with performance pay reframed as contribution- or competency-based pay. Progression was linked to the job holder demonstrating that they could apply particular knowledge and behaviours (i.e. competencies), evaluated in the appraisal process. The best-known example of this approach was in the NHS with the Agenda for Change pay reforms establishing an NHS wide career and pay progression system. In local government as well, a mixture of skill acquisition and demonstrating competence was used to enable progression (IDS 2008b: 8).

In the civil service, the Makinson (2000) report recommended that team-based performance bonuses should be used which provided a link between individual and group performance, seen as more meaningful for employees than organisational performance. According to Makinson, team-based rewards fitted the collective ethos of the group better than individual achievement, while making use of existing benchmark data and dealing with negative perceptions in respect to individual performance-related pay. This encouraged experimentation with team-based rewards in Jobcentre Plus, the Inland Revenue and the Child Support Agency linked to achieving operational targets. A series of evaluations of these schemes, however, were extremely cautious and equivocal about the results. In some cases time spent on incentivised activity increased and bonuses were gained, but this was partly attributed to gaming – the establishment of easy targets – and there was no clear impact on productivity or customer service (Burgess et al. 2004; 2005). The government's enthusiasm for team-based rewards subsequently diminished and attention was re-focused on individual performance pay.

Particular emphasis was placed on the contribution of senior managers, recast as 'leaders' and expected to demonstrate behaviours which facilitated change. In primary and secondary schools, prospective head teachers were required to have gained the National Professional Headship Qualification before they could be considered for a headship. Contribution was most likely to be associated with the use of individual performance pay amongst senior managers in the public services, although these schemes differed markedly from those in the private sector. In local government, chief executives could gain bonuses up to 20 per cent of base pay, whilst amongst senior civil servants it comprised about 10 per cent of salary and in the NHS up to 5 per cent of salary (Hutton 2010: 52). Usually these increases were in the form of non-consolidated bonuses, with rules to limit the number of staff in each category or the overall bonus pot. These bonuses were subject to criticism because they applied across the board, regardless of context; the rationale for awarding the bonus or the criteria used was not always clear; and the prevalence of forced distributions militated against motivation and perceptions of fairness (Hutton 2010: 77).

These criticisms indicated that whilst the language had shifted uncertainties remained about how far practice had altered, and shifted away from, annual incremental progression based on seniority. The Confederation of British Industry (CBI) pointed out that length of service remained the most important criterion for progression cited by 70 per cent of public sector employers, although individual performance was the second most common factor (CBI 2006: 15). The CBI, however, failed to point out the contradictory objectives that public service employers confronted. Employers had attempted to reconcile internal equity (to avoid equal pay problems and address low pay) based on the use of narrow pay bands with the need to develop a performance culture, founded upon the award of additional increments or bonuses, but possibly open to legal challenge. Many senior managers had an ambivalent attitude towards rewarding contribution. In part this reflected a belief that the political nature of public services meant the goal posts would inevitably move rendering managers vulnerable to censure. It also reflected the increased transparency of public sector pay, especially at senior levels, and wariness about being associated with the receipt of bonuses and branded a 'fat cat'. Finally, senior managers, such as head teachers, might be reticent about seeking higher pay given limited resources available to governing bodies to allocate higher pay (Smithers and Robinson 2007: 60–61).

Reforms of pay determination

Civil service

In contrast to the NHS and local government, the Labour government inherited more far-reaching reforms of pay determination arrangements in this part of the public services. Following the creation of semi-autonomous executive agencies in the civil service, the Treasury delegated its direct responsibility for negotiating pay and conditions to individual departments and these agencies. This was followed in 1996 by the abolition of civil service wide pay except for the 4,000 most senior civil servants whose pay was determined by a system of independent pay review. In place of a handful of national agreements, more than 150 new bargaining units were created as each department and executive agency established their own pay and grading structures, leading to variation in pay structures (Kessler et al. 2006). Despite this process of delegation, the bargaining process was tightly controlled by the Treasury. It issued guidance to departments and approved the planned pay awards under the so-called remit process. Treasury 'guidance' severely constrained departmental autonomy, for example in 2007–2008, it stated bluntly, 'Basic awards will be no more than 2%' (Treasury 2007b: para 6.1.3).

In allocating the budget for annual pay increases approved by the Treasury, agencies and departments accorded a high priority to dealing with issues of equal pay. The main civil service trade union, PCS, who represented lower-graded staff called for a return to national collective bargaining. The Treasury appeared sympathetic to aspects of this 'coherence agenda', because delegated pay determination led to wide pay disparities between civil servants undertaking the same work and on the same pay grade, but who worked in different departments (Incomes Data Services 2007). The coherence agenda therefore reflected attempts to join-up government. Departments were encouraged to raise minimum starting salaries, reduce inequalities and limit pay dispersion. This agenda dovetailed with an emphasis on ensuring that pay systems were fair and non-discriminatory and fully equality-proofed on an annual basis. The government, however, faced constraints because the expenditure available to remedy equal pay and 'coherence' problems had been squeezed. Nonetheless, with some caveats, the civil service made progress in implementing the Gender Equality Duty (Business, Enterprise and Regulatory Reform Committee 2008: 31) (see Chapter 4).

A major source of conflict arose from the decision in 2004 to implement the staff reductions recommended by Sir Peter Gershon (2004). This process in conjunction with privatisation and the imposition of pay awards resulted in ongoing disputes in the civil service. Two other factors were significant. First, the remit process was disempowering for trade unions, making it difficult to work in partnership with employers (see Chapter 6). Treasury advice stated that 'Departments should not enter into formal negotiations with Trade Unions until their Remit has been agreed' (Treasury 2007: 5.1.6). Following remit approval, however, there was only limited scope for meaningful negotiations on the pay award. Second, the strategy of the dominant civil service trade union, the PCS, had been influential. A highly vocal critic of Labour government policy, the PCS was much less reticent about putting pressure on the government by industrial action compared to other public service trade unions (Sewotka 2007). This strategy proved effective, not least in reaching a national agreement with the Cabinet Office in 2008 to avoid compulsory redundancies for civil servants who were surplus to requirements (Cabinet Office & CCSU 2008).

The National Health Service

The Labour government published its Agenda for Change (AfC) in early 1999, outlining the case for a comprehensive modernisation of NHS pay systems. The proposals were agreed in November 2002 after four years of negotiations between unions, employers and the Department of Health and implemented between 2004–2006. The AfC structure replaced almost 650 staff grades and numerous complex allowances and working arrangements with harmonised terms and conditions and better career progression. This pay structure was designed to address unequal pay, provide rewards based on skill acquisition and responsibility rather than length of service, and to encourage innovative working practices (Department of Health 1999a; 2004a). The pay structure comprised a single pay spine, divided into nine pay bands and underpinned by an NHS wide job evaluation scheme. Staff were allocated to a pay band on the basis of 'job weight' matched with nationally agreed job profiles or determined by job evaluation locally. Pay progression was no longer based exclusively on automatic service-based increments, at key points being linked to a competency-based assessment of knowledge and skills, termed the Knowledge and Skills Framework (KSF). The KSF process not only underpinned pay progression but equally importantly sought to establish a new culture of career development and work redesign, in particular providing opportunities for low-paid staff to progress. AfC covered all staff with the exception of doctors and dentists, under separate contracts, and some top managers.

The ambitious nature of Agenda for Change resulted in a mixed evaluation of its impact. Criticism centred on widespread scepticism about the Department of Health's claim that AfC would bring about productivity savings of 1.1–1.5 per cent per annum, contributing to savings of at least £1.3 billion over the first five years of its implementation. These savings were to be generated by increased productivity, reduced use of agency staff and reductions in equal pay claims, but there was a reluctance by the Department of Health to specify the precise savings associated with pay reform or to actively realise its benefits (Public Accounts Committee 2009: 10). It preferred to emphasise that pay reform was an 'enabler' of changes in working practices, with mixed evidence on its efficacy in these terms. The National Audit Office (2009: 20) in its survey of 189 NHS trust HR directors reported that over half of respondents, 58 per cent, agreed that AfC had been used to create new roles for nursing staff with nearly half agreeing it would deliver higher quality care. However, the NAO's own visits revealed limited examples of new ways of working.

A further criticism related to the implementation of the KSF which lagged other elements of pay modernisation. It was intended to bolster staff development and ensure that pay progression was based on staff achieving the knowledge and skills required in their post, formalised through an annual appraisal and development process. The NHS Review Body (2008: 74) expressed disappointment at the slow implementation of the KSF. Managers suggested that it was too complicated and time-consuming; in practice salary increments remained virtually automatic, making the KSF irrelevant. Despite these limitations, the skills escalator concept encouraged some modest improvements in skills acquisition for ancillary staff and healthcare assistants (Cox 2007; Kessler et al. 2010). There were other misgivings amongst employers, however, especially about the scope for local flexibility. NHS Employers expressed concern that Agenda for Change was a compliance issue, another target to be achieved, rather than a basis for changes in working practices and improved productivity (NHS Employers 2006).

Although these criticisms had some validity, they tended to underplay the urgent need to address equal pay problems, the level of dissatisfaction amongst managers and staff with the previous structure of NHS pay determination and the legacy of previous attempts to reform NHS pay structures, such as the difficulties associated with nurse clinical re-grading in the late 1980s (Bach 2004; Buchan et al. 1998). Moreover the initial proposals identified the need for 'improved status and higher earnings for those who contribute most to the service' (Department of Health 1999a: 4), so it was somewhat churlish to admonish the Department of Health for pursuing this aim. Pay reform brought benefits for many low-paid NHS staff such as cleaners and HCAs, who gained higher pay under AfC, better annual leave entitlement, opportunities for pay progression and career development. AfC was developed in partnership at national level and implemented on this basis locally, bolstering forms of co-operative working in the NHS (Buchan and Evans 2007). It was also noteworthy that despite continuing criticism of Agenda for Change, only one NHS employer – Southend University Hospital – had opted out and this reflected its prior adoption of local pay and conditions in 2006.

Local government

The 1997 'single status' agreement was greeted by employers and trade unions as a major turning-point for employment relations in local government. A national pay spine, based on a jointly agreed job evaluation scheme, was designed to provide a framework within which each local authority could seek local agreement on a grading structure covering all staff. Alongside the harmonisation of basic conditions such as working time and holidays, the agreement greatly increased the prospect of equality of employment between men and women, as well as between manual and white-collar staff. Over the last decade, however, progress on the local implementation of the agreement was slow; less than half of local authorities achieved the deadline of 31 March 2007 for the implementation of equality-proofed local pay and grading structures (IDS 2008b).

This can be explained mainly by the absence of additional funding provided by central government to meet the cost of moving to single-status pay and conditions compared to the funding available to implement Agenda for Change. This reflected the less generous public financing of core local government in comparison to the higher priority assigned to health and education. The measures proposed by some local authorities to offset the costs of single status – for example, to increase productivity or reduce allowances – invariably were resisted by employees and union representatives. This opposition was exacerbated by the anxieties of some groups of white-collar employees who expected to gain nothing from assimilation onto a single pay spine, and the fears of manual workers that they would lose their bonus payments and allowances, prompting industrial action in a few authorities (IDS 2008c). In addition, some specialist professional groups, such as social workers, emerged poorly from local job evaluation exercises, exacerbating severe recruitment and retention problems (NJC for Local Government Services 2010).

Whilst these problems were not insurmountable, they had to be confronted alongside more immediate priorities, in particular reviewing the quality of services to ensure 'best value' and the subsequent requirement to obtain good ratings in the system of comprehensive performance assessment (Bovaird and Downe 2006). By early 2008, almost half of local authorities had completed pay reviews at an estimated cost of £2.8 billion. These pay structures incorporated many aspects of the modernisation agenda with an emphasis on equal pay and progression based on the acquisition of competencies, and contribution. The main beneficiaries were low-paid women such as carers and cooks. Nonetheless, the obstacles which delayed the implementation of the local government agreement revealed the scope and complexity of the government's pay modernisation proposals and the continuing vulnerability of many public sector employers to equal pay claims.

By contrast, the government celebrated the success of the reforms of the school workforce. The School Teachers' Review Body (STRB), in response to union pressure, played an important role in highlighting key issues of teacher shortages and unsustainable workloads, providing the impetus for government action. The proposed solution known as *Re-modelling the School Workforce* resulted in a national agreement in 2003 amongst the government, employers and school workforce unions, except the National Union of Teachers (NUT), to reform the school workforce and reduce teachers' workload (DfES 2003) (see also Chapter 5). The national agreement outlined a three-year phased process of implementation which included the removal of 24 administrative tasks from teachers, a maximum 38 hour annual limit for covering for absent teachers and guaranteed planning, preparation and assessment time amounting to 10 per cent of normal timetabled teaching time. Implementation of the agreement was undertaken by the Workforce Agreement Monitoring Group (WAMG) comprised of unions, employers and government, demonstrating the value of partnership working. WAMG encouraged further partnership working to bring about employer–union agreement in re-structuring teachers' pay (Stevenson 2007).

The workforce agreement was the trigger for further reforms of the school workforce with all schools required to review their staffing structures. The School Teachers' Review Body supported plans for the abolition of management allowances with proposals developed on a partnership basis under the auspices of the Rewards and Incentive Group (RIG). The main goal of these reforms was to reinforce the link between rewards and performance for teachers who passed through the performance threshold, directing payments at teachers who raised standards rather than those with the greatest administrative burden. Teachers could gain additional income linked to contribution, either in terms of taking on extra responsibilities which resulted in high-quality teaching or by demonstrating excellent results and thereby qualifying for the excellent teacher scheme. The implementation of these proposals was not straightforward and in May 2007 only 34 Excellent Teachers (ETs) were in post. The STRB (2008) remained concerned about the implementation of the ET scheme, especially the positioning of ETs within an increasingly complex pay structure and more broadly the STRB was frustrated by the unwillingness of schools to utilise their existing pay flexibilities to address recruitment and retention and other local priorities.

Conclusion

The Labour government inherited a series of deep-seated problems with the existing systems of pay determination which failed to ensure adequate recruitment and retention, to address equal pay problems or to systematically encourage changes in performance and working practices. *Modernising Government* set out a clear set of principles for pay reform and significant changes in pay systems occurred, but they fell short of the principles set out in 1999. Pay determination in the public sector in terms of process and outcome differed substantially from the private sector and this resulted in much greater compression of wages within the public sector than in the private sector and a smaller element of pay being 'at risk'. Although new public management rhetoric of incentives and performance was prominent, its application was uneven. Essentially the priorities of employers overlapped imperfectly with those of central government.

For the Labour government, sensitive to concerns about equality and staff shortages, the priority was to uplift the remuneration of the workforce, especially the lower-paid, focusing on internal equity within national pay structures. Employers, however, were more concerned with the recruitment and retention of professional and specialist staff with a greater focus on their external worth. Employers also expressed disquiet about the compression of pay structures and limited scope to reward contribution with continuing use of incremental pay progression (CBI 2006). At the same time, employers often proved reluctant to use available flexibilities in existing national pay systems given uncertainties about the response of the workforce, concerns about the availability of resources and an awareness of central government, especially the Treasury, intrusiveness.

It was therefore more straightforward for central government and employers to use the stick of centrally defined and monitored targets to drive through changes in service standards, rather than use the carrot of altered pay incentives, which many staff received without significantly altering their behaviour and working practices. The spread of individual performance appraisal contributed to this trend, although its role in strengthening performance management should not be overstated as its implementation remained uneven and it was not always closely aligned to performance targets. The shortcomings of this approach, however, were evident with staff required to work harder rather than smarter. Consequently, the immediate work experience of most public sector staff was shaped primarily by the priority assigned to key government targets, reinforcing a sense of disempowerment and making staff relatively unreceptive to measures which reinvented the model employer tradition, including higher salaries and policies of work–life balance considered in the next chapter.

4

Employment relations: flexibilities and equalities

Introduction

This chapter focuses on patterns of working, often conceptualised in terms of flexibility, and on workforce equalities, typically seen as embracing the management of equal opportunities and diversity. The two are often associated, most obviously in the case of gender, where enduring differences in the distribution of domestic responsibilities have often produced variation in the take-up of flexible forms of employment between men and women (DWP 2009). Under New Labour, flexibility and equality connected to the modernisation of public services in a number of ways. First, they formed part of a much broader New Labour public policy agenda which embraced public service organisations, along with other employers across the economy. This was a progressive agenda in that it sought a new and radical shift in policy and practice. Over its three terms in government, New Labour enacted more than 20 legislative changes directly related to flexibility and equality. Public policy support for workplace flexibility and equality was designed to strengthen individual employment rights, sitting alongside other developments such as the introduction of the National Minimum Wage, whilst also boosting levels of labour market participation, complementing wider welfare changes, including the use of tax credits to incentivise work (DWP 2010).

Second, workforce flexibility and equality were more directly taken forward by New Labour as elements of public services modernisation. Flexibility supported new forms of service delivery, with moves away from standard working hours, for example, supporting the provision of services at the convenience of the user rather than the producer. Lifestyle flexibilities

73

were also used as a reward, often being included in packages of measures designed to enlist employee commitment to high-quality service provision (see Chapter 3). In a more general sense, the link between equalities and public service modernisation was based on a set of values which suggested that workplace inequalities, whether on the basis of gender, race, age, disability or sexual orientation, were incompatible with modern employment relations. If, as highlighted in Chapter 3, unequal treatment was inimical to a 'modern' public sector pay system, it was certainly not legitimate in relation to any other human resource practice in the public services, for example, recruitment, training, appraisal or career development. There was also a more pragmatic, business case for equal opportunities: they were seen as a means of making the public service (more) attractive as an employer to diverse groups, so addressing labour supply issues and consequently enhancing the efficiency and effectiveness of service delivery.

Third, and perhaps most distinctive was New Labour's attempt to harness flexibility and equality in the provision of public services to a broader, more ambitious agenda related to user engagement with the state. A diverse and adaptable workforce was envisaged as supporting *fairer* service delivery, particularly to communities varying in terms of their social, ethnic and economic make-up. As *Modernising Government* stressed:

> The public service must be a part of, and not apart from, the society it serves. It should reflect the full diversity of society…Addressing this is a top priority. The Government wants a public service which values the differences that people bring to it. (Cabinet Office 1999: 59)

This chapter is mainly concerned with workforce flexibility and equality as they directly related to New Labour's public service modernisation programme, and how their pursuit in the public services was linked to a broader public policy agenda on fairness in service delivery. It is divided into two main parts: the first explores different forms of flexibility across the public services; the second, concentrates on equality as it related to gender, race, disability, age and sexual orientation. In both parts attention will be given to the rationale for New Labour initiatives on flexibility and equality; the range of policies and practices implemented; and their impact on various stakeholders. The chapter argues that under New Labour public service organisations remained relatively progressive in their approach to flexibility and equality. However, adopting a 'harder', target-driven approach and linking policies to a broader fairness agenda, it will be suggested that the government also sought to re-establish its 'model employer' status. How effectively this intent was realised is open to greater debate, with some unevenness in the impact of these policies and practices on the management of public service organisations and on the working lives of public servants.

Flexibilities

Attention focuses on three forms of workforce flexibility. The first is working time flexibility, reflected in the scope to vary hours worked, typically amongst those employed by the organisation on a permanent basis and covering: part time workers and job sharers; more novel patterns, such as an annualised and zero hours contracts; and traditional arrangements, including overtime and shift working. The second is flexibility which facilitates rapid and contingent change in the numbers of workers employed by the organisation through the use of non-permanent forms of employment: casual, short-term contract and agency workers. The third form of flexibility captures those working in an organisation, while being employed by another. Again this would include agency workers but on a larger scale, those engaged in outsourced activities employed by an external organisation, the contractor. Once more this form of working is usually for a fixed period, but it does raise some distinctive employment relations issues.

Working time flexibilities

In general policy terms, New Labour's approach to working time flexibility was presented as supporting the pursuit of a work–life balance agenda. Government policies in relation to such flexibilities were not without their ambiguities. The Part Time Workers (Prevention of Less Favourable Treatment) Regulations, 2000, derived from an EU directive rather than from domestic policy, while the government rigorously sought to retain an opt-out from the Working Time Directive, which allowed workers to choose to work over 48 hours if they wished. At the same time, however, the government implemented a raft of measures to encourage work–life balance: the Working Time Regulations, 1998, and the Flexible Working (Eligibility, Complaints and Remedies) Regulations, 2002, provided employees with young children the right to request flexible working arrangements, rights extended to a wider range of workers under the Flexible Working Regulation, 2006.

In important respects, the public services were ahead of this legislative agenda, with working time flexibilities an established feature of employment in the sector. This reflected the nature of certain services, particularly the NHS, where shift working was common, and the needs of the specific organisations, with, for example, term-time working amongst teaching support workers providing schools with cost efficiencies. Such flexibility was also apparent in the relatively high incidence of part-time working in the public sector. In 1999, around a third of public servants were working on a part-time basis, compared to just under a quarter in the private sector, figures which remained fairly stable over the New Labour period (Mathews 2010: 34). It was a difference largely accounted for by the gender composition of the respective workforces: at this time, close to two-thirds of the public sector workforce was made up of women, compared to around 40 per cent in the private sector (ibid: 32).

Notwithstanding these entrenched practices, a progressive legislative programme on working time made it difficult for New Labour not to promote working time flexibility in the public services. This point was stressed by the Family Friendly Working Hours Task Force (DWP 2009: 9) which recommended that the 'Government continues to lead by example and actively encourage central government departments and other public sector organisations to improve their own practices in terms of designing and managing flexible jobs at all levels'. It was a recommendation that the government was prepared to accept, noting that 'We fully recognize our role as an exemplar of flexible working practices (DWP 2010: 12).'

The rationale for the pursuit of working time flexibility in the public services (and elsewhere) was seen to lie in mutual employee and management gain from the practice. Such flexibility allowed employees to develop working patterns sensitive to their lifestyle choices and domestic responsibilities, while for employers it provided a basis for motivating, recruiting and retaining staff. As noted in an NHS context, 'staff work best for patients when they can strike a healthy balance between work and other aspects of their life outside work'. While in local government Cambridgeshire County Council was showcased as an authority using flexibility to address labour supply issues (http://www.audit–commission.gov.uk/localgov/goodpractice/leadership/Pages/cambridgeshirerecrutimentandrentionissues.aspx). A number of the public service unions were willing to leverage this business case argument in campaigns for working time flexibility. For example, Unison's Work–Life Balance (Undated: 5) campaign launched in 2002 noted that 'The concept of work-life balance, of which flexible working is a part, is that if people could improve the balance between the demands of their work and the demands of their home life they would be more satisfied at work and be more productive'.

New Labour's pursuit of a working time flexibility agenda in the public services needs to distinguish between policy and practice. In policy terms there were signals of the importance attached to such flexibility in different parts of the sector. In the civil service, for example, a work–life balance guide for line managers, stressing that 'A flexible approach to work is essential in a modern Civil Service' (Foreign and Commonwealth Office 2002) was supported by a number of innovative approaches such as a cross-departmental online and job sharing board (http://www.fda.org.uk/Media/whats-new/FDA-supports-new-online-civil-service-job-share-board.aspx) and in certain departments work–life balance frameworks provided various options on working patterns (Foster 2008). One of the most significant policy initiatives, in terms of scale and prescriptive detail, was in the NHS where the Improving Working Lives Standard, developed in 2001 and 'refreshed' by the NHS Staff Council in 2009, made a number of commitments on working time within the context of staff well-being, reinforced by performance targets designed to ensure implementation by Trusts (Department of Health 2000a). Trusts were tasked with developing, and regularly reviewing, with staff input, a specific strategy to address flexible working patterns and supportive, family-friendly policies as a means of addressing the 'long-hours culture' in healthcare.

Across the public services, these initiatives provided staff with enhanced opportunities to take up working time flexibilities. An index of flexibility developed in the Third Work Life Balance (WLB) *Employee* Survey (Hooker et al. 2007: 173), which combined the number of such flexibilities available with a measure for employer encouragement of such working, found that almost a third of public sector employees (30 per cent) worked in 'high flexibility' organisations compared to under a quarter of private sector employees (23 per cent). The WLB *Employer* survey (Hayward 2007: 101) revealed that with the exception of working flexi-time, a higher proportion of public than private sector organisations were offering all other forms of working time flexibility. The contrast was particularly stark in the case of job sharing, with over three quarters of public sector organisations (78 per cent) providing this option, compared to just over a half in the private sector. The survey also revealed that in almost all public service organisations part-time working was available (96 per cent), in over half (51 per cent) staff could work flexi-time, and almost a third (32 per cent) could work from home on a regular basis. Moreover, many working time flexibilities had been introduced under the New Labour government, the second WLB survey in 2003 finding that a third of public sector employers had adopted work–life balance practices in the past three years (Woodland et al. 2003).

Questions remain, however, about practice, that is the *effective* implementation of these policies. Certainly the Third WLB Employers Survey (Hayward 2007: 105) suggested that the take-up of all forms of flexible working time was higher in the public than the private sector: in most public sector organisations part time work was taken up while job sharing and working flexi-time was taken up in around third. The Employee WLB survey (Hooker 2007: 171) revealed that almost three quarters (71 per cent) of public sector workers were content with the hours they worked, while in a survey of Unison members the Work Foundation found that 70 per cent of members were 'very' or 'fairly satisfied with their job, all things considered'(Visser and Williams 2006: 21).

However, there were difficulties in implementing working time flexibilities in the public services, while adverse employee outcomes also emerged. There were claims that opportunities to meaningfully pursue a work–life balance had been driven-out by work pressures. The civil service union, the PCS noted: 'Instead of the Government leading by example and the Civil Service implementing good work life balance policies, the efficiency agenda has led to longer hours ... and withdrawal of opportunities for flexible working. Even where good policies exist workloads prevent people from taking advantage of them' (www.pcs.org.uk/en/resources/welleing_at_work). This view found some support in the Employee Work Life Balance survey, (Hooker 2007: 89) which indicated that a significant majority of managerial (76 per cent) and non-managerial (59 per cent) public servants felt workload had increased compared with three years ago, markedly higher figures than for workers in the private sector where the respective figures were 62 per cent and 34 per cent. Moreover a Unison survey revealed that the 'solutions' offered by public sector employers to work–life balance issues were not always compatible with member needs (Visser and Wlliams 2006: 7).

There were also organisational barriers to the introduction of such flexibilities. A review of recruitment practices in the civil service indicated that almost three quarters of jobs were advertised as full-time positions, although many roles were suitable for part-time staff (Woods 2009). Moreover, there was evidence of inconsistent practice in the use of such flexibilities across the civil service. The Civil Service Manager's Work–Life Balance guide noted that 'Despite a firm commitment across the Service [to] different working patterns ... many managers experience difficulties when they try to put work life balance policies into practice' (Foreign and Commonwealth Office 2002). Indeed a review of the Defra initiative showed an inconsistency in the take-up of flexibilities even within the same department, reflecting differences in line manager sensitivity to such an approach (Foster 2008).

Finally, despite the mutual gains rationale, certain forms of working time flexibility had detrimental consequences for employee working lives. This was particularly the case in relation to term-time working in education; an increasingly common practice under New Labour with the growth in teaching assistant numbers (see Chapters 2 and 5). Lewis (2002) in a review of term-time working, undertaken for Unison, suggested that it was often not a choice but a requirement, depressing earnings opportunities and other entitlements such as holidays and pensions.

Temporary working

If working time flexibilities within the public services under New Labour were presented and often taken forward on the basis of mutual worker and employer gain, temporary working was perceived and deployed in a much more ambiguous way. While temporary working takes different forms, it is generally characterised as precarious, being founded on fixed-term employment. For various stakeholders in the public services, employers as well as employees, such practices generated highly contradictory outcomes (Tailby 2005; Conley 2006).

For public service employers, the use of temporary workers proved an important means of dealing not only with routine and immediate absences but with longer-term fluctuations in labour supply. In this respect public sector employers were no different from employers in other sectors. However, volatility in the availability of staff, particularly amongst professionals, was especially acute in the public services under New Labour, with additional pressures to meet targets for the employment of certain groups, and the need to maintain staff complements to deliver quality services.

There were some differences between parts of the sector in the incidence of temporary working in the context of these contingent needs. In education, the use of supply teachers actually went down over the New Labour period (NUT 2010), partly a consequence of emerging higher-level teaching assistant roles performing the kind of cover work formerly undertaken by these teachers and the establishment of cover supervisor roles. Other sub-sectors faced pressing issues which forced the use of temporary workers. In the NHS, for instance, the implementation of the Working Time Directive had a significant impact on the use of locums and agency clinicians. The Royal College of Surgeons noted an increase in expenditure on such workers from 214 million pounds in 1996–1997 to more than 750 million pounds in 2009–2010 (Royal College of Surgeons in England 2010).

There was also variation by sub-sector in how such workers were used. Kirkpatrick et al. (2009: 10), in a study of agency working amongst nurses and social workers, found that hospitals planned around the use of agency staff, engaging them as a means of coping with 'the ebbs and flows in the demand for services, activity rates and levels of patient dependency'. Local authorities appeared to lack the capacity for such planning, deploying agency social workers in a much more ad hoc and opportunistic way to cover short-term vacancies. Such variation in the use of temporary staff was even apparent in the same part of the public services, the National Audit Office finding that the use of temporary nursing staff in NHS Trusts could range from less than 1 per cent up to 29 per cent (NAO 2006b.)

In terms of outcomes, it might be argued that the use of temporary workers had certain organisational benefits: they were possibly less complacent and keener to impress management with their commitment and energy. However, the deployment of such temporary workers also generated problems for public service employers, threatening aspects of New Labour's modernisation project. Most striking were the cost implications of temporary staff. The cost of long-term agency staff in English social services departments rose from 148 million pounds in 2001 to 255 million pounds in 2005 (Kirkpatrick et al. 2009: 7). In the NHS, expenditure on agency staff peaked in 2001–2002 at around 6.8 per cent of nursing expenditure, a figure which prompted government moves to tighten up the use of such workers. This was reflected in trust performance targets which sought regular reductions in expenditure on agency staff. However, this was a move which tended to re-distribute rather than significantly reduce spending. The NAO reported that between 2003–2004 and 2004–2005 expenditure on agency staff fell by 25 per cent from 330 to 240 million pounds, while over the same period, the amount spent on bank staff increased by 10 per cent from 500 to 550 million pounds (NAO 2006b: 12). At the same time it might be argued that bank workers were better value for money: much cheaper than agency staff and often more familiar with the trust and its routines (NAO 2006b: 28).

In addition to cost, the deployment of any type of temporary worker introduced an element of uncertainty into public service provision with potential consequences for staff management and service quality. In a review of evidence on the consequences of temporary working amongst registered nurses, Mercer et al. (2010) highlighted the added supervisory burden on ward managers, and the failure of ward staff to report poor performance by temporary workers. More striking were the concerns about patient safety highlighted by the NAO (2006b: 30) and reinforced by Department of Health (2007a) findings which suggested the greater the use of temporary staff, the higher incidence of hospital acquired infections. This link between care quality and temporary working was also reflected in witness statements to the Francis

Inquiry into the Mid Staffordshire Foundation Trust (Francis 2010: 40). It was most strikingly illustrated in findings from Lord Laming's inquiry into public services failures which led to the murder of Victoria Climbé by her carers. In all three local authorities dealing with this child, extensive use was made of temporary social workers, often from abroad, in response to recruitment difficulties, with major questions raised about their competence in dealing with the case (Laming 2003: 73).

For public service workers, the use of temporary employment also had mixed outcomes, dependent on the form assumed by the practice, the type of employee and the sub-sector. Temporary workers in the sector sometimes faced less favourable treatment than that received by permanent staff. For example, Ball and Pike (2006), in an RCN commissioned survey of nurses working on a temporary basis, revealed that almost a third (32 per cent) did not have 'access to the professional development they needed'. More significantly, Tailby (2005) linked temporary working to the gendered nature of nursing, suggesting that bank working, in particular, was often a pragmatic response by women to coping with domestic responsibilities given limited hospital support for the work–life balance agenda. Such working was seen by few of these nurses as a satisfactory option, although certainly more attractive than the perceived stress and uncertainty associated with agency working. In the case of supply teachers, temporary working was also often a forced choice, almost a half (41 per cent) of those responding to an NASUWT survey indicating that supply teaching was a means of supplementing their teachers' pensions (NASUWT 2008). Those supply teachers employed directly by the local authority were covered by statutory rules on pay, but the growing number employed by agencies was not protected. As the NUT (2010: 4) noted, 'Many agencies undercut the national pay rates and conditions applicable to teachers employed directly by local authorities and schools.'

However, these negative employee consequences were not universal, some public service professionals valued temporary working. Amongst social workers in local government, agency working was often a deliberate career choice. Kirkpatrick and Hoque (2006) highlighted how agency work amongst social workers, in tight labour market conditions, allowed them to pick and choose their assignments. Moreover, in contrast to supply teaching, the pay rates for social workers employed by agencies were typically much higher than for social workers employed in-house. It was equally clear that agency working was used by social workers to avoid 'workplace politics' and associated stress, particularly acute within target-driven local authority social services departments. In addition, there was the growth of the interim manager role in the public services, a role with some attraction to the individual looking for a more flexible working life. Typically employed on a rolling contract, this role assumed particular significance in 'recovering' local authorities, those judged as 'poor' or 'failing', which sometimes resulted in the removal of senior managers and the need for a quick replacement, specifically to lead change and improvement in the short term (Jas 2004).

Outside contractors

In the 1980s and early 1990s, Conservative governments sought flexibility by engaging the private sector in the delivery of public services, with significant implications for the workforce. Whilst the outcomes for workers were not invariably detrimental, career opportunities sometimes opening-up (Kessler et al. 1999), in the main outsourcing, especially in the form of competitive tendering, introduced greater uncertainty into the employment relationship and placed downward pressure on labour costs (Escott and Whitfield 1995; Conley 2006). The Labour government provided a new rationale for forms of service delivery, a shift from ideology to efficacy in determining the appropriate provider, but in practice this resulted in the continued, indeed the extended, involvement of private, and independent, sector contractors as public service providers, with implications for the management of employee relations.

The involvement of outside contractors in the provision of public services took various forms, each with slightly differing objectives. The first was the outsourcing of discrete ancillary or back office activities, such as catering, cleaning, payroll and facilities management. New Labour softened the approach to this form of outsourcing, replacing CCT with the benchmarking Best Value process in local government (Vincent-Jones 1999), whilst still intensifying pressure to contract-out such activities in later years in pursuit of efficiency savings (see Chapter 5). The second placed publicly funded core services beyond the boundaries of the public sector to be delivered by private or independent sector organisations. Under this form of outsourcing New Labour was seeking partner providers, perhaps better positioned in terms of resource and capability, to increase service capacity; a process reflected in the establishment of the independent sector treatment centres in the NHS. The third stream was a raft of Private Finance Initiatives (PFI) or Public Private Partnerships (PPP). Again inter-organisational networks were being established, with the government in this instance seeking collaborators to renew and maintain the public services capital infrastructure (Allen 2001; Audit Commission 2003; Pollock 2005).

Clearly these three externalisation streams were indicative of the networked model of public service provision outlined in Chapter 2, with significant consequences for the management of the workforce. These consequences were in part related to the traditional employee relations agenda, the impact on pay and other terms and conditions of employment. In general, there were claims that externalisation or the commodification of public services eroded or degraded such terms and conditions (Whitfield 2006: 72), a view encouraging considerable union opposition to externalisation in any form (Unison 2008a). The evidence base suggested a more nuanced picture. More specifically, New Labour progressively sought to safeguard the treatment of public service workers employed by outside contractors, driven by concerns about service quality and by expediency in the context of union pressures.

Bach and Givan (2010) have stressed the role played by the government in re-regulating employment relations in the context of outside provision of public services. The Care Standards Act, 2000, set out minimum standards for care in private and independent sector nursing homes, which included aspects of workforce management such as staff training and qualifications (Care Quality Commission 2010a). In the public sector, the government stressed the importance of maintaining worker terms and conditions of employment as outside contractors competed to provide public services. As Tony Blair noted:

> We want to ensure that when services are contracted out, it is not done on the basis of poorer terms and conditions of employment of staff. One of the things that we have learned over the past few years, not only under this Government but under the previous Government, is that if the impact of contracting out is simply to undermine the terms and conditions of staff, it will not usually lead to better services. (Hansard 2001)

The Transfer of Undertakings (Protection of Employees) Regulations protected the main terms and condition of those workers transferred to a private provider. The major gap in the protection lay with workers employed after any transfer, who could be employed on inferior terms and conditions giving rise to a 'two tier workforce'. Ruane (2007), in her study of ancillary health-care staff working under a number of PFI arrangements, highlighted the scale of inequality arising in such circumstances. This issue was addressed in local government with the introduction of the Best Value Code of Practice on Workforce Matters in 2003, extended to the rest of the public sector as part of the Warwick Agreement in 2005 and then confirmed as applying to re-tendered contracts. This did not prevent debate on the efficacy of these Codes, Unison in particular, contesting their value and coverage. In a survey conducted in January 2008 it found that well over half their branches (59 per cent) claimed that they had not been consulted by their employers on the Code, with just half (42 per cent) more significantly revealing that the Code had yet to be applied by their employer (Unison 2008b).

Notwithstanding these union concerns, the residual protection of substantive terms and conditions of employment encouraged alternative employer approaches to the control of labour costs: employing fewer people, working harder. Studies by Ruane (2007) and Grimshaw and Hebson (2005) highlighted the alacrity with which private providers reduced staff and made redundancies following the service transfer. They similarly noted an intensification of work, tight performance requirements and close monitoring invariably being embedded in the service contracts. This is not to deny some contingency in the treatment of public service staff following their transfer to the private sector. These same studies revealed that there were variations in how employers managed the transfer both in procedural and substantive terms. Moreover, through a series of case studies in health and local government, the Involvement and Participation Association (2010) highlighted how outsourcing on a partnership basis could safeguard working conditions. In these instances a collaborative approach secured union recognition agreements and the smooth implementation of the Code of Practice on Workforce Matters. Unison (2008: 4) could also point to instances where local authorities, such as Newcastle, Dudley and Haringey, had included 'TUPE-plus' clauses in their contracts, and the example of the Greater London Authority which required contractors to pay no less than £7.20 an hour for all directly and indirectly employed staff.

Externalisation had more novel consequences, beyond the traditional preoccupation with terms and conditions of employment. Networked organisational arrangements added a new complexity to workforce management, reflected not least in the disruption of the normally dyadic relationship between worker and employer. As noted, provider partnerships involved a range of independent organisations, possibly from different sectors of the economy and with their own workforces, engaged or contracted to provide the same or often complementary public services.

Researchers have drawn attention to a range of distinctive issues arising in such circumstances (Marchington et al. 2005; Coyle-Shapiro et al. 2006; Bach and Givan 2010; Grimshaw et al. 2010). These have included matters related to the management of worker identity and commitment: where do worker loyalties lie if, for example, they are working in a public sector organisation but employed by another, the provider contract company? They have concerned employee voice and communication: how and to whom do workers express their views in such circumstances? They have related to staff training and development: where does the responsibility for such support rest, with the commissioner or the provider?

In the specific context of contract-provider relations, there is strong evidence to suggest that contract employees working in a public service organisation are sensitive to their treatment both by the commissioner of their services, and by their direct employer, the contract firm or agency (Coyle-Shapiro et al. 2006). These workers reciprocated fair treatment by both parties with positive service behaviours. However, these complex employment relations issues within networked organisational arrangements often appeared to be marginalised, overlooked or perceived by managers as too challenging (Marchington et al. 2005; Grimshaw et al. 2010). Although contracts with providers might import certain public service norms into the treatment of users and staff (Bach and Givan 2010), the commissioning process establishing partnership or outsourcing relations rarely extended to 'softer' employee relations issues. Despite participation in partnership projects, respective networked organisations remained discrete and independent entities, typically driven by their own, self-seeking business and human resource management goals and strategies and unwilling or unable to develop more integrated approaches to the treatment of staff.

Equality and diversity

Legacy

In many developed economies, the public services have been presented as the source of 'good practice' on equal opportunities (Byron 2010: 437). An emphasis on transparency and accountability in public sector bureaucracies has encouraged procedural fairness, reflected not least in the development of policies designed to deal with workforce inequalities. There has, however, been considerable debate about the efficacy of formal policies on this aspect of employment. Jewson and Mason (1986) were amongst the first to question the effectiveness of a liberal agenda based on procedural action, particularly relative to a more radical agenda based on outcomes, and a longer-term agenda seeking to address structural and systemic causes of unequal treatment. A liberal agenda was seen by the authors as a flawed means of addressing the disadvantage many social groups still faced in engaging with notionally fair procedures or the informal power relations still underpinning them.

In Britain, the history of equal opportunities in the public services has mainly been taken forward on the basis of a procedurally driven liberal agenda. This is not to ignore fluctuations in the sector's approach to equality over the years. It was indicative of the narrow view taken of equal opportunities in the public sector during the interwar years that Stampe (1930: 47), in an article published in *Public Administration*, could define equal opportunity as ensuring that 'men shall be trained and tested so that each shall have [an] adequate chance to develop and disclose their potentialities.' However, in the 30 years following the Second World War, this emphasis on procedural fairness, along with the attempts to deal with the most striking substantive examples of discrimination, mainly on grounds of gender and race, prevailed. Corby (2007) noted measures, particularly in the civil service, to address equal pay and sex discrimination well before any statutory requirements; while in local government attempts were made to address such issues through contract compliance, ensuring the inclusion of equal opportunities principles in procurement policy.

The Conservative governments of the 1980s and early 1990s pulled back from such an approach with legislation prohibiting contract compliance and budgetary constraints limiting the scope for local authority action. These moves were linked by some to a new public management agenda inimical to equal opportunities in the public sector. Cunningham (2000) stressed the different ways in which NPM worked against the effective management of equal opportunities. These included an emphasis on competitive values, making adherence to equal opportunities contingent on the 'business case', along with new power relations in disaggregated organisational structures allowing the development of divergent practice and limiting the space for specialist equal opportunities managers to address such issues. Indeed for Dickens (1999: 11) the cost-based, market-driven rationale for diversity within the context of NPM marked a move away from 'bureaucratic personnel-driven equal opportunities initiatives' and the consequent surrender of the public sector's claim to 'good employer' status.

The resilience of equal opportunities policies and practice during this period of Conservative government should not, however, be overlooked. On the cusp of New Labour taking office, formal equal opportunities policies were near universal in the sector (Dex and Forth 2009). In a more detailed analysis of the WERS 1998 data, Hoque and Noon (2004) found that equal opportunities approaches in the public sector were much less likely to constitute an 'empty shell' than in the private sector: formal policies tended to be supported by and given meaningful effect in specific practices. Throughout the period of Conservative government some parts of the public sector, particularly in Labour-controlled local authorities, (Coyle 1989) continued to pursue and deepen their equal opportunities, albeit in the context of the financial pressures exerted by central government; while in the final phase of Conservative government, targets and action programmes were introduced to deal with the employment of women and minority groups in the civil service (Corby 2007).

General approach

New Labour's approach to equality and diversity in the public services marked a departure from past practice. There were aspects of continuity, but these were often reconfigured and combined with genuinely novel elements to produce a new, hybrid programme for action. There was an extension of the equalities agenda to cover a broader range of social groups. On taking office, equality concerns were mainly limited to gender, race and disability. The Labour government added new strands: religion/beliefs, sexual orientation and age (NAO 2004). These six strands informed broader public policy and legislative change, affecting public service organisations along with others in the economy.

The government also sought to reclaim the title of 'model employer' on equal opportunities. New Labour was aware of its past reputation in this respect. As *Modernising Government* asserted, 'The public service has a strong tradition of fairness. It is committed to achieving equality of opportunity.' (Cabinet Office 1999: 59). This model employer aspiration was echoed in different parts of the public services. In the equalities statement Vital Connection, the NHS set out its goal 'to ensure that [it] is a good employer in achieving equal opportunities and fair outcomes at the workplace' (Department of Heath 2000: 19). Similarly the Local Authority Equality Standard (I&Dea 2007) referred to the importance of local authorities adopting 'good practice', while the NAO (2004) in its review of diversity uses 'good practice' to evaluate performance of public service organisations in this respect.

Of course, the nature of this 'model employer' approach still remains open. It was the move away from a bureaucratic proceduralism to a business case model which led Dickens (1999) to suggest that the public sector had forfeited its right to 'model employer' status. Was the model employer claim by New Labour solely rhetorical? If not, did New Labour move away from a business case model based on a managerial notion of diversity? If so, was this a return to the liberal agenda of bureaucratic proceduralism or a new approach providing an alternative rationale for good employer status?

Certainly diversity management as a means of relating employee differences to business need remained woven into government rhetoric. Gus O'Donnell, Secretary to the Cabinet and Head of the Home Civil service in a speech entitled 'The Modern Civil Service' (2006) asserted that 'Diversity is more than a moral imperative – it is also a business imperative ... By improving diversity we are broadening our talent pool as well as gaining greater insight into the society we serve.' This implies that the business case approach to equalities was partly related to expediencies, in particular the need to address the recruitment and retention of staff. Similarly Options for Excellence (Department of Health 2009a: 35) suggested that dealing with the 'poor image' of the social work profession and its high vacancy and turnover rates involved 'sending out a clear message that the social care sector is characterized by diversity, with a multitude of people who work in and use that service.'

At the same time, New Labour's approach marked a partial break with the business case model. While diversity management's preoccupation with employee uniqueness seemed to resonate with the government's person-centred values, substantive policy and practice was rooted in more traditional assumptions, which viewed inequalities in public service sector employment as stemming from membership of social categories: the six equality strands highlighted. More profoundly, the government's approach was underpinned by a value-based emphasis on equality as a means of addressing and furthering community inclusion. New Labour policy on equalities and diversity in the public services was driven by the Macpherson Report (1999) on the police handling of the Stephen Lawrence murder, published early on in the period of New Labour government. This provided the impetus for a much *stronger and broader* approach to equalities and diversity in the public services informed by the 'rightness' of delivering quality services to diverse communities (Cabinet Office 1999).

The *stronger* approach, moving New Labour closer to Jewson and Mason's radical agenda, was based upon the more extensive use of output targets to achieve equality aims. In local government and healthcare, equality was linked to standards with clear requirements on the design, implementation and outcomes associated with equalities policies. These features were reflected in the Workplace Employment Relations Survey, 2004, carried out in the early stages of this stronger approach. Equalities targets, monitoring and review practices were more likely in public than in private sector organisations. Indeed, more than a quarter of public sector workplaces (27 per cent) were found to engage in equal opportunities measurement compared to 14 percent of private sector workplaces. The proportion of public sector workplaces using special procedures to attract applicants from ethnic minorities had fallen, but in the context of the other findings, it might be argued that this was illustrative of the shift from a 'bureaucratic personnel driven' approach, to one based on harder outcome measures (Kersley et al. 2006; Walsh 2007).

The *broader* approach was reflected in the attempt to integrate equality and diversity in the public service workforce with the delivery of public services sensitive to diverse communities. Macpherson's exposure of 'institutional racism' within the police force highlighted the tragic consequences of embedded discriminatory public service structures and systems: the failure to adequately respond to and investigate the murder of a black youth. This link between workforce and service equality was summarised by the Treasury in its departmental equality scheme: 'Diversity is about how we do business as well as the people we employ' (Treasury 2010: 5). It was this connection which opened up a new set of diversity issues for public service organisations, encouraging a focus on how public servants engaged with diverse communities: employee preparation and capabilities in this respect. As the Local Government Workforce Strategy, 2010: 7 noted: 'In many areas there has been an increase in ethnic diversity. As part of making sure that they understand their customer needs and priorities, councils have to make sure that the services they provide are sensitive to the needs of their citizens.' It was an agenda which also connected public service organisations to a range of new stakeholder groups: community-based organisations representing different identity groups, and regulatory bodies with a responsibility to further and protect equalities in various contexts.

The most obvious representation of a stronger *and* broader approach to equalities under New Labour lay in the equalities duties placed upon public service organisations. The first of these duties related to racism, prompted by the findings of the Macpherson inquiry and introduced in the Race Relations (Amendment) Act, 2002. It was followed by the Disability Duty, which came into force in December 2006, and the Gender Duty taking effect in April 2007. These changes placed a general duty on public bodies not only to eliminate unlawful discrimination, but also to actively promote equality (Equality and Human Rights Commission (EHRC) 2009). These general duties were supplemented by a series of specific duties, including the need for public bodies to prepare equality schemes giving effect to the general duties, to monitor and assess the impact of the scheme, and its associated practices, on relevant stakeholders. The equality duties were underpinned by statutory codes of practice and enforced by the EHRC, set-up by the Equality Act, 2006. The culmination of this process was the development of Single Equality Schemes (SES) across the public services, typically bringing together the three duties – gender, race and disability – into a combined and integrated statement. This was an acknowledgement not only of the link between workforce and service diversity, but also of the possible interface between different forms of inequality. As the Department of Health (2007b: 7) noted, the reasons for its

SES included 'a recognition that inequalities are rarely experienced in isolation but are often interdependent.'

Action and impact

Against this general backdrop, different initiatives were taken in various parts of the public services to address equal opportunities and diversity, with some unevenness of treatment and progress across the six equality strands suggesting some care in claiming unqualified 'model employer' status. These initiatives are now considered by exploring developments respectively in the civil service, the health service and local government.

The civil service

The civil service had a long tradition of procedural fairness which can be traced back to the introduction of open competition in recruitment following the Northcote Trevelyan Report in 1854. It was perhaps the well-entrenched nature of such policies which limited the perceived need for the development of equalities and diversities agenda in the civil service during the early period of Labour government. Initial interest in this agenda under New Labour focused on employment targets at the upper levels of the civil service. As part of the Comprehensive Spending Review 2004, targets were set for women in the senior civil service and top management posts (TMP), for those from Black and Minority Ethnic backgrounds and with disabilities. As can be seen from Table 4.1, these were quite ambitious targets, raising the proportion of women in the senior civil service (SCS) and top management posts from around a quarter to a third, and doubling the proportion of those with BME backgrounds and disabilities. A review of progress in 2008 revealed only one Department, Communities and Local Government on course to hit all four targets, with the Equalities Office, unable to respond to the review because a workforce data base was not in place. Indeed it is clear from Table 4.1 that departments fell somewhat short of some of the targets, although this should not detract from the noteworthy increases in the proportion of women at the upper echelon of the civil service, or from the achievement of BME and disability targets.

In 2005, a more broadly based approach to equal opportunities in the civil service was launched under the heading *Delivery in a Diverse Civil Service* and underpinned by a ten point plan. It was an approach founded upon the

Table 4.1 Civil service employment equalities targets

%	April 2003 (actual)	Target set in 2004 to be achieved by 2008	Oct.2009 (actual) (2005 Figures)	New Targets set Feb 2010 to be achieved by 2013
Women in the senior civil service (SCS)	26.4	37.0	35.0 (29.1)	39.0
Women in top management posts (TMP)	22.9	30.0	27.9 (25.5)	34.0
BME in the SCS	2.4	4.0	4.0 (2.8)	5.0
Disability in the SCS	1.8	3.2	3.0 (2.9)	5.0

Source: Office for National Statistics Various and Cabinet Office, 2005 and 2008

'rightness' of creating a civil service which reflected the diversity of the community and the value of drawing upon the 'talent' of such a community to improve service delivery (Cabinet Office 2005a: 1). The ten points included an extension of target-setting for the employment of women and minority groups to lower grades, which fed into the senior civil service. Departments were required to set their own targets, and develop a plan to achieve them. The infrastructure for such policies and practices was strengthened with the appointment of board level departmental Diversity Champions and the creation of a Diversity Champions' Network. It was an approach further developed within the context of the equality duties, leading to the formulation of *Promoting Equality, Valuing Diversity: A Strategy for the Civil Service in 2008* (Cabinet Office 2008b).

These policies appeared to meet with some success, certainly if measured by the achievement of employment targets: by 2008 more than half (53 per cent) of those employed in the civil service were women compared with 46 per cent of those employed in the UK; the percentage of civil servants with BME backgrounds had risen from 5.7 per cent in 1997 to 8.3 per cent in 2007, the proportion with disabilities increasing from 3.1 in 2001 to 6.7 per cent in 2007. (Cabinet Office 2008b: 4). In a more general context, Greene and Kirton's (2008) study of equality and diversity in a government department found that often line managers failed to fully understand or apply the relevant policies. However, these policies were positively viewed, with 'very little criticism from any of the stakeholder groups'. Moreover, they proved to be resilient: while often an early 'victim' of cuts, in this department downsizing was accompanied by attempts to safeguard equalities and by the adoption of appropriate procedures, such as the undertaking of an equalities assessment exercise.

The National Health Service

There was a sustained public policy interest in the promotion of workforce equality and diversity in the NHS. This was partly driven by a 'business' need to address labour supply problems, NHS Employers suggested that managing diversity should become 'core business' (NHS Employers 2009). It was also based on a perceived 'model employer' obligation, the NHS being presented by policy makers as having a 'unique responsibility' to match the policies and standards of the 'best employers' (NHS Executive 2000: 19). More specifically, the importance attached to workforce equality and diversity was apparent in a number of overlapping but discrete initiatives, ranging from general statements of policy and principle to more specific and robust practice.

The earliest initiative, *Positively Diverse,* pre-dated the election of the New Labour government, being launched by Bradford Community Health NHS Trust in December 1995. On assuming office, however, this initiative was taken up by New Labour and broadened in terms of purpose and coverage. It was associated with more general developments in employment relations within the NHS, supporting an approach which valued and involved staff as set out in the first NHS HR plan under New Labour (see Bach 2004). As such Positively Diverse was positioned as a culture-change tool, rather than as a more narrowly conceived mechanism seeking to address workforce equality (NHS Executive 2000: 9).

The first stage of the programme, completed by 2000, engaged 37 healthcare trusts and organisations in auditing policy and practice on equality and diversity, providing the basis for action, and a model which might be followed across the NHS. In the wake of the Macpherson report, this work was reinforced in various ways. The government paper *Looking Beyond Labels* (Department of Health 2000b) sought to deepen employment opportunities for people with disabilities in the NHS. It was framed by the broader Vital Connection (Department of Health 2000c: 2) initiative which encouraged a more strategic approach underpinned by equality indicators tied to the award of the Improving Work Life Standard. All NHS organisations were required to publish an 'Equality Statement' as part of their Annual Report. National targets were set for ethnic minority and women representation at board level, respectively at 7 per cent and 40 per cent by the end of March 2004. If the appointment of the first National Director of Equality and Human rights in October 2004 assumed symbolic significance, the inclusion of equality as one of the six core dimensions of the NHS Knowledge and Skills Framework, in the same year was a more tangible attempt to embed sensitivity to diversity into performance across the NHS workforce.

There are limited time series data to assess fully the impact of these policies and practices on the treatment of staff. In terms of workforce composition, the NHS was always a predominantly female workforce. In 2009, over 80 per cent of the non-medical workforce was female. The BME community was also traditionally well-represented in healthcare employment. A report on the NHS workforce in London (Hutt and Buchan 2005), for example, found that 37 per cent of the NHS non-medical workforce in London was from minority ethnic groups compared to 28 per cent of the working population in the area. Indeed over the period of New Labour government the proportion of the NHS non-medical workforce with a BME background appeared to have increased from 7.3 per cent in 2000 to 13.7 per cent in 2009 (NHS Information Centre 2010). However, these figures often blur the distinction between indigenous British BME healthcare workers and migrant employees. This is an important distinction given the significant, albeit fluctuating, increase in use of migrant workers in the NHS, particularly in registered nursing. While the proportion of nurses trained overseas remained small, in the early New Labour years, the number of overseas trained nurse registrants increased rapidly as a means of meeting targets on nurse numbers, reaching a peak in 2001–2002 at around 15,000 (Bach 2007; 2010).

In terms of policy implementation, there were difficulties, particularly in terms of communication. For instance, a Healthcare Commission survey of all Trusts in England found that only seven had all the required information under the Race Relations (Amendment) Act readily accessible, with nearly a third of trust websites having none of the required information (Millar 2006). More striking, some healthcare employees faced ongoing inequity of treatment on grounds of gender and minority status. A report by the Equal Opportunities Committee of the BMA (2004a: 19), based on the experience of doctors, concluded that racism towards minority ethnic doctors was 'still prevalent' and that those with disabilities or chronic illnesses were 'often stigmatized'. Moreover the report highlighted the disproportionate distribution of males and females in senior medical career grades: 76 per cent of consultants were men. In the absence of other data, it is difficult to assess whether these experiences can be generalised across the NHS workforce. Certainly annual Trust staff surveys over the period indicated low levels of perceived discrimination: in 2005 just under 6 per cent of employees had experienced discrimination in the last 12 months, with little change in this figure in 2009. This is not, however, to overlook a residual degree of perceived discrimination revealed by this survey, most commonly on grounds of race. Indeed, if, as likely, those reporting ongoing discrimination come from an ethnic minority, significant concerns remain.

Local government

In policy terms, the local government sector responded relatively quickly to the equalities agenda. This might well reflect a legacy of progressive equal opportunities policies in this sub sector, and their resilience even during the period of Conservative government. Moreover, in contrast to slow progress made by local government in responding to pay inequalities, this broader equalities agenda, touching on other aspects of the employment relationship, was less resource-intensive, and as framed by New Labour, complemented the sector's interest in community-building. A Commission for Racial Equalities designed Best Value standard, 'Race Equality Means Quality', was developed into a broader Equality Standard for Local Government which embraced gender and disability as well as race.

Established in 2001 on the basis of a partnership between the various bodies seeking to advance equal opportunities, this standard was similarly integral to various Best Value measures. In line with the goals underpinning the equality duties, the Standard was seen as central not only to ensuring the implementation of equality practices in relation to the workforce, but as essential to the delivery of quality services to the whole community. The Standard sought to establish a holistic performance management framework which mainstreamed equality within service provision (I&Dea 2007). As one local authority, the London Borough of Richmond, noted in a briefing paper, 'The aim (of the Standard) is to create a culture in which managers and staff will question and challenge assumptions about their services and re-assess them on the basis of equality and diversity' (http://cabinet.richmond.giv.uk/mgConvert2PDF.aspx?ID=3270).

Following a review, the Standard was revised in 2006, clarifying certain elements and extending it to the three remaining equality streams: sexual orientation, age and religion/belief. While the equalities duties had not been broadened to these streams, national anti-discrimination legislation had been. The revision, however, left the standard's core framework largely the same, a series of strategic themes – Employment and Training: Leadership and Corporate Commitment; Consultation, Community Development and Scrutiny; and Service Development and Customer Care – different measures and outcomes being associated with each (I&Dea 2007).

If local government's policy response to the equalities was immediate and sustained, the efficacy of these approaches remained more difficult to judge because of limited research. Creegan et al. (2003) highlighted some concerns amongst minority ethnic workers in local government about the design, implementation and impact of race equality policies in the sector. A survey of staff in one local authority revealed that over three quarters of those from minorities agreed that discrimination remained a problem in the council. These concerns were acute amongst women with a BME background suggesting the combined effects of gender and ethnicity on treatment. Moreover, there was consensus that a lack of knowledge and engagement by line managers compromised the effectiveness of these policies. However, some care is needed in generalising from the views of staff in one authority, while it is unclear how the timing of the research interfaced with the introduction of the Equality Standard in local government.

Research on the treatment of Lesbian, Gay and Bisexual (LGB) workers in local government in the context of national legislation to deal with discrimination provided a mixed picture of progress. Colgan et al. (2009) found that an emphasis on monitoring and targets was perceived by employees as having some effect in addressing discrimination, with authorities also seen as increasingly mainstreaming such matters. Nonetheless, there were residual problems, with around a quarter of LGB workers still experiencing discrimination, higher than in the private sector and challenging the public sector's reputation for 'good practice' in this area. Again the findings of this research might have been overtaken by subsequent developments: soon after the local authority standard was extended to cover sexual orientation. At the very least, however, this research, as well as the work on race, suggests some caution in assuming the efficacy of policies and the consistent treatment of employees across the six equality strands.

Discussion and conclusions

Against a broader public policy backdrop, it has become clear that New Labour governments were committed to flexibility and equality across the public services workforce. The chapter explored the public policy rationale for this commitment, how it was translated into policy in different parts of sector and with what affects on various stakeholder groups, in particular employers as well as employees from the different equality strands. Although flexibilities and equalities, as part of the employment relations domain, were originally linked to the work experience narrative, the chapter has also highlighted how policies and practices in these respective areas relate to the model employer and institutional infrastructure narratives. More generally the chapter revealed how New Labour's hybrid network governance model of public service fed into some of these policies and practices, with significant implications for employee relations.

The rationale for New Labour policy on flexibility and equality revolved around the balance between an instrumental, contingent business case for these practices and a more principled approach, founded upon a particular conception of certain values such as fairness. This balance, in turn, was linked to the status of the public sector as a 'model employer'. Some commentators (Dickens 1999) have questioned the business case model as the basis for such a claim, and New Labour's approach to flexibility and equality was informed by an explicit pragmatism and expediency. The modernisation agenda could not be delivered without an adequate supply of committed workers. Flexibility and equality were positioned as a means of addressing difficulties in recruiting, retaining and motivating public service professionals in particular. Such an approach was not without its drawbacks for employers, attention being drawn to the high costs, in financial and service quality terms, associated with for example the use of temporary working. But, there were suggestions that a number of policies related to flexibility and equality generated benefits, a more diverse workforce, for example, engaging more efficiently with diverse service users.

It was also argued, however, that New Labour's approach to flexibility and equality was driven not only by instrumental values, but by a more positive set of principles. Flexibility, connected to a work–life balance agenda, and the prevention of discrimination against women and minority groups in employment which was seen as incompatible with modern public services. More distinctive was the positioning of these policies as the vehicle for social justice, not only in relation to the workforce, but to how this in turn ensured fairness in service delivery. The workforce not only needed to be diverse but capable of delivering services to diverse communities. It was an approach the government implemented through the equalities duties placed on public service organisations, a proactive and holistic approach to workforce and service equality.

If this more principled approach, albeit blended with elements of the business case model, provided a basis for New Labour to re-assert model employer status for the public sector, the form and coverage assumed by its policy and practices provided further support for this claim. Public service organisations remained more likely to have policies and practices in these areas than private sector organisations, reflected, for example, in the more ready availability of working time flexibility. It was, however, the move to a robust, outcomes-based approach which provided a new legitimacy for the claim. This was especially the case in relation to equality, with grounds for suggesting that New Labour had moved away from Jewson and Mason's liberal agenda towards their radical one.

An approach combining equalities duties with a more radical, outcomes-based diversity agenda, betrays features of New Labour upstream, hybrid model of public service provision. The equalities duties connected with the network features of this model. Public service organisations were required to reach out more to diverse communities, developing a collaborative approach with them to ensure that their workforces were capable of delivering services in a manner sensitive to these community needs. The more explicit outcomes approach, mimicking the government's broader approach to performance management, is also related to features of the new public management. Thus, equality standards, and indeed some aspects of the work–life balance agenda, were underpinned by targets and by a prescriptive procedural infrastructure to ensure compliance with the relevant objectives. The approach ran the same risks as those associated with this broader auditing regime as highlighted in Chapter 3; flexibility and equality becoming onerous, paper-driven, box-ticking exercises adding to workplace pressures, and undermining the aim of mainstreaming equality. At the same time, it arguably represented an attempt to cut through the systemic disadvantage which formally fair procedures concealed, forcing public service employers to achieve more concrete results.

If there were strong grounds for suggesting a distinctive rationale and approach to flexibility and equality, *the impact* of these policies and practices on employees' working lives remained more contested. The consequences of policies seeking to establish flexibility and equality might be presented in different ways. The first views these developments as simply benign, with certain policies and practices failing to penetrate or affect the working lives of public servants. For example, working time flexibilities were available but simply not taken up. The second regards some of these initiatives as irrelevant, incapable of dealing with the deep-seated, structural features which give rise to inequalities. Despite attempts to set employment targets, the ongoing occupational segregation within the public services workforce on the basis of gender and ethnicity might well reflect such features (BMA 2004a; Hicks et al. 2005; Mathews 2010).

The third sees these developments as detrimental, especially to employees. For example, some claimed that the opportunities to take up welfare-oriented working time flexibilities had been forced out by work pressures, whilst forms of temporary working, for instance bank and agency working by nurses, generated stress and uncertainty. These flexibilities and others related to outsourcing were presented as emerging from the neo-liberal values underpinning New Labour, a residue of the new public management. Certainly the government had sought to protect substantive terms and conditions of employment in this context, but this had often driven employers to seek cost efficiencies through workforce reductions and work intensification. These negative outcomes were also associated with instances of poor implementation. A number of studies drew attention to the barrier presented by line managers, particularly apparent in parts of local government and the civil service, blunting the impact of policies and possibly perpetuating forms of discrimination. More profoundly, a distinctive employee relations agenda revolving around worker identity, voice and development in new flexible, networked relationships, had typically proved too challenging for organisations still fixated on short-term goals and targets.

The fourth picture presents these developments in a more positive light, generating benefits for different stakeholders. Under New Labour public service organisations remained ahead of those in the private sector in terms of flexibility and equality. The procedural infrastructure was more developed, with the emergence of new employee relations actors such as the EHRC responsible for monitoring and enforcing the equalities duties. Positive flexibility continued with more lifestyle working options available to employees. Moreover, there was limited evidence of expressed employee concern with these issues: in general workers were content with working patterns, while discrimination against employees was perceived as low. Indeed, there was even some evidence to suggest that a target-based approach had begun to dilute some aspects of occupational segregation.

5

Work relations: professions, roles and ways of working

The New Labour programme of public service reform was deeply embedded in attempts to alter work relations in the sector. From the outset national policy makers recognised that new forms of service delivery had major implications for job roles and ways of working. If service provision was to become more person-centred, providing greater user voice, independence, control and choice, it followed that the organisation of work would also require radical change. As Lord Warner, then Minister of State for NHS Delivery, noted in relation to health and social care:

> Those who use our health and social care services expect better and speedier access to services, more flexible and integrated services and to be more involved in the decisions about the treatment and care provided for them ... (Employers) need to encourage innovation and new working practices across professional and staff groups. Equally, staff who work in health and social care must appreciate the inevitability of continuing change and that flexibility in the way we deliver services will be the norm. (Department of Health 2005a: 1)

An interest in work relations – the nature, allocation and regulation of employee tasks and responsibilities – has long been integral to the study of the employment relationship (Gospel 1992; Martin 2003). In general, however, it has not figured prominently in the research literature on employee relations in the public services. This might be seen to reflect the absence of collective bargaining on such issues. In general, a bureaucratic model of public service delivery fixed job roles and prescribed work activities, while any developments associated with work organisation often fell within the remit of managerial prerogative or of professional self-regulation. Thus, it is striking that one of the more sustained streams of research on work relations in the sector has been founded on a labour process model, centred on methods of managerial control and worker resistance beyond formal institutional collectivism (Ironside and Siefert 1995).

Under New Labour, work organisation became increasingly central to *collective* worker–employer relations in the public services. The government was prepared to bring the management of the professions and of work organisation into the arena of joint discussion. It was also determined to (re-)establish an explicit link between 'effort' and 'reward', collectively bargained improvements in remuneration only being agreed on the basis of a reciprocal revision to working practices as a means of improving employee efficiency and effectiveness. Indeed some of the bitterest conflicts of this period, exemplified by the extended fire fighter dispute of 2002–2003, revolved around the trade-off between union pay demands and government calls for revised working practices (Seifert and Sibley 2005). At the same time, many of the attempted changes in public service work relations under Labour took place outside of the formal collective bargaining machinery, encouraging an interest in new actors, processes and outcomes.

Public policy developments under New Labour constituted no less than an attempt to completely re-shape work relations in the public services. Dedicated projects were launched to develop new roles and ways of working in all parts of the sector, while the contribution of different occupations was systematically reviewed. These moves generated a pressing workforce training and development agenda, as well as the need for a re-designed infrastructure to regulate the newly constituted workforce. Such attempts to uproot entrenched working practices inevitably threatened well-established job jurisdictions and interests, at the same time subverting established procedures for the management of work relations. These challenges were rendered all the more acute by tensions in New Labour attempts to change work relations.

This chapter maps out changes in work relations and explores these tensions. It is divided into six main parts. Five of the sections concentrate on closely related but analytically distinct themes informing New Labour's attempt to re-shape work relations: public service professionals, new (non-professional) roles, new ways of working, the service user and a re-designed supportive infrastructure. The sixth provides an overview, presenting changes in work relations in the different parts of the public services and assessing the consequences of these changes for different stakeholders.

The professions

The efficacy of any attempt to re-shape work relations in the public services was dependent upon addressing the role of the professional. Professionals in health, social care and education have long been core to the public service workforce. In 2009, more than half of the 1.3 million NHS workforce was professionally qualified, including some 140,000 doctors, around 417,00 nurses, midwives and health visitors and over 150,000 qualified scientific, therapeutic and technical staff (Health and Social Care Information Centre 2010); in primary and secondary education there were some 420,000 qualified teachers; while on a smaller, but still significant, scale there are over 50,000 social workers in local government (Eborall et al. 2010: 59). Indeed the distinctiveness of the public service workforce in these terms was reflected in the fact that almost half (44 per cent) of the workforce in public services had at least one degree or were at NVQ level 5, compared with barely a quarter (24 per cent) in the private sector (Audit Commission 2002: 9).

The importance attached by New Labour to the professional was apparent in the fact that few, if any, of the core professions escaped formal scrutiny. Teachers were one of the first to receive attention, with the White Paper 'Teachers Meeting the Challenge' (DfES 1998) raising themes reinforced by the then Secretary of State for Education Estelle Morris in an influential speech 'Professionalism and Trust' (DfES 2001). Nurses and midwives were reviewed twice: once under 'modernising nurses careers' (Department of Health 2006a) and then under a commission established by Gordon Brown as Prime Minister (COI 2010), whilst health visitors were also subject to a re-examination (Department of Health 2007c). The working practices of NHS consultants and GPs were considered as part of the re-negotiation of their contracts, respectively agreed in 2003 and 2004 and post-graduate medical training was completely re-structured under 'modernising medical careers' (Department of Health 2003a; Department of Health 2005b; Tooke 2008). A task force was set-up to review social worker roles (Department for Children, Schools and Families 2009), along with a New Ways of Working programme undertaken by the National Mental Health Institute in England (NIME) which assessed the consultant psychiatrist role (BMA 2004b; Department of Health 2005c).

The public service professions presented New Labour with a dilemma. Preceding Conservative governments had viewed the traditional professions as epitomising 'producer capture' of service delivery with their inflexible and self-serving protective work practices. New Labour showed little signs of distancing itself from this perspective. Tony Blair famously referred to the 'scars on his back' from confronting 'vested interests' in pursuit of public service reform and 'the legacy of professional domination of service provision' (Blair 2004). This critique of the professions was given added weight by a crisis of professional legitimacy following a series of failures in professionals practice: the Victoria Climbé case; the unauthorised retention of children's organs by clinicians at Alder Hay hospital; the shortcomings highlighted at the Bristol Royal Infirmary in the quality of children's cardiac surgery; and the murder of elderly patients by the GP Harold Shipman.

At the same time, New Labour was aware that the effective implementation of public service reform resided not only in the commitment of public service professionals but also in their capacity to deliver it. This capacity had been severely undermined by the demoralisation resulting from the sustained vilification of certain groups under Conservative governments and, partly related, by recruitment and retention difficulties, especially acute amongst such groups as social workers, teachers and nurses. Other developments had also reduced professional capacity: for example, the European Union Working Time Directive had forced a revision of hours worked and tasks performed by junior doctors.

New Labour's response to these dilemmas was a form of 'tough love': a recognition of and an attempt to protect the distinctive contribution made by the professional to service provision, but accompanied by a re-assessment of the rationale and form assumed by this contribution. It was an approach captured in the government paper on children's services, Every Child Matters (ECM), (DfES 2003: 10) which noted: 'We want to value the specific skills that people from different professional backgrounds bring, and we also want to break down the professional barriers that inhibit joint working, and tackle recruitment and retention problems.'

The 'love' shown to the professions assumed various forms. In general, the government sought to provide space for the professional to concentrate on the technical and specialist essence of their role and reward this front-line contribution (Chapter 3) rather than spend time on 'burdensome' routines. Workforce re-modelling exercises explicitly attempted to free up the professional in these terms. The Workload Agreement in primary and secondary education, 2003, was principally designed to allow teachers more time for high-quality marking and preparation (DfES 2002: 5). This approach also underpinned the re-structuring of the wider childcare workforce structure (Department of Health 2009a: 31). Drawing lessons from the Workload Agreement, the Children's Workforce Strategy (H.M. Government 2005: 47) noted the government's intention to 'support employers and local service planners to remodel the workforce to enable social workers to concentrate on the complex work that needs their skills.'

The gentler side of the government's approach was further reflected in the provision of opportunities for role development, often involving the extension or the deepening of professional skills and responsibilities. This was most evident in the development of registered nurse roles. Regulations were loosened to allow nurses independently to dispense a wider range of medication: in 2009, there were around 48,000 nurse prescribers in the UK (Lomas 2009). Moreover, new, advanced practitioner and consultant roles enabled nurses to specialise and lead. An RCN (2005) study of over 700 nurses performing such new roles found that most had been introduced in the last four years, with 60 per cent of respondents being the first to fill them. These moves were reinforced by raising entry standards into quasi professional groups such as teachers, nurses and social workers, with the intention to turn them into all-graduate professions.

This support for and enhancement of the professional was, however, tempered by a 'toughness', displayed in a number of ways. There was an attempt to impose a much more flexible approach to service delivery, involving a weakening of the exclusive performance of certain traditional professional tasks. Indeed, there was a strong undercurrent within New Labour's workforce reforms that capability rather than status should determine task performance: 'Increasingly (health and social care) employers will plan around competence rather than staff group or profession' (Department of Health 2006b: 186).

In education, this weakening of professional jurisdiction saw the delegation of certain, albeit limited, whole class activities, such as classroom cover, to higher-level teaching assistants under the Workload Agreement. This generated considerable concern amongst the teachers' unions and contributed to the NUT's refusal to sign the agreement. In social care the establishment of the Lead Professional role, co-ordinating activities in complex childcare cases, was opened to any profession with a stake in the case, challenging the pre-eminence of the qualified social worker. In the NHS, healthcare assistants were given increasing scope to deliver direct patient care (Kessler et al. 2010). This challenged nurse provision of the holistic care, a traditional pillar of nurse claims to professional status, generating debate within the RCN about whether nurses were 'too posh to wash'. As the Chief Nursing Officer (2004) in the NHS warned,

> I believe that we are guilty of seeing caring as lower status as reflected in our keenness to delegate caring aspects of our role to others. Our actions fail to legitimise

the value of caring – as nursing develops we tend to take on the roles and tasks from the medical profession.

The search for flexibility was also accompanied by an attempt to re-shape the substance of the professional role. There were some signs of an insidious leaching away of the professionals' authority. For example, the re-modelling of the mental healthcare workforce, revolving around the difficulties in recruiting consultant psychiatrists, involved a re-allocation of tasks, pointedly presented not so much as a delegation by the professional but as a re-distribution of responsibility (Department of Health 2005c). In a more constructive vein, there were moves in social care to develop a professional model based on social pedagogy, involving a more holistic, personal approach to work with young people (Cameron et al. 2010). The most striking prospective changes in the professionals' role were related to the personalisation agenda and increasingly became articulated as a form of 'New Professionalism'. The notion of a 'New Professionalism' emerged at the backend of the Labour government and was designed to capture a re-orientation of professional activities. At its core was a partnership relationship with the service user:

> New Professionalism rests on a redefinition of the relationship between professionals and citizens. Professionals are no longer simply accountable to their managers or the Government. Users of public services and other citizens should have the primary role, empowered to demand service improvements where performance falls below expectations and bring more of their own expertise, time and energy to solving problems collaboratively with professionals. (Cabinet Office 2008a: 33)

It was an approach most meaningfully articulated in Putting People First (Department of Health 2007d) setting out the government's plans to reform adult social services, which envisaged the social worker in adult social care acting less as an assessor and a care manager and more as an advocate, a navigator or a broker.

New roles

Under Labour governments new roles emerged in two main guises. The first was as a series of recast roles, involving the re-configuration of tasks performed and responsibilities held by an established occupation. The second was as a range of original roles, creating an occupation performing genuinely novel activities, tasks not previously undertaken.

Recast roles

The recasting of roles has already been highlighted in the case of public service professions, but it assumed a particularly prominent, and partly related, form in the case of support workers. Such support roles, working alongside the professional, appeared to proliferate under New Labour – the healthcare assistant, the teaching assistant, the maternity support worker, the physician assistant, and the social worker assistant. While some of these support roles were often long established within their respective sub-sector workforces, they were increasingly developed to address a range of public policy goals. As noted, they were central to re-modelling exercises, providing the capacity to relieve professionals of routine burdens. They were also seen as a substitute, encroaching on more traditional professional tasks, a process apparent in the dilution of skill mix (the ratio of professional to non-professional staff) (Thornley 2000). Assistants were further viewed as a way of addressing recruitment and retention difficulties amongst professionals: the role was presented as a stepping stone to becoming a registered professional, part of a 'grow your own' approach (Malhorta 2000). Moreover, assistants were seen to add to service quality: for example, the teaching assistant provided an additional classroom resource to support individual pupils and deliver 'catch-up' programmes. As the government noted: 'Increased numbers of better trained support staff will in their own right enrich the experience of pupils' (DfES 2002: 6).

The importance attached to these support roles varied in different parts of the public services. In primary and secondary education, they were closely associated with the pursuit of New Labour's public policy goals, in particular raising teaching standards and pupil attainment. This was reflected in a dramatic increase in the number of teaching assistants: in the first decade of New Labour government the numbers in this role increased from 61,000 to 177,000, a 200 per cent rise, the number of teachers rising 10 per cent from 399,000 to 440,000 over the same period (http://news.bbc.uk/1/hi/education/7462691.stm). The Community Support Officer (CSO) role in the police force was also presented as key to a broader public policy agenda designed to improve crime prevention and detection. CSOs were established to undertake neighbourhood liaison activities, at the same time releasing warranted police officers to concentrate on dealing with more serious criminal activities (Cooper et al. 2006). In healthcare, however, the support worker role developed in a more organic fashion. Certainly the healthcare assistant became an essential part of the primary and secondary healthcare workforce: over the New Labour period the number of workers supporting clinical staff rose from 222,000 to 284,000. However, these roles were less explicitly related to the NHS modernisation project, with limited evidence to suggest that they were used as a strategic resource (Kessler et al. 2010).

Novel roles

As striking as the emphasis placed on support and other recast roles was the emergence of genuinely novel roles in the public services, roles which had not previously existed on any scale. These new roles were in part the product of planned and co-ordinated national initiatives designed to give effect to the principles of public service modernisation. For example, the Skills for Care New Type of Worker (NToW) programme in social care supported new roles in 20 pilot sites, explicitly designed to support service user voice, choice and control (Kessler and Bach 2011). Similarly, the NIMHE New Ways of Working project in mental health (Department of Health 2005c) developed a variety of new roles to further service quality and access, including fostering the emergence of graduate primary care mental health worker (Strain et al. 2006) and the 'gateway' worker (Department of Health 2003b). The NHS Modernisation Agency, 2001–2005, organised some 30 role redesign projects under its Changing Workforce Programme. Amongst the important roles to emerge from this programme were the Support, Time and Recovery (STR) worker and the Emergency Care Practitioner (ECP). The STR worker role was specifically designed to promote social inclusion by supporting those with mental health difficulties in the community, with over 3,000 post holders in place in 2006 (Department of Health 2007e). The ECP was a generic role developed in response to the increasing pressures faced by Emergency Departments and to manage unsuitable demand for emergency care. The ECP 'brought the hospital to the patient' (SfH 2007). The role operated in a different context: for example, working in Out-of-Hours Services or as an ambulance paramedic with extended skills.

In central government, the Jobcentre Plus Personal Adviser provided a further example of a novel role closely associated with strategic developments and purpose. Established as an executive agency of the Department of Work and Pensions in 2001, Jobcentre Plus brought together the job search activities of the Employment Service with welfare support role undertaken by the Benefits Agency. The Personal Advisor was developed as the key role within this merged entity, balancing apparently bespoke guidance to the individual job seeker with the more punitive, control activities required to dispense state benefits (Rosenthal and Peccei 2007).

Over time, however, novel roles began to develop as a more ad hoc and opportunistic response to difficult or pressing issues. For instance, with educational attainment proving a 'sticky issue', the government launched a two-year (2006–2008) pilot in twenty local authorities to support a new school-based Parent Support Advisor role designed to foster greater parent engagement in their child's education. In 2009, there were almost 2,500 such advisors operating in schools across the country. Similarly in acknowledging that one in five mental health in-patients were from BME backgrounds, the government promoted a Community Development Worker role to raise awareness of mental health well-being in the BME community(Department of Health 2005d). As hospital-acquired infection began to take its toll, the NHS (Department of Health 2000d) developed a housekeeper role. Seeking to improve nutritional and cleaning standards, particularly as set out in the Department of Health's Essence of Care Plan, 2001 (Department of Health 2001a), there were around 5,000 ward housekeepers in post in a third of trusts by 2003 (May and Smith, 2003).

New ways of working

New ways of working in the public services under Labour governments concentrated on the enactment of tasks and responsibilities within established occupational boundaries, rather than on their re-allocation across new professional and non-professional work roles. These new ways of working were shaped by three broad aims: community engagement, service integration and cost efficiency.

Community engagement

Labour governments were keen to develop ways of working which supported a shift from closed institutions to ones that were more open to community participation. Schools played an important role in community engagement with 'extended schools' opening up their facilities to pupils, their families and the community to provide breakfast clubs, after-school clubs and other activities, eroding the boundaries between the school and the wider community. It was envisaged that the general community would become the main location for public services, particularly in health and social care. This shift was driven in part by expediency, community-based care often being lower cost than more institutionalised support, an important consideration within the context of an ageing population. It was also underpinned by an evidence-based belief that health and social care users often preferred this type of service (Department of Health 2005e).

New ways of working were a means of engaging often hard-to-reach community members in need of public service support. For example in mental health and social care emphasis was placed on the development of Assertive Outreach Teams. Both the NHS Plan (2000) and the National Service Framework for Mental Health stressed the importance of these teams as a means of addressing those with severe and enduring mental health difficulties, the government committing itself to establish 170 such teams around the country. Along similar lines, the Family–Nurse Partnership (FNP), emerged from the Government's report 'Reaching Out – An Action Plan on Social Exclusion' (Hall and Hall 2007). Comprising a series of 10 FNP pilot sites across England in 2007–2008, this health-led model involved intensive home visiting from pregnancy through to two years of age by qualified nurses. Each nurse had a caseload of 25 families, with evidence to suggest high take-up and some effectiveness in providing support to families (Barnes 2010). Yet other examples highlighted how new ways of working were designed to sustain care in the community for as long as possible. For instance, the Crisis Resolution and Home Treatment approach, as set out in the Department of Health (2001b) Mental Health Policy Guidelines, provided a 'rapid response to mental health crisis in the community with the possibility of offering comprehensive acute psychiatric care at home until the crisis is resolved' (National Institute for Mental Health in England 2001c: 7). It was an approach which achieved some success in reducing in-patient admissions (Jethwa 2007).

Integration

The development of more integrated ways of working was a government response to the oft repeated user frustrations of dealing with a range of different public services. Perhaps more profoundly, it was a means of addressing the risks associated with the vulnerable user falling between 'the cracks' left between different services, tragically highlighted in the case of Victoria Climbé (ECM 2003: 21). Integrated ways of working were encouraged by the development of national frameworks covering various conditions and client groups including cancer, children, coronary heart disease, chronic obstructive pulmonary disease, long-term conditions, mental health, older people, renal services and stroke. These revolved around care or service pathways, and at senior decision-making levels stimulated whole systems planning and the joint commissioning of services. Unsurprisingly, children's services were at the forefront in developing integrated service provision. Every Child Matters paved the way to the establishment of Children's Service Departments in local authorities, bringing together children's social care and education services, and the more belated emergence of Children's Trusts. As the government noted:

> We want to see services delivered around the needs of the child, not around the specialism of a particular practitioner or agency.... We want to see (staff) working in a new way, where working across professional boundaries and sharing information about a child's need is the norm. (H.M. Government 2007: 19)

One of the most significant initiatives undertaken under the umbrella of ECM, illustrative of attempts to draw-in partner organisations in new ways of working, was the creation of Sure Start Children's Centres. Initially focused on areas of deprivation, some 3,500 of these centres were finally established nationwide by 2009, as part of an extended school or within the community. They provided a space for the delivery of 'wrap around care' for under-fives, delivered by a range of occupational groups employed by public, private independent sector providers. As the NAO noted in a review of these centres:

> Centre managers and staff (were) working in challenging ways, often new to their professional discipline. (NAO 2006c: 9)

The growing emphasis on team working within the public services further supported this drive towards more integrated ways of working. The team became a key unit of work organisation within discrete employing units, for example the school, or at even more refined levels such as the hospital ward. The importance of team working can be traced to workforce re-modelling, the re-distribution of tasks across a wider range of occupational groups and the heightened contribution of new work roles calling for more flexible and co-ordinated working. The team was also crucial in engaging those from across different parts of the public services. This was illustrated in mental health where the National Institute of Mental Health in England (NIMHE) developed an approach and toolkit, Creating Capable Teams, designed to develop multi-disciplinary teams which cut across health and social care. The emphasis on team working also reflected a shift away from the New Public Management's emphasis on 'heroic' individual leadership towards a more distributed form of leadership involving staff across an organisation. The benefit of a distributed style of leadership was heavily promoted in schools by the National College for School Leadership (2008).

Efficiency

While the second- and third-term Labour governments heavily invested in the public services, they retained a strong interest in value for money, not only in response to traditional scrutiny mechanisms, but also reflecting a broader policy and electoral interest in controlling expenditure. These concerns were reflected in efficiency-driven changes in the structure of the civil service. The Lyon's Review, 2004, (Lyons 2004) recommended the relocation of some 27,000 civil servants from London to the regions, while the O'Donnell review provided the basis for the merger of the Inland Revenue and Customs into a single department HM Revenue and Customs (O'Donnell 2004). These reviews formed the backdrop to Sir Peter Gershon's (2004) wider ranging review of efficiency savings across the public services, often seen in more loaded and provocative terms as seeking to reduce back office 'waste' in the sector, albeit with the aim of allowing front-line services to retain their capacity. The review set a target of £21 billion of efficiency gains to be made across the sector, prompting the government to place a requirement on all public service organisations to make year-on-year savings. This search for efficiency was reinforced in the Comprehensive Spending Review, 2007, which sought annual 3.0 per cent savings across the public services.

The pursuit of these efficiencies had a number of consequences for ways of working in the public services (see also Chapter 4). In 'back office' terms, they encouraged the development of shared services – payroll, HR support, procurement – on the assumption that pooled activity rendered economies of scale (Cabinet Office 2005b; Varney 2006). It was an approach which attracted some interest, a review of practice in local government suggesting between a quarter and a third of local authorities were involved in the creation of shared back office services and joint procurement, with a similar proportion considering such an option (PricewaterhouseCoopers 2007: 6). In front-line terms, the search for efficiencies was apparent in operational re-structuring. The government drew attention to private manufacturing models of 'good practice', particularly those founded on the principles of lean production, revolving around identifying customer value, organising production around a given value stream, and ensuring a continuous product flow without defects.

Although there was much debate about whether the principles of lean production could be transferred to the public services (Radnor and Boaden 2008), a prescriptive agenda emerged (Bhatia and Drew 2006) and more significantly changes in work organisation under this banner were instituted across many parts of the public services. Some applied the 'lean' label loosely to any generalised attempt to make efficiency savings. For example, the

London Borough of Merton's lean programme was described by its Director of Transformation as a review of all services 'to ensure that we are minimizing waste and maximizing efficiency' (Pope 2010). Others instituted more substantive change under the 'lean banner'. The Department for Work and Pensions presented its 'Lean Journey' in terms of 'customer focus' and 'continuous improvement' (Select Committee on Work and Pensions 2007: para. 87–94). The PCS was more inclined to view it as a crude means of reducing costs through job cuts, as they noted, 'DWP claim that Lean is about improving the customer experience and not about job cuts. PCS members have however not been fooled by the language used' (http://www.pcs.org.uk/en/department_for_work_and_pensions_group/dwp-news.cfm/id/998CE8B1-B1C1-4F61-84C36B484318949B). The NHS provided the most dynamic and sustained site for the implementation of lean principles. The NHS Institute for Innovation and Improvement (NIII) developed a 'Productive Series' seeking to provide guidance on how these principles might be given effect in different parts of healthcare: the productive ward, community hospital and operating theatre (NIII 2010).

The service user

Under New Labour's modernisation, the public service user became a key actor in the regulation of work relations. The unfettered sovereignty of the 'customer', rhetorically associated with the marketisation of the public services during the Conservative period of government, was replaced by the citizen-consumer (Clarke et al. 2007), a more nuanced construct which suggested different forms of user engagement in service provision. Notwithstanding the tensions in this construct (Clarke 2005; Rosenthal and Peccei 2007; Carey 2009; Needham 2010), the New Labour 'consumer', supported in public policy terms by the user-centred and choice agenda, assumed the individual's right to direct involvement in the delivery and design of personal services. As a 'citizen', and community member, the user might gain both a voice in the broader social consequences of service provision, alongside a civic responsibility to reciprocate in various ways the support provided by the state. These individual and collective dimensions of service engagement might be mapped onto different forms of user involvement in work relations distinguishing the levels of such involvement: societal, organisational or workplace; the form assumed: co-design, production or supervision of a service; and the impact on decision making: short or longer lasting, binding or advisory (Bellamere 2000; Alford, 2009).

The citizen voice: abstract and benign?

A raft of New Labour initiatives provided a collective voice by engaging service users at the organisational level, particularly in the design and operation of services, albeit mainly on a consultative basis and with limited binding effect. These initiatives mobilised the service user as a member of the public or as a citizen with access to universal public services, through involvement in community-based forums or networks. The Best Value regime introduced under the Local Government Act, 1999, established a statutory duty on local authorities to consult with service users and carers, while the Health and Social Care Act, 2001, placed a new obligation on NHS institutions to make active arrangements to involve and consult patients and the general public in the planning, development and operation of services (Department of Health 2004b; Department of Health 2004d). Moreover under the Local Government and Public Involvement in Health Act, 2007, local authorities were given £84 million to set-up Local Involvement Networks. The general public's enthusiasm for such initiatives was, however, limited and their impact upon public service providers questionable: an Audit Commission survey found that three quarters of best practice authorities failed to link the results of consultation to decision-making processes (Kelly et al. 2002: 25). These initiatives were complemented by individual voice mechanisms, for example a strengthened right to complain at provider level, reflected in the establishment of a patient advice and liaison service in every NHS trust, supported by the creation of an independent complaints advocacy service.

Client consumer groups: focused and more potent?

Collective voice mechanisms assumed a more refined form in relation to particular client groups: users not so much as a member of the public, but as a consumer with specific service needs – those with chronic health conditions, the elderly, those with mental, learning and physical disabilities. Steps were taken to engage these groups at the societal level, particularly in the development of public policy as it related to service development. Different client groups were encouraged to develop a narrative on the kind of services they wanted (Beresford and Halser 2009). This stream of user engagement fed into work relations directly, with various attempts to involve service users in reviewing different work roles, ascertaining the value they placed on different worker skills and behaviours (Branfield and Beresford 2006). In developing the 2020 Children and Young's People's Workforce Strategy, for example, some 140 documents presenting children and young people's views on the social care workforce were evaluated (DfCSF 2008). Indeed there were examples of user views affecting tangible outcomes: thus, the Support, Time and Recovery worker was presented as a role developed to address an expressed need for social inclusion amongst those with mental health difficulties.

User-driven services

This focus on citizen-consumers as comprising distinct client groups with particular needs provides a firmer foundation for understanding the involvement of the user as an actor beyond the more generalised, relatively reactive, low impact collective and individual voice mechanisms. Bolder, more proactive and meaningful forms of involvement were captured by the term 'user driven public services', defined by the House of Commons Public Administration Select Committee (2008: 9) as a service:

> [a]ctively involving the people using services, in their design and delivery. [Such services] entail drawing upon the expertise, views and perspective of service users to complement the skills and input of service professionals. User-driven services go beyond user consultation and representation.

The development of user-driven services was taken forward under the government's personalisation agenda, extended across most of the core public services – health, social care and education (Leadbeater 2004). It was equally clear that the traction established by this agenda varied by client group, reflecting the uneven capacity of such groups to engage with it. The advance of user-driven services was most marked among select groups within social care, particularly those with physical and learning disabilities, and to a lesser extent amongst those with certain chronic health conditions.

The progress made in social care reflected a long history of collective interest aggregation and mobilisation amongst these groups, highlighted by the Independent Living Movement of people with physical and sensory impairment and the Inclusion Movement of those with learning disabilities (Tyson et al. 2010: 11). The most recent campaigns launched by these groups revolved around a social model of care, explicitly adopted by the government (Department for Health 2007d), which viewed disabilities as exacerbated by the constraints imposed by established social systems and therefore alleviated by their re-structuring in user-sensitive ways.

New Labour attempts to develop user-driven services informed by the principles of personalisation were most marked in two related policy initiatives: direct payments and individual budgets. Direct payments had the longer and more deep-rooted provenance. Under the provision of the Health and Social Care Act, 2001 and from April 2003, local authorities were under an obligation to offer the vast majority of social service users money instead of arranging services for them. Between 2002 and 2008, the number of recipients of direct payments rose from around 8,000 to almost 114,500 (Eborall et al. 2010: 25). While direct payments related to social care money, individual budgets brought together different income streams, providing users with personal options as to how the composite monies might be used: as a direct cash payment; or as services commissioned by the local authority; or as services brokered on the individual's behalf. In 2006, pilots in 13 councils across the country were set-up to implement individual budgets, along with self-support projects taken forward by 100 local authorities, in collaboration with the influential voluntary sector interest group In Control, covering around 2,300 users and carers (Glendinning and Challis 2008).

Building upon this preparatory work, the Putting People First concordat signed in December 2007 provided £520 million of ring fenced funding for an adult social care programme built on personal budgets (Department for Health 2007d). Indeed the breadth of this commitment to user engagement in service delivery in social care was reflected in Putting People First's commitment to be 'The first public service reform programme which is co-produced, co-developed, co-evaluated and recognises that real change will only be achieved through participation of users and carers in every stage.'

These and other initiatives to develop more personalised public service provided opportunities for the user to act as an actor in work relations in a number of guises:

User as Worker. There were examples of the user doubling-up as a worker. In these instances, the boundary between the user and worker collapsed, the user becoming a provider of their own care. In health and adult social care, an example was highlighted of young black men with mental health problems becoming paid employees in exploring the quality of the service provided for their condition (Kessler and Bach 2011). On a more significant scale, the health service promoted forms of self care. As Cottam and Leadbeater (2004: 16) noted, 'The front line of healthcare is not where professionals dispense their knowledge to the patient but where people look after themselves.' This was illustrated by the NHS Expert Patient Programme (Department for Health 2009b), mainstreamed between 2004 and 2007, providing training for patients with a range of chronic conditions- diabetes, asthma- to self administer care with considerable financial savings (Community Interest Company 2010).

User as Employer. One of the more striking developments of this period saw the service user becoming the employer. Direct Payments, in particular, provided the funds for users to employ their own personal assistant, evidence suggesting that in 2008 there were some 76,000 individuals working as assistants in around 125,000 roles (individuals often worked in more than one assistant role) (IFF Research 2008). Research suggested that the overwhelming majority of service users were satisfied with their personal assistants with most (80 per cent) being confident about their employer responsibilities. However, this form of employment also fragmented the domiciliary workforce and lead to the employment of female, often migrant, workers in largely unregulated, low skilled and low-paid work (ibid).

User as Partner. As noted, many of the developments around personalisation were predicated on a partnership relationship between the public service professional and the user or carer. The user was to be seen less as a passive recipient of assessment and care packages and more as an active contributor to the development of services sensitive to their needs. The elevation of the user to partner challenged a range of entrenched systems and values founded upon the authority of the professional. However it raised question marks about the users' ability to turn the rhetoric of personalisation into reality. As Carr notes (2004: 14) in a review of the evidence on user involvement: 'Power issues underlie the majority of identified difficulties with effective user led change... exclusionary structures, institutional processes and attitudes can still affect the extent to which service users can influence change'.

A supportive infrastructure

The Labour government's attempt to develop new roles and ways of working in the public services, and to involve the service user as an active stakeholder, was predicated on the establishment of a supportive infrastructure, a set of institutions and systems which would facilitate and ensure their efficient and effective enactment. This infrastructure comprised four elements: principles, capabilities, planning and regulation.

In different parts of the public services principles were needed to underpin the enactment of new roles and ways of working. This element reflected the need for a simple transparency, not least for the benefit of service users, as to the distribution of responsibilities and tasks across the public service workforce. As the government noted in its white paper Youth Matters

(DfES 2005: 72), 'Young people are often confused about the roles and responsibilities of different professions. We will aim to create greater coherence by establishing very clearly the skills and competencies that people in the workforce have in common- and those that make them distinct.' Similar concerns were expressed about the general social worker role: 'The distinct role of social workers in modern public services is unclear' (2009: 7 DfCSF). This element encouraged the development of principles to underpin the performance of work roles, particularly important in the provision of care which cut across different parts of the public service sector. For example, the Department of Health articulated core principles formulated by Skills for Health and Care to support those working to establish self care (Department for Health 2008b).

New roles and ways of working also necessitated the identification and re-evaluation of requisite capabilities, and as already implied there was a strong emphasis on the development of competencies often linked to the National Occupation Standards underpinning the system of National Vocational Qualifications retained by New Labour. The government noted in Youth Matters (2005: 71), 'We believe that, in the future, the focus should be on skills and competencies needed to deliver services for young people rather than on organisational employment structures that have led to a proliferation of new, specific roles in responses to individual initiatives'. It was a view echoed in the healthcare context, where it was noted that 'Increasingly employers will need to consider competence rather than staff group as the basis for workforce planning.' (Department for Health 2005a: 1). Indeed, this flexible use of capabilities was reflected in the NHS Knowledge and Skills Framework which underpinned Agenda for Change. As the preamble to AfC noted, 'The signatories to this agreement will accordingly work together to meet the reasonable aspirations of all the parties to … assist new ways of working which best deliver the range and quality of services required, in as efficient and effective a way as possible, and organised to meet the needs of patients' (Department for Health 2004a: 2).

This emphasis on competency was accompanied by the second element of the new infrastructure, the attempt to develop new and shared capabilities which reflected the provision of more integrated services. Most striking in this respect was the common set of skills and knowledge devised by the Children's Workforce Development Council (2010), covering information sharing, multi-agency working and supporting transitions. A similar initiative was taken in mental health where 'ten essential shared capabilities' were developed (Department for Health 2004c) including working in partnership, respecting diversity and promoting recovery.

The third element was reflected in attempts to map and plan for the skills and capabilities needed to deliver new roles and ways of working. The main vehicle for this process was the sector skills agreement, brokered by the appropriate sector skill council. Sector skill agreements captured the deals reached between public service employers, education and training providers, funding agencies and government, on the development of future skills and qualifications. By 2008 these agreements had been reached by the main sector skills councils covering the public services- Skills for Health, Skills for Care and Children's Workforce Development Council.

This planning for skills and capabilities was also linked to a broader agenda designed to improve access to the professions and more generally to enhance the supply of new skills. The government commissioned report by Sir Alan Langlands (2005) on gateways into the professions was deepened in the health service with the creation of the Widening Participation Unit in the Department of Health, seeking more integrated career pathways for support staff in the NHS. The most prominent initiative in this respect was the development of the Department for Health (2001d) Skills Escalator, introduced with the suggestion 'that in theory, staff can progress from cleaner or porter to consultant or chief executive'.

The final element of the infrastructure was a sharpening and extension of workforce regulation, the framework for ensuring that employees were suitably qualified, maintained their capabilities, and behaved in appropriate ways. In general, regulation was perceived as key to ensuring and signalling service quality, but more specifically it connected to debates on service user risk. Certainly strengthened regulation was seen as needed to address the concerns generated by the failures of professional practice highlighted earlier; however debates on risk engaged with broader questions related to the potential vulnerability of service users in the context of new ways of working and new work roles across the public service workforce: if work relations were being re-shaped, then safety assurances under these new arrangements became essential.

Parts of the public services had long been subject to relatively tight forms of regulation. In healthcare, core professions had traditionally been covered by regulatory bodies founded upon on the establishment and maintenance of a register of capable practitioners. There was some fine tuning across these traditionally regulated groups: for example, the Nurses and Midwives Council published a new Code of Conduct in May 2008 (NMC 2008) providing revised guidance standards on how registered nurses should respond to changes in the delivery of nursing care. There were, however, attempts to extend regulation to a much greater swathe of the public service workforce.

This extension embraced professional groups hitherto not subject to a regulatory model based on registration. The General Teaching Council was established for teachers and the General Social Care Council (GSCC) for social workers and the wider social care workforce. These developments were not particularly contentious; they pandered to the professional aspiration of these groups for more complete occupational closure, while in the case of teachers, regulation rooted in Qualified Teacher Status already was fairly tight. The regulation of social workers assumed some importance, reflecting greater uncertainty about the nature and boundaries of the role, and indeed the government provided statutory support for the protection of the 'social worker' title as a necessary prelude to registration (Department for Health 2003c).

Less straightforward was the extension of regulation to non-professional groups. The growing importance of support roles with low barriers to entry, delivering care to the most vulnerable members of the community, raised concerns about service user well being. McKenna et al. (2004) asserted that 'the increasing reliance on healthcare assistants raises serious quality and safety questions'. Such worries were echoed in a survey of chief executives in health and social care organisations, over half (52 per cent) feeling that there was a 'considerable' or 'moderate' risk from the use of support workers (Saks and Alsop 2007). As a mean of allaying such fears, there was strong support for such regulation from key representative organisations: for example, both the RCN and Unison lobbied for the regulation of healthcare assistants.

For the government, however, such regulation created dilemmas. It imposed certain rigidities on the development of new roles and ways of working, regulation assuming a stable configuration of tasks and responsibilities as the basis for imposing entry conditions and monitoring performance. As the 2020 Children and Young's Workforce strategy noted (Department for Children, Schools and Families 2008: 22): 'Regulation and registration are the means through which Government seeks to influence the quality of parts of the workforce, however it is important that regulation requirements do not create inappropriate barriers to progression through the workforce or to deployment of staff in integrated ways.' More specifically in the wake of the Health Professional Council taking on the regulation ambulance paramedics in 2003, the Head of Operations at the South Central SHA is reported to have stated: 'We have got to the point where we do not have enough qualified paramedics because of the registration and education changes' (Nursing Times. Net 7 Oct. 2008). This tension between flexibility and risk encouraged consideration of 'lighter touch' forms of regulation for these non-professional groups, for instance employer-led regulation, a model finally adopted for the regulation of HCAs in Scotland, and forms of licensing, perhaps applicable to personal assistants in social care. Yet, when Labour left office, significant parts of the public services workforce remained unregulated. A model for regulating HCAs in England had still not been agreed, while the roll out of regulation beyond social workers had made little headway.

Overview and discussion

Patterns

In presenting the cross-cutting patterns characterising New Labour's attempt to re-shape work relations across the public services, sensitivity is needed to highlight variations between different parts of the sector. Table 5.1 draws upon the main elements of work relations as discussed, to provide an overview of developments by sub-sector. It highlights the streams of activity which relate to education, children's and adult social care, mental health and the NHS. This is a more complex picture than the disaggregated analysis provided in some other chapters that concentrate on developments in a limited number of discrete bargaining units. Indeed, a challenge faced by policy makers and practitioners in changing work relations in a given service area was the engagement with workers from different bargaining units employed on different terms and conditions. Indeed, Table 5.1. still fails to capture some of the more refined streams of activity, for example specific initiatives taken to address work relations amongst those working with older people and those with learning disabilities. There were also overlapping developments- hence the arrows in the table: for example, mental healthcare is provided by the NHS *and* social services; while children as well as adults will have learning and physical disabilities.

Before considering sub-sector variations, it is worth summarising some of the shared features of change in work relations highlighted by Table 5.1. The first such feature relates to the rationale for change. New roles and ways of working reflected in part a pragmatic response to staff shortages amongst professionals, to deal with difficult or stubborn issues and to motivate staff in ways which encouraged service quality. However, new forms of work organisation were also driven by a strategic purpose, which sought to re-shape work relations in ways which supported and gave effect to the principles of public service modernisation: personalisation, user voice, independence and control. Lending meaning to these principles involved not only addressing the role of the profession, developing new roles and ways of working, but ensuring that employees had the capabilities to deliver on this agenda and that the regulation of the workforce was appropriately modified.

Table 5.1 Developments in work relations by sub-sector

	Local Government				National Health Service
	Education	Social Care		Mental Health	
		Children	Adults (incl. elderly, physical/ learning disability)		
Core professions	Teachers	Social Workers Occupational Therapists	Social Worker Care Manager Occupational Therapists Rehabilitation Officers	Social worker Consultant Psychiatrist	Consultants GPs Nurses Health Visitors Dentists Allied Professional Groups
New and recast roles	- Teacher assistants - Invigilators - Behaviour managers - Career advisers - Learning mentors - Cover supervisors - Parent Support Adviser - Business managers/ bursars -Facilities managers	-(Budget holding) Lead Professional - Pedagogue -Personal Advisers	-Broker - Navigator -Advocate	-Graduate Primary Care Mental health worker - Psychological associate - Associate Mental health practitioner -BME Community Development Worker -STR Worker	- HCAs -Physicians Assistants -Specialist/Practice/ Consultant Nurses -Assistant Practitioners -Modern Matrons -Community Matrons -Housekeeper - ECP

New ways of working	- Workforce re-modelling -Extended school	- Work force re-modelling -Children's Services/Trusts - Local Safeguarding Children's Boards -Children's Centres		-Capable Teams -Assertive outreach - Crisis resolution. -Home treatment	-Self-care/Expert Patient - Ward teams - Lean/Productive Working -Families-Nursing Partnership -Lean production
Support Systems	-Developing people to support learning; A skills strategy for the wider school workforce (TDA, 2006) - Framework of Professional Standards (GTC, 2007) - General Teaching Council	- CWDC: Integrated qualifications framework, - CDWC: Common Core of Skills and Knowledge, 2005 - Early Years Professional - CDW Sector Skills Agreement	-General Social Care Council -Social Worker Protected Job Title	- Creating Capable Teams, 2007 - The Ten Essential Shared Capabilities August (DH, 2004c) -New Ways of Working for Everyone-Implementation guide, 2007	-Agenda for Change -Knowledge and Skills Framework -Skills Escalator - Productive Series-10 High Impact Changes - Skills for Health, Sector Skills Agreement -Common Core Principles to Support Self Care, (DH, 2008)

The second feature connects to the involvement of a much broader range of actors in the regulation of work relations across the public services. Whereas in the past work relations had often been seen by the traditional stakeholders in employee relations (trade unions, management and the government) as outside the collective bargaining agenda, under New Labour they became the subject of negotiation. The scale of the changes in work relations had profound implications for the employment experiences and working lives of public servants, drawing trade unions into a concern with such changes. This reform agenda led unions into a broader interest in public policy. For example, Unison (2010) commissioned a report on personalisation, highly critical of the funding provided for this initiative. The government linked the traditional union preoccupation with pay and conditions to working practices, whilst also being prepared to confront professional self regulation, so opening up for discussion traditionally protected work arrangements.

The role of these actors was reflected in collectively bargained agreements which embraced changes in work relations and covered significant swathes of the public services workforce: the new contracts respectively for consultants and GPs, the Workload Agreement covering workers in primary and secondary education and Agenda for Change embracing much of the NHS workforce. Moreover, public service unions and professional associations were re-integrated into the policy making 'establishment' in the ongoing regulation of work relations, for example the signatory trade unions joined with local authority employers and government in a working group to monitor the Workload Agreement and in broader terms unions and professional associations were typically represented on the various tasks forces and commissions to explore aspects of work relations.

Equally noteworthy was the engagement of a new set of actors in the regulation of public service work relations. Workforce regulatory bodies assumed increasing importance in the framing and structuring of work relations, seeking to maintain work standards, typically through a process of registration, linked to the achievement of formal qualifications and maintained through continuing professional development and adherence to a Code of Practice. A range of intermediary institutions, sponsored by, but at arm's-length from, government, supported new work relations. These institutions sought to facilitate the integration of service provision. For example, the Care Services Improvement Partnership, part of the Care Services Directorate at the Department for Health between 2005 and 2008, took responsibility for a number of cross-cutting programmes such as Putting People First in adult social care. Others institutions were engaged in progressing the capabilities agenda, essential to the delivery of new roles and ways of working. The sectors skills training councils in health, social care and justice as well as the Children's Workforce Development Council and the Teachers' Development Agency, formulated occupational standards for new and evolving roles while co-coordinating workforce development. Perhaps the most important new actor to participate in the organisation of work relations was the service user, reflected in the public policy emphasis placed on co-design, – production and –monitoring.

Framed by these patterns across public services, Table 5.1 also highlights some important differences of approach and emphasis within different parts of the sector. Change in work relations displayed some sensitivity to contingent factors including the size and complexity of the workforce, public policy objectives, and the characteristics of the user groups. More specifically, the contours of change in each sub-sector was as follows.

In *education,* change was underpinned by a re-modelling exercise, designed to free up and support the teacher as the key professional, and given effect in the Workload Agreement. Re-modelling created a more diverse school workforce with a range of new or enhanced roles, but the teaching assistant assumed particular prominence as a vehicle for pursuing a range of policy objectives in schools. Alongside re-modelling, the Every Child Matters agenda came to assume considerable importance, reflected not least in the notion of the extended school seeking to engage children in a range of extra-curricular activities either side of the normal school day.

In children's social care, the ECM agenda was the main driver for change, with the development of inter-agency working emerging as the predominant feature of the new work relations. This was particularly reflected in the development of Sure Start Children's Centres designed to provide wrap around care for early year's children, delivered on a partnership basis with a range of providers and necessitating new ways of inter-disciplinary working. ECM also had important implications for workforce roles, with the growing importance of the Lead Professional and the application of a new common assessment framework.

Adult social care was most directly affected by New Labour's personalisation agenda, reflected in the emergence of direct payments and individual budgets. The Putting People First strategy deepened the commitment to this approach. It was in this sub-sector that user engagement in work relations was most fully developed: client groups, such as those with physical and learning disabilities as well as older people, were able and willing to participate in service design and delivery. The impact on work roles and ways of working was reflected in the growing cadre of personal assistants employed by users, and in the re-evaluation of care manager and social worker roles.

In *mental health*, workforce re-modelling became central to change in work relations as a means of addressing depleted professional capacity. In addition, team working was developed as a key dimension of work organisation, a function of the range of services drawn upon to provide mental healthcare. There was also an emphasis on the establishment of more robust community-based services, particularly based on outreach and crisis resolution, an area of development which overlapped with the government's social inclusion agenda.

In the *health service*, the re-shaping of work relations defied easy generalisation. The public policy drive towards primary relative to secondary healthcare impacted on work relations with the growth of new community roles, such as the community matron, and new ways of working such as the Family–Nurse Partnership approach. In secondary healthcare, developments were characterised by incremental shifts in occupational boundaries, the most noteworthy seeing nurses take on more specialist and technical tasks, leaving healthcare assistants to play a more significant role in the provision of direct care. These were accompanied by more explicit attempts to break down traditional occupational barriers and develop new work roles. Such attempts were supported by new systems agreed in Agenda for Change, although their effective pursuit is questionable, reflected not least in the low take-up of new assistant practitioner roles (Spilsbury and Studdard 2009).

Process and outcome

While New Labour's attempt to re-shape work relations displayed a latent coherence, and perhaps a strategic intent, the effective implementation of changes in work organisation and the achievement of related policy goals remains open to greater debate. Given the time and resources devoted to changing work relations, the gains and benefits were not always readily apparent or conveyed. In short, the positive outcomes of change often seemed less than the sum of the parts. Various factors might explain this situation. Despite some unifying characteristics, the process and the evaluation of change was fragmented. New Labour was quite meticulous in piloting and assessing new roles and ways of working to provide an evidence base for practice. Indeed this assessment often revealed significant gains from change for different stakeholders. But the approach to evaluation remained diffuse and uneven, rendering it difficult to present an integrated and transparent picture of accrued benefits. More significantly, Labour's programme of change in work relations was riddled with tensions, impacting on the workforce and users in contradictory ways.

For the workforce the pace and nature of change generated uncertainties and pressures. Much of the momentum for change came in Labour's second and third terms, coinciding with major investment in the public services after holding to the Conservative's public expenditure plans in the early part of its first term. Whilst this left a ten year period to re-shape work relations, it is questionable whether even this was sufficient to embed change on the scale outlined. Moreover, for the public services professional, in particular, the 'toughness' of government policy often crowded-out the 'love'. For certain professional groups change provided benefits in terms of rewards and status: nurses were given the opportunity to develop their roles, while GPs worked under new contracts which yielded considerable financial returns (see Chapter 3). However, these gains were often at the expense of a growing insecurity about professional identity as new work roles began to challenge their traditional jurisdictions. More generally professionals typically found that the 'space' created by workforce re-modelling was taken up less by cherished core tasks, and more by a new set of burdensome routines associated with the target culture (see Chapter 3).

For some this degradation of work was seen to characterise developments not only amongst professionals but across much of the public service workforce. As the efficiency agenda began to assert itself and 'lean' techniques emerged in some parts of the sector against the backdrop of performance measures, commentators highlighted the Tayloristic features associated with these forms of work organisation (Mooney and Law 2002). The increased use of support workers fed into these debates with suggestions that in straying into professional terrain such workers were being exploited as 'cheap labour' (Thornley 2000; Stevenson 2007). Others took a more nuanced view, suggesting that the workforce consequences of change in work relations were somewhat more ambiguous. For example, research on support workers in education, social care and health (Bach et al. 2007; Kessler et al. 2007) revealed the difficulties faced by such workers as their roles developed: the poor management of their performance, the limited training opportunities and the frustrated career aspirations. It suggested, however, that some aspects of working life had been enriched with new and extended roles generating high levels of job satisfaction and a strong commitment to the job and the organisation.

The consequences of changes in work relations for the service user were also sensitive to tensions within New Labour's broader modernisation project. In part this was reflected in research on the consequences of change in work relations for service users. There was evidence from various sources which called into question user gains. For example, users often found it difficult to breakdown the power of the professional (Carr 2004). Moreover, the most rigorous study on the role of the teaching assistants, contested their contribution to pupil attainment (Blatchford et al. 2009). At the same time the evaluation of particular initiatives often highlighted the value placed on them by the service user: for example, those with direct payments and individual budgets welcomed the greater freedom; service users engaging with the new roles developed in social care by the Skills for Care New Type of worker programme usually saw them as meeting an important need and providing more accessible care and support (Kessler and Bach 2011); while patients found dealing with healthcare assistants easier and less intimidating than engaging with health professionals (Bach et al. *forthcoming*; Kessler et al. 2010).

Against the backdrop of uneven research evidence, there were powerful general influences fuelling a less positive user response to change. In part New Labour became a victim of its own rhetoric. In stressing consumer rights, such developments in service delivery came to be viewed as a right rather than a 'hard won' benefit that is the product of considerable investment in new work relations. Indeed, this sense of entitlement deepened, as New Labour achievements became tainted by continued and high-profile failures in organisational and professional practice.

Whether isolated instances or not, these failures were symbolically significant, calling into question just how far public services had improved. Between 2005 and 2009, many patients were perceived to have died 'unnecessarily' at the Mid Staffordshire hospital, a trust which had met many of its performance targets and been awarded Foundation Trust status. Moreover, with tragic irony and a macabre symmetry, after the intensity of effort and resource devoted to improving the provision of children's service under ECM, the New Labour period ended as it had begun with the murder of a child-in-need, Baby P. The shortcomings highlighted by this case were framed by Lord Laming's review of progress on child protection when he noted (2009: 11) that although there had been considerable progress in inter-agency working:

'There remain significant problems in the day to day reality of working across organisational boundaries and cultures, sharing information to protect children and a lack of feedback when professionals raise concerns about a child. Joint working between children's social workers, youth workers, schools, early years, police and health too often depends on the commitment of individual staff and sometimes this happens despite rather than because of, the organisational arrangements.'

6

Industrial relations: employee involvement, partnership at work and trade union renewal

Previous chapters have identified the shifting agenda of employee relations with work relations becoming far more central to public service employment relations, supported by reforms of pay determination and the strengthening of performance management. It would be misplaced, however, to suggest that industrial relations – trade union and employer relations – and other forms of employee involvement had moved to the fringes of public service employee relations. Controversy surrounding private sector involvement in public service delivery and unease about the target culture indicated the importance of engaging staff in public service modernisation and raised important questions about the extent to which the Labour government viewed trade unions as social partners (Bach 2002). Two main standpoints can be discerned which reflect different perspectives on the Labour government's modernisation agenda and the prospects for employee involvement, social partnership and trade union renewal.

The first, prominent amongst industrial relations scholars, is a degradation perspective, hostile towards the modernisation agenda. This perspective equates modernisation with neo-liberalism and a new public management characterised by competition, marketisation and tight monitoring of performance to satisfy the requirements of discerning customers and employers (Mooney and Law 2007; Worrall et al. 2010; Whitfield 2006). The scope for public service reform to accommodate and be influenced by the views and interests of the workforce is heavily circumscribed. Systems of employee involvement including partnership at work are irretrievably inscribed with a neo-liberal agenda, and trade unions are not viewed as legitimate partners. Such a perspective implies that at best the Labour government regarded the workforce and trade unions as marginal to public service reform and at worst they were perceived as vested interests defending outmoded forms of service delivery and narrow producer interests. These commentators are therefore dismissive of government initiatives to encourage employee involvement and partnership, seeing them as an attempt to incorporate the workforce and their representatives into participating in their own work intensification and loss of professional control (Bain and Taylor 2007; Stevenson and Carter 2009).

A second perspective, which could be termed engagement, whilst remaining cautious about trade union and workforce involvement with modernisation was more positive about New Labour's public service reform project. It viewed the inclusion of trade unions in policy making and the endorsement of partnership as an important departure from previous Conservative governments, providing some scope for trade union influence (Bacon and Samuel 2009; Farnham et al. 2003). These perspectives were closer to an analysis of New Labour which emphasised a shift towards forms of network governance and engagement with a range of stakeholders. As Ludlum (2004: 74) stated: 'it is impossible to exaggerate how important increased direct access to ministers has been', exemplified by regular quarterly meetings between senior trade union leaders and the Prime Minister after 2000. It was argued that trade union involvement in workplace modernisation created scope for mutual gains because all stakeholders had overlapping interests. New Labour was seeking to provide high-quality public services and this objective could be furthered by improving staff working lives and generating increased staff commitment. Encouraging 'voice' – two-way communication mechanisms which assisted employers, employees and their representatives in understanding each other better and resolving their differences – had been viewed as providing benefits to all parties. Bacon and Samuel (2009) highlighted the extent to which partnership agreements were predominantly public sector phenomenon and suggested that because of high levels of union density, public sector unions gained more from partnership than their private sector counterparts. In addition, the prevalence of communication and involvement practices was much higher than in the private sector, indicating concerted attempts by employers to involve staff (Bach et al. 2009). Some analysts went further claiming that the emergence of partnership represented an attempt to reinvent the model employer tradition and develop a new accommodation with organised labour (Stuart and Martinez Lucio 2000).

This chapter starts by outlining the government's approach to employee involvement and partnership, highlighting the reasons for its approach. Trends in employee involvement and partnership at work are then examined before moving on to an examination of how trade unions engaged with partnership at work and other strategies they adopted to increase their membership and influence the modernisation agenda.

New Labour and industrial relations

The increasing concentration of trade union membership in the public services indicated that New Labour's approach to industrial relations would be especially significant for the public service workforce. In the 1997 election manifesto Tony Blair set out his reasons for why New Labour would govern differently from previous Labour governments, establishing a different relationship with the trade union movement (Labour Party 1997). The role assigned to trade unions was shaped by the importance that New Labour attached to globalisation and the centrality of enhancing the competitiveness of the British economy. This approach required modernised public services which equipped citizens for a more uncertain and competitive world (Bach 2002).

New Labour invoked a particular industrial relations settlement in which 'there will be no return to flying pickets, secondary action, strikes with no ballots or the trade union law of the 1970s' (Labour Party 1997: 3). The reference to the 1970s clearly signalled that trade union militancy, epitomised by the winter of discontent in 1978/9, which contributed to the Conservative electoral success of Mrs Thatcher in 1979, would not be tolerated. Instead the relationship with the trade unions would be placed 'on a modern footing where they accept they can get fairness but no favours from a Labour government' (Labour Party 1997: 2). This entailed strengthening of individual employment rights but there was a reluctance to promote collective voice and to encourage collective bargaining (Dickens and Hall 2010). The Labour government tilted towards a unitarist perspective in which it was assumed that employers and employees shared common interests and worked together effectively, but this was tempered by a recognition that the workforce required minimum standards to ensure fairness at work (McIlroy 1999). The Labour government was much more wary of bolstering collective rights, not least because of Tony Blair's own ambivalent attitude towards the trade union movement (Smith and Morton 2001; Taylor 2001).

This did not preclude a role for public service trade unions, but it was to take the form of partnership at work in which employers and trade unions would co-operate to achieve mutual benefits and implement government reforms. This was especially important in a public sector context in which the trade unions had an important role in interpreting managerial reforms for employees. For example, in the case of the attempts to decentralise pay determination in the early 1990s, the health sector trade unions forcefully articulated a concern that local pay would lead to lower pay, a fear that resonated with their members, reinforcing opposition to pay reform (Bach and Winchester 1994).

Partnership, however, was defined loosely and was not confined to trade union–employer partnerships. The Labour Party (1997: 17) expressed its support for 'a variety of forms of partnership' which could include forms of direct partnership with employees in the absence of trade union involvement. Partnership could complement but not substitute for the direct relationship between line managers and employees because 'many employers and employees will continue to choose direct relationships without the intervention of third parties' (Department of Trade and Industry 1998: 1.9). Trade unions, in a similar way to the Labour Party itself, were to be rebranded and encouraged to work with government 'to achieve our shared goals of committed, fair, efficient and effective public services' (Cabinet Office 1999: 12).

Public policy: staff participation

The priority attached to involvement and partnership at work was intended to fulfil a number of government aims and to respond to a series of challenges inherited by Labour on taking office in 1997. A high priority was to address severe recruitment and retention problems for public sector professionals and to respond to a widespread perception of a public service in crisis. Survey data from registered nurses, a high-profile occupational group, reported that more than a third of respondents agreed that 'I would leave nursing if I could' and around half agreed that 'I feel under too much pressure at work' (Smith and Seccombe 1998). These concerns were backed up by threats of industrial action and other sanctions against government policy. In 2001, the usually divided and squabbling teacher unions passed identical motions in support of a 35-hour week, backed up by a campaign of industrial action (Stevenson and Carter 2009).

The government responded to this malaise by advocating more staff participation. The NHS was in the vanguard of these developments because controversial market reforms under the Conservatives had left a legacy of distrust between managers and the workforce, especially professionals, which the Labour government feared could jeopardise further reforms (Bach 2004).

The NHS White Paper ,'The New NHS', published within months of the 1997 election, acknowledged the importance of staff involvement, which in the past had 'not been a high priority', but pledged a new approach 'to better valuing staff' spearheaded by a taskforce on staff involvement (Department of Health 1997: 50–51). Many of these policies were targeted at individuals, although an emphasis on partnership and involvement was intended to alter the culture of NHS employee relations. The government viewed partnership as a means to make the NHS 'the employer of first choice', but also signalled that managers would expect union-based or direct forms of involvement to focus on fostering flexible working and service improvements (Cabinet Office 2004).

The government's NHS HR strategy was set out in *Working Together* (Department of Health 1998). The proposals were relatively modest in terms of staff involvement, focusing on developing an involvement policy, including relevant questions in each trust's annual staff survey and reviewing induction arrangements. It still represented a significant departure for government because it was the first time that the NHS had set out a detailed approach to employee relations. Doubts were expressed, however, about how far this guidance provided a sufficient incentive for staff involvement to become integral to the core concerns of senior management. In a survey of 75 trusts, 'reviewing staff involvement' and 'establishing a partnership agreement' were the lowest priorities in terms of progress on 13 HR goals (Industrial Relations Services 1999: 5–6).

Partly because of the difficulties of persuading employers, the government took every opportunity to set out the business case for involvement (see Cabinet Office 2004). The NHS taskforce report pointed to private sector best practice and used almost evangelical language to persuade sceptical employers that staff involvement works:

> We have seen the research evidence. We have talked to employers in the NHS and outside the NHS who are demonstrating that it works. We have no doubt...that employers in the NHS who involve staff in decisions, planning and policy making: improve patient care through better service delivery; manage change more effectively; have a healthier, better motivated workforce and reduce staff turnover (Department of Health 1999b: 3–4).

A similar if somewhat more muted emphasis on staff involvement was used in local government and the civil service. As part of the local government Best Value regime, which replaced periodic market-testing, local authorities were expected to engage in a continuous process of performance review designed to improve quality, efficiency and encourage partnership working with a range of stakeholders. Government guidance on Best Value emphasised the importance of involving the workforce not only because their support was viewed as critical to successful implementation, but because they brought a valuable perspective on how services were perceived and how they could be improved (Department for Transport, Environment and the Regions 1999). The *Modernising Government* White Paper noted that 'we want staff at all levels to contribute to evaluating policies and services, and to put forward ideas about how they might be improved' (Cabinet Office 1999: 57). In the civil service, the Cabinet Office worked closely with the Council of Civil Service Unions in reviewing diversity, pay and performance management systems and prior to the introduction of the revised Senior Civil Service (SCS) competency framework in 2001, all members of the SCS had the opportunity to comment. Agency chief executives also strengthened forms of direct staff involvement and the use of staff opinion surveys increased (Farnham et al. 2003).

The main focus of staff involvement was to encourage employers to improve recruitment, retention, sickness absence and staff morale. The Labour government also established new funding streams and institutional innovations to reinforce this agenda. In 2003, the government set-up the Public Services Forum (PSF), chaired by a Cabinet Office Minister, which brought together government, employer and trade union representatives. The PSF, utilising specific taskforces, addressed controversial issues relating to pensions, the two-tier workforce, skills and procurement and produced a toolkit – *Drive for Change* – intended to engage trade unions and the workforce in service improvement (Cabinet Office 2008a).

An important dimension of social partnership was the promotion of trade union involvement in workplace learning. This represented a broadening of the role of trade unions in public service modernisation, reflecting a more general widening of the employee relations agenda, discussed more fully in Chapter 5. An important innovation was the establishment of the Union Learning Fund which supported novel union learning activity and which led to the establishment of Union Learning Representatives (ULRs). Their main role was to encourage members to take up learning and training opportunities and to enable trade unions to broaden the activist base of trade unions. The 2002 Employment Act placed Union Learning Representatives on a statutory basis and government funding in excess of £10 million per annum enabled around 100,000 learners a year to access training, including many low-paid public service workers with aspirations to advance (Keep et al. 2010).

These innovations focused on the interdependence between actors and provided a degree of autonomy for networks to flesh out state policy. Some aspects of service delivery, particularly those underpinned by the use of targets, remained highly prescriptive, but in many areas of industrial relations, with more diffuse outcomes, a network governance orientation was adopted. This approach involved establishing the main principles and direction of reform, engaging a variety of stakeholders to try and establish consensus around the way forward, bolstered by incentives to reach agreement (Newman 2001). The Local Government Pay Commission, established after the 2002 strike in local government (Kessler and Dickens 2008), the NHS Social Partnership Forum and several institutional innovations in education (e.g. the Workforce Agreement Monitoring Group and the Rewards and Incentives Group) were notable examples of this approach. The deliberations of the Low Pay Commission and the Migration Advisory Committee also had implications for the pay and composition of the public service workforce. The range of stakeholders was extended with private sector employer associations and third-sector organisations represented within many partnership forums, although business stakeholders were invariably better represented than trade unions (Howell 2004). While, unions remained wary that the language of partnership could disguise the extent to which they were participating in reforms which harmed their members' interests, the development of partnership working and other forums for union engagement suggested that trade unions were gaining access to policy making in a way that eluded them under previous Conservative governments.

Trends

To what extent did the Labour government's emphasis on employee involvement translate into developments at the workplace? It is customary to differentiate between direct and indirect involvement. Direct involvement involves individuals or groups of employees focused on information sharing, communication and operational work matters using staff surveys, team briefings and suggestion schemes to elicit staff views. Indirect involvement is collectivist and representative and can include more strategic management decisions, raising questions about the limits and use of managerial power. Within the public services employee involvement was underpinned by a long-standing tradition of collectivism, associated with joint consultation arrangements and more recently forms of partnership at work. Indirect consultation also operated at multiple levels. The analysis of pay determination in Chapter 3 indicated that the public sector had a long tradition of pay and conditions being jointly regulated at national level by collective bargaining or pay review bodies. There was also widespread consultation at the workplace via the establishment of joint consultation committees with membership drawn from representative trade unions. It was the increasing combination of direct and indirect involvement, involving a wider range of stakeholders which characterised developments over the last decade.

The most authoritative data derives from the comprehensive Workplace Employment Relations Survey (WERS) which has surveyed workplaces on a regular basis since 1980 with surveys in 1998 and 2004, providing insights into the first half of New Labour's tenure. Public service workplaces had dense systems of employee involvement and the nature of this 'voice' differed markedly from that of the private sector. In particular public sector workplaces were much more likely to have representative forms of voice than the private sector. Although union-only voice had declined in both the public and private sectors, its incidence was around twice as high in the public sector over the last quarter of a century (Willman et al. 2009: 103). In 2004, 33 per cent of public sector workplaces with more than 25 employees had a joint consultative committee (JCC) compared to 21 per cent in the private sector. Nonetheless the number of JCCs meeting once a month fell significantly between 1998 and 2004 (see Table 6.1). In the economy overall, whereas 33 per cent of managers suggested that JCCs were 'very influential' in 1998, this figure had fallen to 23 per cent by 2004 (Willman et al. 2009: 105).

In terms of direct voice mechanisms, the public services provided more information to staff and the use of two-ways systems of involvement such as problem-solving groups was generally higher, encouraging more active employee involvement (Bach et al. 2009). As Table 6.1 indicates many of the main forms of direct voice increased in the public sector between 1998 and 2004 and the incidence of these mechanisms was higher, with the exception of suggestion schemes, than in the private sector. Case study and other workplace data provided a more contextualised picture, giving a better insight into staff involvement and highlighting a shift from a focus on traditional systems of indirect involvement towards a preference for direct engagement with the workforce and an indifference towards engagement with trade unions (Bach 2004). An in-depth study of three NHS trusts reported that managers had developed an impressive array of top-down communication mechanisms with the proliferation of newsletters, staff magazines, summaries of board meetings and face-to-face briefings by the chief executive and other senior managers. But as managers focused on achieving their waiting time and financial targets, the scope for staff to shape workplace developments was constrained. Although differences emerged between the trusts, the staff opinion survey

Table 6.1 Incidence of representative and direct voice types in Britain, 1998–2004 by sector

All workplaces	1998		2004	
Representative Voice:	Public	Private	Public	Private
Any on-site JCC	39	24	33	21
On-site JCC that meets at least once a month	31	19	22	15
Direct Voice:				
Regular meetings between senior management and the workforce	44	34	54	36
Newsletters	64	44	66	56
Suggestion schemes	38	30	33	36
Briefing groups	61	49	77	70
Problem-solving groups	49	36	39	28
Provides information about:				
Investment plans	62	49	58	46
Establishment's financial position	79	60	80	58
Organisation's financial position[a]	63	63	58	60
Staffing plans	82	52	83	61

Note: [a] Workplaces that belonged to a larger organisation. All values represent percentages. Figures are for all workplaces with 25 or more employees.

Source: WIRS/WERS data cited in Bach et al. 2009: 325 and Willman et al. 2009: 108.

data indicated that increased employee involvement to influence clinical developments remained a key demand. In general, staff expressed scepticism about senior management's interest in workforce perspectives and noted difficulties in gaining feedback on their suggestions (Bach 2004). Allen (2001: 30) in her study of ward sisters concluded,

> The extent to which sisters had difficulty in getting their voices heard was a marked feature of all [focus] groups. There were opportunities to attend meetings, but most sisters said that they were so busy that they rarely found time to attend meetings in which they could express their concerns. Others felt that the composition of the meetings was not conducive to encouraging the full and frank exchange of views which they would have welcomed.

These sentiments were reflected in national NHS staff opinion survey data which indicated limited change over the decade. In the first national annual staff survey conducted in 2003, 34 per cent agreed (37 per cent disagreed) that 'managers here try to involve staff in important decisions', and in response to the question 'communication between management and staff is effective', 31 per cent agreed (37 per cent disagreed) (Healthcare Commission 2004). The questions in the staff survey have altered, so the results need to be treated with some caution. But in 2007, in response to a similar question Do'[s]enior managers here try to involve staff in important decisions?' 23 per cent of staff agreed or agreed strongly and 22 per cent agreed or strongly agreed that 'communication between senior management and staff is effective' (Healthcare Commission 2007). These results have remained stable since 2007, although in some areas of HR policy there were signs of improvement, for example, accessing training and development opportunities (Care Quality Commission 2010b). Staff survey data reinforce case study evidence which indicated that despite considerable effort to improve communication, staff perceptions had not altered significantly. NHS officials were sufficiently concerned about the 2007 results that the national Social Partnership Forum identified staff engagement and job satisfaction as priority areas to be addressed. Research on 'what matters to staff in the NHS' highlighted widespread frustration and commented that many staff 'see the NHS serving a business agenda driven by financial considerations and irrelevant targets. This frustration, it appears, is driving a feeling of alienation' (Department of Health 2008a: 22).

Similar national-level employee data are not available for local government, despite almost all local authorities conducting annual or bi-annual staff surveys (Local Government Association 2009). Rotherham Council was typical, employing 13,500 staff and undertaking a full staff opinion survey every two years, along with a 300 strong panel of staff to gauge staff opinion on organisational change every three months (Suff 2008). More generally, the introduction of Best Value arrangements was intended to encourage staff engagement, but a survey of 389 Best Value lead officers cast doubt on this assumption. In terms of the benefits of Best Value, it was noticeable that workforce benefits such as 'staff morale' and 'relations with in-house unions' received the lowest scores in terms of the improvements brought by the Best Value process and there was little basis for the government assumption that Best Value would encourage union–management partnerships (Roper et al. 2005).

In the civil service, until 2010, individual departments undertook their own staff opinion surveys. One of the largest (around 70,000 respondents) was carried out in the Department for Work and Pensions (DWP) with results benchmarked against other central government departments. Civil service staff opinion surveys differ from those in the NHS, so comparisons are only indicative, but the data suggest that in terms of involvement staff are generally less dissatisfied. The results for the DWP could be expected to be worse than the results for central government overall, as many low-paid staff are required to achieve demanding targets and often dealt with difficult customers in challenging circumstances (McCafferty and Mooney 2007). In the 2009 DWP survey, which used a traffic light system, the single red light high priority area for action related to 'I have the opportunity to contribute my views before changes are made which affect my job'. Only 31 per cent of respondents agreed with this statement (the central government average was 44 per cent). This represented an improvement from results in 2006 and 2008 when only around a fifth of staff agreed or strongly agreed with this statement but it was still well below the standard expected (65 per cent).

In 2010, for the first time, the civil service systematically started to use one survey instrument (the Civil Service People Survey) across the whole civil service replacing separate exercises in each department. The key results, with comparable benchmark figures, are reported in Table 6.2. The most striking findings were the poor perceptions of senior management with low scores for leadership and managing change, but career development and perceptions of pay and benefits were also rated poorly. The latter in particular may well have been influenced by uncertainties over future pension arrangements and the announcement of a pay freeze for the majority of civil servants. Although staff were generally clear about what was expected of them, only a third felt involved in relevant decisions. Overall employee engagement was 56 per cent, a 2 per cent decline since 2009.

The Labour government's emphasis on staff involvement encouraged employers to communicate and involve staff, as the widespread use of staff opinion surveys testifies. Despite the different instruments used to garner staff feedback across sectors, the results were not especially encouraging for managers and the workforce. The WERS employee survey data provided a sector-wide assessment of employees' evaluations of the degree to which managers were viewed as open to employee influence. In terms of how good managers were at responding to suggestions from employees or workplace representatives, 44 per cent of employees in the private sector rated their managers as 'good' or 'very good' compared to 40 per cent in the public sector. The same gap (41 per cent in the private sector compared to 37 per cent in the public sector) emerged when private sector employees were asked about their satisfaction with their involvement in decision making at their workplace. Overall, these results suggested that although there was a trend towards increased employee involvement, it does not seem that increased incidence was necessarily being translated into effective staff engagement. These findings, however, focused predominantly on direct involvement and the Labour government also put considerable emphasis on indirect involvement, especially social partnership.

Table 6.2 Selected results from Civil Service People Survey: 2010 benchmark results by theme (in bold) and individual item (in italics). All values represent percentages

	2010 Bench mark	2009 Bench mark
My work:	**71**	**75**
01 I am interested in my work	89	90
04 I feel involved in the decisions that affect my work	49	56
Organisational objectives and purpose:	**81**	**81**
07 I have clear understanding of my organisation's objectives	84	84
08 I understand how my work contributes to my organisation's objectives	80	82
My line manager:	**64**	**64**
B11 My manager is open to my ideas	77	78
B15 I receive regular feedback on my performance	60	60
B18 Poor performance is dealt with effectively in my team	37	38
My team	**77**	**76**
Learning and development:	**43**	**50**
B22 I am able to access the right learning and development opportunities when I need to	55	63
B24 There are opportunities for me to develop my career	28	39
Inclusion and treatment:	**73**	**74**
B26 I am treated fairly at work	78	79
B28 I feel valued for the work I do	60	62
Resources and workload:	**73**	**72**
B30 In my job, I am clear what is expected of me	82	81
B35 I have an acceptable workload	62	60
Pay and benefits:	**37**	**37**
B37 I feel that pay adequately reflects my performance	38	36
B39 Compared to other people doing a similar job in other organisations I feel my pay is reasonable	31	33
Leadership and managing change:	**37**	**38**
B44 Overall I have confidence in the decision's made by my organisation's senior managers	36	36
B45 I feel that change is managed well in my organisation	27	27
B48 I have the opportunity to contribute my views before decisions are made that affect me	32	34
Employee engagement:	**56**	**58**
B50 I am proud when I tell others I am part of my organisation	55	56
B54 My organisation motivates me to help it achieve its objectives	36	38

Notes: Based on 325,119 responses (74 per cent median response rate across 103 participating organisations) in 2010. The result for each theme is calculated as the % response to all the questions belonging to that theme (including questions excluded from Table 6.2). For each theme, the 2010 and 2009 benchmark is the median of the results for all participating organisations (2010 =103; 2009= 98 organisations). *Source*: Cabinet Office 2010a (Abbreviated).

Partnership at work

An important component of modernisation was an effort to move away from the adversarialism and industrial strife, often referred to as 'the British disease' in the 1960s and 1970s. From the early 1970s, as trade union membership grew strongly amongst non-manual public sector workers, strike activity became a predominantly public sector phenomenon (Dix et al. 2009). Government endorsement of partnership working was intended to inject a more consensual dynamic into public service industrial relations and implied that trade unions opposed to partnership were failing to modernise: 'Forward-looking trade unions know that the future is about partnership, and are leading the way in a number of projects' (Office of Public Service Reform 2002: 21).

Partnership had a broader symbolic importance closely linked to the preference for network governance, indicating that a variety of stakeholders, especially service users but also staff, were to be included in service planning and delivery. The Involvement and Participation Association (IPA), a major advocate of partnership, and the Work Foundation linked with prominent stakeholders, including the Advisory Conciliation and Arbitration Service (ACAS), the Trade Union Congress (TUC) and the Department of Trade and Industry (DTI), to galvanise support for partnership at work. Financial assistance was made available by the DTI partnership fund, expertise and best practice was shared by ACAS, and the TUC set-up a Partnership Institute to facilitate partnership working (Martinez Lucio and Stuart 2002).

Although the government did not view partnership as limited to accords with trade unions, in practice partnership agreements were almost exclusively located in organisations with union recognition. Consequently the public services with high levels of trade union density and a long tradition of negotiation and consultation featured prominently with an estimated two million public sector employees covered by partnership agreements by 2007 (Bacon and Samuel 2009). Around a third of all agreements in the UK were accounted for by the 'Health and Social Work' sector with public administration comprising a further 20 per cent of agreements (Bacon and Samuel 2009: 239–240). This pattern was replicated amongst successful bids to the DTI partnership fund in which the public services were the largest recipients of funding, overwhelmingly drawn from the NHS and local government (Terry and Smith 2003). Partnership agreements occurred at sectoral level, such as the agreement between the civil service unions and the Cabinet Office (2000), and at individual employer level with many partnership agreements concluded by NHS trusts, some civil service agencies and a smaller number of local authorities.

Based on principles established by the TUC (2002) and actively championed by the IPA, agreements typically involved the partners recognising the legitimacy of each partner and a commitment to work together to achieve mutual benefits. Differences of interest were acknowledged but seen as secondary to a shared interest in organisational success. This in turn required a broader dialogue between employers and trade unions which extended beyond a narrow focus on terms and conditions of employment. Typically trade unions were provided with undertakings on employment security, or at least the avoidance of compulsory redundancies, but expected to contribute towards enhanced efficiency and flexibility. The relationship between trade unions and employers was usually characterised as consultation rather than negotiation with pay and conditions established in a different forum which might be at national level (e.g. pay review bodies). Partnership offered employers the prospect of developing a more productive relationship with trade unions, enabling them to manage change more effectively. Trade unions anticipated that endorsing partnership working would increase their legitimacy, providing opportunities to influence employer policy and workplace practice. Despite some misgivings amongst employers and trade unions, within the public services, both parties felt under pressure from government to endorse partnership working (Stuart and Martinez Lucio 2008; Tailby and Winchester 2005).

National partnership arrangements

Because the term 'partnership' has often been ill-defined, a variety of arrangements have been labelled partnership agreements. As noted in Chapter 3, reforms of pay and working conditions in the NHS and in schools were negotiated on a national basis between government, employers and trade unions. The label 'partnership' was attached to these national agreements because of the commitment to involve national and local trade union representatives in joint implementation, for example NHS trade union representatives had a crucial role in local job evaluation. The broader remit of these agreements which extended beyond pay and conditions to incorporate skills, job roles and contribution was in keeping with a focus in partnership agreements on improving organisational effectiveness. A different form of national partnership was the establishment of sectoral institutions. In education, this was effective because the Workforce Agreement and Monitoring Group (WAMG) had high level stakeholder involvement and a clear remit to monitor the implementation of the 2003 national workload agreement, and it issued high-profile guidance on good practice to assist with local implementation. Schools, as relatively small employers with little HR expertise, increasingly independent of their local education authorities and required to publish their revised workforce structures, ensuring transparency and accountability, were generally receptive to national guidance on complex workforce issues (Hammersley-Fletcher and Adnett 2009; Hutchings et al. 2009; Ofsted 2007).

The NHS experience with its national Social Partnership Forum represented a marked contrast. The Forum's establishment stemmed from a blizzard of NHS policy documents advocating involvement and partnership (Department of Health 1998; 2002; 2004a), but a blunt assessment of its achievements, undertaken by the pro-partnership IPA (2008: 1) concluded that the Forum:

> appeared to stand alone as a piece of architecture, had little access to ministers or senior Department of Health officials, and had no means of tasking other bodies or monitoring the outcomes of its deliberations…Health officials did not regard the partnership arrangements as intrinsic to managing change.

The IPA reported that employers were unsure of the relevance of a national forum whilst trade unions felt that major policy announcements were made without reference to them.

The Forum was re-launched in 2007, chaired by a minister, and started to have more impact. It was instrumental in shifting policy towards the NHS being the 'preferred provider' for health services, a controversial decision that upset independent and third-sector providers (Timmins 2010). Despite this temporary renaissance, in contrast to partnership working focused on school workforce re-modelling, the remit of the NHS Social Partnership Forum remained ambiguous and there was little awareness of its existence. Consequently the form and outcomes of partnership varied substantially between sectors. These differing experiences resonate with Kelly's (2004) argument that in essence two main forms of partnership agreement exist with employer-dominated partnerships, tilted towards employers and advancing their agenda, compared to labour-parity agreements in which there is a more even balance of power between trade unions and employers.

Workplace practice

The experience of workplace partnership highlights five main issues. First, some employers and workplaces are more receptive than others to partnership working, and even receptive contexts are vulnerable to changes in circumstances. A legacy of adversarial relations and a recognition of the need to improve working relations has sometimes provided the catalyst to alter industrial relations. In the NHS a common pattern was a recognition that existing joint consultative committees had ceased to function effectively and had become mired in addressing relatively trivial operational issues, requiring outside facilitation such as ACAS (Bach 2004; Stuart and Martinez Lucio 2008). Although dissatisfaction with existing industrial relations could sometimes prove a catalyst for change, amongst ambulance trusts, with a long history of adversarial industrial relations the scope for partnership working was very limited (IPA 2008). It was often the commitment of specific senior managers and their trade union counterparts which had operationalised partnership working, and this created an obvious risk that partnership working might evaporate as individuals or circumstances altered. In local government, Martinez Lucio and Stuart (2007) tracked one partnership agreement which proved highly vulnerable to managerial turnover and the loss of organisational memory. In the civil service, the partnership agreement signed in 2000 was not renewed when the Department for Work and Pensions was established as the successor to the Benefits Agency, reflecting altered managerial judgements about the benefits of partnership working (Martin 2010).

Sufficient union capacity is a second important influence on partnership working. For trade unions, their ability to recruit sufficient union members to act as union representatives is a key challenge with implications for union membership which extends beyond their involvement in partnership arrangements. As Darlington's (2010) review of workplace organisation confirms there has been a substantial reduction in the number of workplace representatives in recent years. WERS 2004 data indicated that in public sector workplaces with union recognition, 63 per cent of workplaces with 25 or more employees had a workplace representative, a marked decline from the figure of 71 per cent in 1998 (Charlwood and Forth 2009: 77). Waddington and Kerr (2009: 49) reported similar findings based on Unison branch data, noting that about 30 per cent of Unison members reported the absence of a union representative at their workplace. It was not simply the absence of representatives but the limited time available to union representatives to become involved in partnership arrangements which proved a barrier to participation, especially when set alongside other priorities in supporting union members at the workplace. The increased workload involved in attending meetings could leave workplace representatives feeling overwhelmed (Munro 2002: 283) and nurses, amongst others, were often reluctant to participate in partnership and other staff involvement arrangements because their absence would leave colleagues short-staffed (Bach 2004).

Third, managers also faced dilemmas and their involvement in partnership arrangements was often influenced by the commitment of top managers and the wider context in which they operated. In the case of the NHS, corporate HR managers endorsed staff engagement conscious of the central government emphasis on staff involvement and the targets they were expected to achieve. This agenda was rarely endorsed with the same level of commitment by other senior or middle managers as they struggled to reconcile a series of seemingly contradictory commitments. Managers were under pressure to enhance patient throughput and reduce waiting times whilst expected to enhance the quality of working lives of staff, a more diffuse goal than their budgetary targets (Bach 2004; Tailby et al. 2004). Overall, the IPA (2008: 21) concluded that partnership was not 'embedded in the NHS culture...there remains a need to convince some chief executives and managers that partnership is a helpful process that will take staff along rather than a delaying tactic by unions.'

A fourth consideration relates to the implications for the workforce. An important starting point is the extent to which employees are aware of partnership arrangements. In a case study of one large hospital trust, few employees who were interviewed realised that partnership arrangements existed in the Trust. Staff opinion survey responses indicated that only 19 per cent were aware of the existence of joint consultation arrangements with only 10 per cent aware of who represented them within this forum (Tailby et al. 2004: 408). Similar uncertainties about the awareness and process of partnership working were highlighted in local government (Richardson et al. 2005).

It is not simply the lack of trade union capacity which limited partnership working, but also a reticence to endorse partnership working if the benefits for union members were unclear. Although the authority of a trade union and its senior workplace representatives were often enhanced with more vibrant consultation arrangements, the corollary was that relations with members and other representatives became more distant, eroding the scope for union activism (Danford et al. 2002). This was not inevitably the case with the civil service partnership agreement benefiting the union by increasing facility time, enabling representatives to exert more influence with management over working conditions (Martin 2010). The suspicion remained, however, that partnership working was designed to incorporate trade unions into a process of change to the detriment of the workforce. As Richardson et al. (2005: 714) commented in their study of local government: 'This approach focuses more on partnership as an agreement between the employer and trade unions rather than as a process involving employees'.

The clear implication is that union participation in partnership arrangements was a sign of union weakness which could debilitate unions and leave workers exposed to unfavourable outcomes such as work intensification and reduced job security (Richardson et al. 2005). Many accounts were relatively cautious and had difficulty identifying clear outcomes – positive or negative – which could be attributed to partnership working. In the public services some modest benefits in terms of an improved climate of workplace employment relations, the construction of an agreed approach to issues such as bullying and harassment, or enhanced training provision were noted, but these outcomes seemed to confirm Bacon and Samuel's (2010) argument that the aims and provisions of partnership agreements lacked ambition. Not surprisingly the prospects and commitment to partnership working fluctuated. Just as the initial high expectations of public service reform became tarnished, a similar process occurred with partnership which also lost its allure. Few public service employers actively abandoned partnership agreements, but forms of collective consultation played a less central role in employee relations, leaving aside specific change projects such as reforms of pay determination. Although partnership indicated a commitment by government to involve staff in the modernisation process, trade unions could not rely on partnership to boost their membership and influence.

Trade unions and modernisation

Partly because of a continuing process of union mergers, the 14 trade unions with more than 100,000 members comprise around 85 per cent of British trade union membership (Certification Office 2010: 24). The vast majority of these trade unions draw their membership predominantly from the public services with the main exceptions being UCATT and USDAW whose membership is concentrated in the construction and retail sectors respectively (see Table 6.3). Unison is the largest public service industry trade union with more than 800,000 members in local government, around 400,000 members in health and a significant membership in other parts of the sector. PCS represents the majority of lower-paid workers in the civil service and Prospect recruits amongst technicians and specialists, such as scientists working in government. In education, many of the largest trade unions are occupational unions including the trade unions for classroom teachers (i.e. the rival NUT and NAS/UWT), and in health the RCN, representing nurses, and the BMA, representing doctors, are influential stakeholders.

Table 6.3 Membership of trade unions with more than 100,000 members in Great Britain at 31/12/2009

	Male	Female	Total
Unite	1,120,290	354,274	1,474,564
Unison	419,875	917,375	1,337,250
GMB	310,562	278,435	588,997
Royal College of Nursing[a]	36,098	356,854	392,952
National Union of Teachers	89,213	286,737	375,950
Union of Shop, Distributive and Allied Workers	159,752	212,108	371,860
National Association of Schoolmaster/Union of Women Teachers	86,285	224,983	311,268
Public and Commercial Services Union	120,001	178,585	298,586
Communication Workers Union	171,008	41,319	212,327
Association of Teachers and Lecturers	52,545	157,771	210,316
British Medical Association	73,913	59,444	133,357
University and College Union[b]	59,608	55,505	115,113
Union of Construction Allied Trades and Technicians	109,279	2,119	111,398
Prospect	77,437	23,154	100,591

(a)Figures for year ended 31/03/10 (b) Figures for year ended 31/08/09

Source: Certification Officer AR21 Returns. Available at http//www.certoffice.org/Nav/Trade-Unions/Active.aspx

Irrespective of union mergers, an important characteristic of public service unionism is the existence of many specialist trade unions which have contributed to very high levels of trade union membership amongst occupations such as nursing and teaching. The existence of multiple trade unions attests to the divergent views of how these interests can best be represented and also contributes to fierce competition for members. Specialist occupational trade unions highlight their ability to identify and advance the professional interests of their membership, but this can prove resource-intensive. By contrast the challenge for large general unions, such as Unite and the GMB, which have grown through a series of mergers, is to ensure that the distinctive occupational identities of their members are recognised within union structures (Bach and Givan 2004).

Although public sector trade union density remained relatively high and nearly four times the level of the private sector (57 per cent compared to 15 per cent) (Achur 2010), this represented a significant decline from the level of 84 per cent in 1980. Workplace Employment Relations Survey data indicate that in sectors such as education two-thirds of employees remained union members. By contrast, in health the sub-sector with the lowest density, there was continuous decline between 1980 and 2004 from 85 per cent to 48 per cent union density (Bach et al. 2009). Declining density reduced union legitimacy with employers and union members. It also compromised effectiveness by reducing union visibility and making it more difficult to recruit workplace representatives, risking the hollowing out of union structures. Even more significant was that it encouraged employers to consider non-union channels of representation. The Local Government Employers' Organisation highlighted their concerns in 2003, in their evidence to the Local Government Pay Commission:

> The relative decline in union membership in the sector is becoming an issue. In whole swathes of southern and rural England, membership levels have fallen to a point at which it is difficult for councils to be confident that the union speaks for the workforce as a whole. Overall, membership appears to have fallen below 40% of the local government service's workforce, to judge by the number balloted for the 2002 industrial action (cited in Kessler 2005: 120).

Re-structuring as part of the modernisation agenda intensified these challenges. The fragmentation and outsourcing of public services required unions to follow their members into the private and voluntary sectors to maintain membership levels and to recruit new members. This was not straightforward as unions had to deal with a proliferation of more geographically dispersed employers, which was resource-intensive. This placed a large workload on local activists who also needed to be competent and confident enough to deal with a variety of employers and adjust to a private sector, less procedurally orientated, culture of industrial relations. As Waddington and Kerr (2009: 31) point out in relation to Unison, branches were originally conceived as being based on a single employer (i.e. a health trust or local authority) but 45 per cent of branches dealt with more than ten employers and around 17 per cent handled in excess of 51 employers. Existing public service workplace union representatives were often indifferent to outsourced workers, which risked creating an impression amongst potential members that these unions were not welcoming to private sector employees. This difficulty was exacerbated when union representatives were unable to use their facility time to recruit or represent workers employed by outsourced contractors (Bach and Givan 2008). Consequently the modernisation agenda by encouraging a more dispersed and fragmented set of public service providers, a more variegated workforce structure (Chapter 5) and a more diverse set of employment arrangements (Chapter 4) fractured union membership and created enormous challenges for trade unions in developing a shared identity amongst their membership.

Trade union responses: organising and community unionism

Public service trade unions recognised these challenges and identified possible responses (Heery et al. 2003), although their sense of urgency was muffled by the expansion of the workforce and relief that a lengthy period of hostile Conservative government had ended. The Labour government favoured unions developing partnerships with employers, but trade unions also examined the experience of organising, drawing on the experience of the USA and Australia. The term 'organising' signified attempts to reach out to new constituencies, encouraging member activism, and developing durable forms of workplace organisation. This straightforward label, however, concealed a highly charged debate about the objectives, techniques and effectiveness of organising (de Turberville 2004; Carter 2006; Heery and Simms 2008). For public service trade unions the main priority was not to secure new recognition deals, but to increase density where union members were already present, so-called in-fill recruitment. Some public service unions also broadened their organising campaigns, often using the language of social justice, to develop links with community groups and build local coalitions for change.

Initially, attention focused on the merits of organising versus partnership as a strategy for union renewal. John Monks, the TUC General Secretary, advocated a dual strategy of partnership with good employers and organising of bad employers, but it remained uncertain how feasible it was for a trade union to pursue seemingly incompatible policies (Heery 2002). Subsequently debate revolved around the practice of organising and a shift away from viewing organising as a single coherent model (de Turberville 2004). Public service re-structuring by devolving more responsibility to workplace managers has been viewed as creating opportunities for local activism and 'bottom-up' renewal (Carter 2006; Fairbrother 1996). A contrasting view suggested that effective organising required some top-down activity which Heery (2006) referred to as 'managed activism'. This included employing specialist organisers or integrating organising work into existing roles of full-time officers, often backed up by recruitment and other targets.

Many trade unions with public service membership were influenced by the shift towards organising. In the civil service the Public and Commercial Services (PCS) union under its left-leaning general secretary, elected from the workplace, explicitly rejected partnership and the Labour government's modernisation agenda. PCS established a dedicated national organising department with over 20 national organisers, agreed a national organising strategy which tracked membership levels by civil service department, and identified priority areas for action, such as focusing on the recruitment and involvement of young members and black members. It also focused on ensuring more accurate data on membership levels and set targets for density or membership growth. To encourage involvement and to make the role of union representative less onerous, unions were distributing this work amongst more people. PCS sought a recorded distributor of union communications in every workplace (PCS 2010).

Organising, however, was not straightforward as it required trade union commitment to invest scarce resources in organising activity and a change of culture within trade unions; complicated further by trade union reliance on voluntary representatives to recruit and retain new members. This was not necessarily the priority of overstretched representatives or full-time officers struggling to deal with the individual problems of existing members. The increased workload of organising activity was often unappealing. This was especially the case when trade unions sought to reach out to new constituencies and sectors such as migrant workers and the third sector. Full-time officers struggled to accommodate the increased workload associated with organising, resented the recruitment targets established for them, and had to tread carefully to encourage rather than direct workplace representatives to embrace the organising agenda (Bach and Givan 2008; Waddington and Kerr 2009). Although some trade unions pointed to increased membership as a result of organising initiatives (Bryson et al. 2010), the fragility of organising success was evident (Hickey et al. 2010).

These uneven results encouraged some broadening of organising strategies to involve a wider range of campaigning organisations and service users under the rubric of community unionism, influenced indirectly by the emphasis within the modernisation agenda on the priorities of end users. By building alliances with community groups around common concerns in particular localities it was intended to raise the profile of union campaigns and transform demands for improved pay and conditions into community concerns of social justice (Tattersall 2010). The best-known example was the living wage campaign of London Citizens, an alliance of faith, labour and community organisations based in the East London. It targeted the *clients* of low-wage contract cleaning firms who through their procurement decisions effectively set the wages of these staff and achieved success in improving the wages and conditions of outsourced cleaning staff in East London hospitals (Wills 2007). The challenge of community organising, which remains small scale, is to reconcile the tensions between the different priorities of trade unions and community organisations. Campaigning organisations may often view existing service provision and the working practices of union members or potential members as part of the problem which needs to be changed. Trade unions are concerned to build union organisation and membership as well as achieve a positive outcome for the workforce, whilst campaigning organisations are focused predominantly on improving wages. Mistrust between trade unions and community groups can create tensions over the financing and accountability of campaigns, especially if union resources are used for campaigns which may benefit rival trade unions (Wills and Simms 2004).

For many public service trade unions with a membership built around a professional identity, focusing on professional support delivered nationally rather than at the workplace, the language of social justice and highlighting workplace grievances may be incompatible with their ideology and organisational approach. For these reasons, organisations such as the nursing union, the Royal College of Nursing, identified different strategies to increase membership. The changing composition of the workforce brought about by the modernisation agenda with big increases in assistant type roles and managerial posts encouraged unions to broaden their membership base and encourage into membership occupational groups which were excluded or had a low priority in the past. For example, the Royal College of Nursing opened up its membership categories to focus more attention on the recruitment and professional support provided to healthcare assistants. The Secondary Heads Association extended its membership from head teachers to incorporate the leadership group in schools, including non-teachers such as bursars within the reconstituted Association of School and College Leaders (Bach and Givan 2004).

Influencing government

Trade unions also looked to their traditional link with the Labour Party to exert influence and to advance trade union interests. Howell (2001, 2004) contends that this process of political exchange between social democratic parties and trade unions is in terminal decline and that the fundamentally liberal market character of the UK economy provided little scope for gains from New Labour. John Monks, the TUC General Secretary, famously complained that trade unions were often regarded by the government 'as embarrassing elderly relatives at a family get-together' (Observer June 20 1999). It is certainly the case that the Labour Party's constitutional reforms in the 1990s weakened union influence over party policy, but despite some success at diversifying funding, the trade unions remained a key source of finance. With Labour Party membership falling rapidly from the late 1990s, public service trade unions not only provided financial support but also invaluable staff and other resources to mobilise labour supporters during election campaigns (Shaw 2008).

Most trade unions pragmatically engaged with the government through a variety of partnership and other forums, but at the same time campaigned vigorously against aspects of government policy (Murray 2003). Many campaigns sought to highlight the consequences for service users and pointed out the absence of 'joined- up' thinking by government. For example, in encouraging the recruitment of overseas health professionals to stem UK shortages, trade unions highlighted the contradiction between an ethical foreign policy and encouraging 'brain drain' amongst health professionals. These campaigns achieved tighter regulation of overseas recruitment alongside a commitment to develop a self-sufficient workforce, advancing their members' interests (Bach 2007). Trade unions also made greater use of legal challenges to slow down, modify or overturn government policy.

A key priority for public service trade unions was to end the Labour government's support for the Private Finance Initiative (PFI) and to curb its enthusiasm for the private provision of public services (Bach and Givan 2005). In addition to mounting well-resourced national campaigns, the trade unions inflicted a series of defeats on the Labour Party leadership at the 2002 and 2003 party conferences. These efforts unsettled but failed to deflect the leadership from supporting PFI and the trade unions focused on ending the two-tier workforce. The government had already pledged to end the two-tier workforce in local government, but with an election pending it conceded the phasing-out of the two-tier workforce which amounted to a major union achievement, and even more significantly indicated that public service unions could achieve a degree of re-regulation of the labour market (Bach and Givan 2010).

As Heery (2005) pointed out trade unions have been able to secure more concessions close to general elections and on issues which required trade union co-operation, such as public service re-structuring and changes in pension provision. These issues formed an important part of the 2004 Warwick Agreement which included 67 pledges for implementation during a third term of Labour government (Unite-Amicus 2005). These commitments included 19 specifically linked to public services and were usually quite specific such as 'Agreement to tackle unequal pay in local government including gender segregation' or 'confirmation that PFI does not require transfer of staff'. Reflecting the shift to network governance, there was some scope for trade unions to influence policy and implementation. This was evident, for example, in the scope for trade unions to monitor the two-tier code, the enhanced role of the Public Services Forum in workforce development, and plans to explore healthcare assistant regulation. This did not preclude government acting unilaterally, for example increasing the public service pension age from 60 to 65, highlighting the fragile and contested nature of any union advances.

Conclusion

Two differing perspectives of New Labour's industrial relations agenda were noted at the beginning of the chapter. The first, which we termed a degradation perspective, was dismissive of New Labour policies and the scope for employee and union involvement, whilst the second, which we termed an engagement perspective, suggested there had been more scope for employee involvement and trade union influence. Our analysis indicates that the second perspective resonates more closely with the policy priorities of New Labour, with attempts to engage staff and rehabilitate 'modern' trade unionism. An enhanced emphasis on staff involvement not only signalled the importance of valuing staff but also communicated required performance standards and reiterated an expectation that the workforce would contribute actively to public service modernisation. By invoking partnership at work, the government also sought to enlist trade unions in reforming public services.

These policies, however, were frequently undercut by the requirements of the audit culture with the immediate work experience of most public service staff shaped primarily by the priority assigned to key government targets, limiting staff engagement. Moreover decaying workplace trade union structures and workload pressures made it difficult for trade unions to take advantage of opportunities to influence developments at the workplace. This workplace context often made staff unreceptive to government attempts to involve them in modernisation and distrustful of senior managers. Partnership was certainly on the agenda but this did not erase a long-standing legacy of adversarialism in many organisations which co-existed uneasily with attempts to adopt forms of partnership working. Employers responded to this altered climate of employment relations and adopted a dual strategy, strengthening forms of direct employee involvement whilst not precluding trade union involvement if unions were receptive to working in partnership to further employer and government objectives.

Trade unions faced a series of dilemmas in responding to the consequences of the modernisation agenda, but in contrast to analysts who favour a degradation perspective, it is important not to conflate continuing trade union decline solely with the policies and practices of New Labour. The government sought to enlist trade union support, providing resources, increased legitimacy and involvement in national and local forums to encourage trade union acquiescence in a more centralised and managerial conception of workforce reform. This strategy brought some benefits to trade unions at the national level when access was translated into influence, and overlapping interests could be accommodated, for example, in reforms of employment and work relations. On other issues, notably private sector involvement in public service delivery, it proved more difficult to accommodate union concerns. Nonetheless, the Labour government, although seeking a more arms-length relationship, could not risk breaking the link between trade unions and the Labour Party and made a series of concessions in the Warwick Agreement. Public service trade unions therefore remained important institutional actors at the national level, and forms of network governance provided some opportunities to reinforce their position, although this varied between sectors. At the workplace, however, a more troubling picture emerged for trade unions and public service union density and organisation continued to decline. A muted sense of crisis amongst public service trade unions was insufficient to engender radical changes in policy, and despite some commitment towards organising, implementation proved difficult and the impact has been limited. Union renewal remained elusive.

7

Targeted change: New Labour, new employee relations?

Analytical framework revisited

During three terms in government between 1997 and 2010, the modernisation of the public services was at the heart of the New Labour project. The management of the sector's workforce was crucial to the effective pursuit of such a reform programme, suggesting that any assessment of New Labour in office needs to take account of employee relations in the public services. The primary aim of this book was to explore change in employee relations driven by New Labour's public service reform agenda: the extent, nature and handling of this change, and its consequences for actors with a stake in the employment relationship: workers, managers, services users and policy makers. The approach adopted to examine these issues was underpinned by an analytical framework comprising a number of elements. These sought to provide a basis for mapping and understanding developments. They also attempted to re-orient the research literatures both on public services employee relations and on public management, and to bring to the fore the distinctive nature of workforce management in the sector.

The *first* element suggested a relationship between the form assumed by New Labour's modernisation agenda and the management of the public services workforce. There was scope to debate the nature of this relationship, but scholars in the respective fields of study had paid limited attention to how the mechanisms adopted for the delivery and the management of the public services interacted with the substantive and procedural regulation of employee relations. The result was an analytical deficit in both literatures:

in public management, limited regard paid to the most important resource to be managed in the public services, the staff; and in employee relations, an uneven consideration of how the details of public policy development constrained and shaped the management of the sector's workforce.

If this first element sought to provide an explanatory dimension to public services employee relations, the **second** was designed to map any change in such relations over the New Labour period. Drawing on the general employee relations literature (Gospel 1992), it was suggested that the employment relationship had often been seen as enacted within different domains, focusing on employment relations, the management of the individual employees' terms and conditions; work relations, the distribution of employee work tasks and responsibilities; and industrial relations, the collectively determined aspects of employment. Debates within the mainstream public sector employee relations literature had tended to concentrate on narratives which, whilst interfacing with each of these domains in various ways, closely connected to one in particular. A 'model employer' narrative had explored the distinctive form assumed by the state as employer. It linked to the industrial relations domain, a function of the collective institutions traditionally underpinning the 'model employer' approach in Britain. A work experience narrative had assessed the quality of working life, with a particular interest in the balance between degradation, which de-skilled, cheapened and intensified employment, and enrichment, which provided career opportunities, the fulfilment of various personal aims and fair rewards. It connected to the employment relations domain, focusing on the treatment of the individual employee. An institutional infrastructure narrative had considered the range of actors involved in the regulation of the employment relationship, along with the systems and structures ordering their interactions. Whilst there were important connections between this narrative and the industrial relations domain, it was suggested that it might more usefully be linked to the work relations domain, a domain which raised the possibility of engagement with a far wider range of actors and institutions than those traditionally found in industrial relations.

The third element again focused on explanation, seeking to understand the detail of the emergent patterns of public services employee relations within these domains. Whilst the broad public policy developments highlighted above might relate to the contours and general character of employee relations in the sector, this third element sought to explain the texture or more refined detail of such relations. Potential explanatory weight was placed on structural and operational differences between the various parts of the public services. The principal focus throughout the book was on employee relations in local government, including education and social services, healthcare and the civil service. Clearly these sub-sectors shared a responsibility for the delivery of publicly funded services, subject to systems of statutory regulation and political accountability. Nonetheless in organisational terms they differed along a number of dimensions, for example the character of the services delivered and therefore the user groups addressed and the type of worker employed; the forms of governance and, as a consequence, the lines of accountability to central and municipal government; public policy priority and as a result levels of finance and resourcing; and funding mechanisms and so the scope independently to generate revenue and investment streams. New Labour's modernisation might plausibly have had a standardising influence on patterns of employee relations across the public services, leading to some convergence in policy and practice. However, to the extent, that there was variation, these sub-sector differences might well have been significant.

Drawing upon the findings presented in the preceding chapters, the discussion here returns to these different elements of the analytical framework to review and analyse the nature and consequences of any change in public services employee relations under New Labour. The chapter is divided into sections which relate to the framework. The first explores the relationship between New Labour's general public policy agenda, particularly as it related to the modernisation of the public services, and employee relations in the sector. The next section explores each of the substantive narratives in turn – model employer, work experience and institutional infrastructure – relating them to the appropriate employee relations domains. The last section turns to New Labour's employee relations legacy in the public services, and to the future of such relations. This involves assessing the sustainability of any change in employee relations implemented by New Labour, particularly within the context of the public policy direction established by the Conservative-led coalition government, which succeeded New Labour.

In reviewing and assessing the material presented in the preceding chapters, this chapter will make a number of claims. The first suggests the analytical value of exploring the relationship between public policy and the management of public services employee relations, particularly in understanding workforce developments during the New Labour period. The hybrid or layered model of public service delivery enacted by New Labour, combining elements of the new public management and network governance, was closely connected to attempts to re-shape employee relations, and accounted for some of the resulting tensions. The second asserts that New Labour attempted to re-establish the government's status as a 'model employer', although the effective achievement of this goal is open to greater debate. The third argues that New Labour sought to re-shape the institutional infrastructure underpinning employee relations in the public services, particularly reflected in the weight placed by the government on changing the sector's work relations. While there were important institutional changes in the industrial relations domain with, for example, attempts to develop partnership arrangements with the trade unions, there was a shift in the 'centre of gravity' in employee relations away from industrial relations to work organisation with the encouragement of new actors and institutional spaces. The fourth proposes certain contradictions in the employees' experience of public service modernisation, a reflection of the ambiguities intrinsic to New Labour's reform programme. For some employees, the reform agenda enriched aspects of working life, but this often co-existed with, and sometimes drove-out, less positive aspects of working life, leading to a degree of residual worker disillusionment with the New Labour project. The final claim stresses the fragility of New Labour changes to public services employee relations, certainly within the context of the Conservative-led Coalition's public services reform programme.

Public services reform and employee relations

This study has been predicated on a close relationship between the principles and practice of public service provision and the management of the sector's employee relations. There are grounds for arguing that over the post-1945 period employee relations concerns have informed and been integral to policy formation on public service reform. With the employee contribution intrinsic and central to the provision of most public services, any upstream decisions by policy makers on the delivery of such services were likely to display some sensitivity to and be informed by certain assumptions about the workforce and its management. At the same time, it might be suggested that there are profound downstream consequences for employee relations, which flow from upstream decisions taken by governments to reform the public services. In the case of the preceding Conservative and the New Labour governments, public service reform was seen both to drive and be driven by employee relations concerns, but the form assumed by these developments significantly varied between the respective governments.

It will be recalled that under the Thatcher and Major governments the link between public service provision and workforce management was rather crude, leading to a short and narrowly conceived employee relations agenda. For the Conservatives, the public services workforce, in many respects, was incorporated into upstream concerns. Ideological values prompted attempts to weaken collective industrial relations in the sector as an end in its own right. In a more strategic sense, the Conservative's emphasis on customer-driven public services was founded on the need to address perceived 'producer capture'. However, a reliance on markets to achieve these goals resulted in government disengagement from workforce management. This is not to deny the government's role in seeking to implement aspects of the prescriptive NPM agenda – disaggregating provider units, strengthening the general management cadre, championing private sector management techniques and denigrating 'all things public'. Nonetheless, these were policy initiatives designed to develop the markets needed to re-balance customer–producer relations, market forces 'naturally' disciplining the workforce. In practice, the uneven stimulation of such market forces in the public services merely undermined staff morale, created labour supply problems, so reducing service quality, with the collective institutions of public service industrial relations proving more resilient than the government expected.

The findings presented in our study suggested a very different relationship between the reform of public services provision and workforce management under New Labour. Certainly the New Labour's public services reform agenda was not founded on a clean-break with the past. It has been argued that this agenda took forward, and in some respects deepened, aspects of the Conservative's new public management. These were, however, combined with features of network governance to establish a distinctive layered or hybrid model of public service delivery. It was an upstream approach which created a long and a much more broadly drawn employee relations agenda with the government as active rather than passive agent.

More specifically, it was noted that there had been much debate about the pressures driving New Labour's reform agenda and more particularly the form taken by it. There were two main types of pressure, which could be framed in different ways. There was a set of domestic pressures associated with what New Labour saw as a potentially disillusioned and discontented 'middle class', which might retreat from public to private sector service provision. This risked generating a crisis of fiscal legitimacy, a noteworthy segment of the community paying taxes for services they did not use, and demanded a radical overhaul of the public services, with a particular focus on service quality. There was also a range of pressures associated with globalisation, with modern public services essential to the competitiveness of the British economy. This required state support for the development of the country's educational, health, welfare and transport infrastructure. The drive to reform the public services in the face of these pressures was often positioned by New Labour as the pursuit of traditional values in a 'modern setting': the safeguarding and development of public services free at the point of delivery, fit for purpose in a 'new global age' (Shaw 2007). At the same time, however, this programme was open to a critique suggesting its support for the neo-liberal project – for global capital and extended markets – and, therefore, its flight from long-standing Labour principles (Hay 1999; Garrett 2000; Coates 2001).

These competing views were often rooted in very different perspectives on the form assumed by New Labour's public services reform programme. For some this programme was imbued with an institutionalism deeply rooted in network analysis. While Rhodes (1998 and 1997) stressed a long-standing trend towards networks as the basis of public service delivery, Bevir (2005) associated this form of delivery much more specifically with New Labour, linking it to a number of explicit policy choices. Government-supported networks were seen as a response to service fragmentation and the hollowing out of the state, whilst, at the same time, providing an alternative to markets as the source of innovation, flexibility and dynamism. For others, the New Labour's public services reform programme remained mired in the principles and practice of the new public management. This was reflected in a continued reliance on markets and contracts (Jordan 2010), and associated with the commodification of public services (Whitfield 2006).

Against the backdrop of these polarised views, we have argued that New Labour established a hybrid model of public services, founded on a series of dualities: on the one hand drawing from a network governance model of service provision and on the other from the new public management. These dualities are set out in Figure 7.1. It can be seen that the former element of each duality relates to network governance and the latter to new public management. The first duality relates to the *citizen-consumer*. New Labour's model of public service delivery was driven by customer choice, voice and control, representing a continuation of the consumerist principles associated with the new public management: services needed to be responsive to customer circumstances and needs. However, these principles were tempered by a conception of the user as a citizen (Clarke et al. 2007). The citizen was embedded within a network of local relationships, generating a range of reciprocal obligations: an obligation to take advantage of the opportunities provided by the state; an obligation to make choices respecting the rights of others; and an obligation to invest in and provide a return on local social capital, for example, engaging in community activities and, if the need arose, contributing to the care and welfare needs of others.

The second was a *partners–markets* duality. New Labour retained, and to some extent deepened, the new public management's emphasis on market

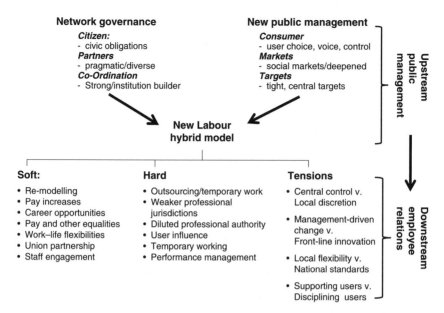

Network governance

Citizen:
- civic obligations
Partners
- pragmatic/diverse
Co-Ordination
- Strong/institution builder

New public management

Consumer
- user choice, voice, control
Markets
- social markets/deepened
Targets
- tight, central targets

Upstream public management

New Labour hybrid model

Downstream employee relations

Soft:
• Re-modelling
• Pay increases
• Career opportunities
• Pay and other equalities
• Work–life flexibilities
• Union partnership
• Staff engagement

Hard
• Outsourcing/temporary work
• Weaker professional jurisdictions
• Diluted professional authority
• User influence
• Temporary working
• Performance management

Tensions
• Central control v. Local discretion
• Management-driven change v. Front-line innovation
• Local flexibility v. National standards
• Supporting users v. Disciplining users

Figure 7.1　New Labour's Upstream and Down Stream Choices

principles. Certainly there are grounds for arguing that these were the principles of a social rather than a fundamental market kind (Gamble 2009), seeking to use competitive forces to organise relations between commissioners and providers in pursuit of various public policy goals. However, the continued progress towards the creation of semi-autonomous provider units, with the creation of Foundation Trusts in the NHS, school academies in education and the re-configuration of some civil service executive agencies, accorded with new public management market-creating principles, seeking to lend greater meaning to the notion of user choice.

More distinctive was New Labour's attempt to create markets based on a partnership of service providers, a feature which owed more to a network governance approach. Partnership is broadly defined here to reflect the active encouragement of a diverse range of providers, whether working together or independently to deliver services alongside government. Certainly, the nurturing of diversity in service providers was not only designed to foster user choice. It sought to improve service quality, especially in conditions of chronic failure: academies, for example, were seen as a radical or 'last chance' response to schools regularly branded as 'inadequate'. However, New Labour's emphasis on a diverse range of partners involved seeking-out providers from different parts of the economy. The Conservatives' privileging of private sector service was replaced by an openness which saw public and independent sector organisations (re)emerge as viable and legitimate providers. Presented as a more pragmatic, less ideological, approach to service delivery, New Labour consistently extolled the virtues of a diverse set of provider partners, suggesting that the final choice of deliverer depended on appropriateness, circumstances and need.

This diversity of provision established the basis for the third duality: *co-ordination-targets*. Network governance implied an important role for the state in managing networks of providers, but it was a light-touch role, with the government acting as coordinator, supporting collaborative forms of public service delivery from across various parts of the public services or from different sectors of the economy. New Labour adopted this co-ordinating role, supporting and sponsoring partnerships between different providers and across health, education and social care. This was reflected in such initiatives as education and health action zones where consortia of providers in an area were encouraged to work with and learn from one another and Every Child Matters with the integration of children's services. However, in pursuing a range of social, political and economic objectives, this co-ordinating role hardened into central control. New Labour re-imported elements of the new public management, principally reflected in the government's retention and strengthening of a targets-based performance management regime as the primary means of ensuring co-ordination. Such a regime was seen as an effective way of ensuring transparency in organisational performance, a prerequisite for informed user choice. It was also a useful means of demonstrating improvement in service quality, essential to retaining middle-class commitment to the sector. Moreover it was a strong guarantor of government authority and value for money given the high levels of investment made in the services.

One of the book's central arguments has been that this hybrid model of public service provision was closely related to the management of the sector's workforce. The model generated a deep and extensive employee relations agenda, which New Labour pursued with determination and some coherence: the government was aware of the downstream workforce consequences of its modernisation agenda, and was willing to address them. This agenda was, however, 'Janus-faced', with soft and hard dimensions, sensitive to the sometimes competing needs of the model's dualities. New Labour praised, nurtured and supported the public service workforce. This was not a return to the provider dominance seen by some as characterising state bureaucracies. However, in contrast to the new public management of the preceding Conservative government, New Labour was acutely aware that public service quality based on NPM consumerist sentiments relied on the commitment and capacity of the workforce: the ability to recruit, retain and motivate staff as well as to provide them with the necessary skills and capabilities.

There was a significant degree of expediency running through the soft, workforce capacity agenda, not least a consequence of the legacy of demoralised employees and skill shortages, both particularly acute amongst the public service professions. This expediency influenced the handling of various substantive employee relations issues in the sector: the boosting of pay and earnings; the attempts to foster and support workplace equalities; the re-modelling of workforces in education, social care and mental health; the encouragement provided to union partnership, staff engagement and work–life balance.

The softer side of the government approach was, however, harnessed to a harder, somewhat more confrontational agenda, as the workforce was nudged towards greater receptivity to consumer choice, voice and control. The support provided by government to the public services workforce had to be reciprocated: occupational jurisdictions needed to be loosened; more flexible forms of temporary and extended working adopted; pay linked more closely to individual and team performance; users accepted more as partners in service design and production; and the community embraced as a site for the delivery of an increasing range and volume of service.

The clearest indicator of the link between New Labour's upstream model of public services provision and employee relations was the government's willingness to play the role of institution builder to support the substantive soft–hard employee relations agenda. The government underpinned the diversity of service delivery, the patchwork of different provider partners from within and beyond the public service sector, by performing a proactive, coordinator role in employee relations. There was strong support for multi-agency, cross disciplinary work, particularly reflected in changes to working practices prompted by Every Child Matters and the re-organisation of service provision for those with mental health problems. Moreover the government devoted considerable energy and resource to the development of bodies to regulate the workforce as occupational boundaries became more fluid and novel roles emerged, and to ensure adequate provision for workforce training and development given the need for new generic capabilities and skills.

At the same time, it was suggested that this hybrid model of service provision nurtured downstream employee relations tensions and contradictions. The most striking might be related to the targets-based performance management regime, where a network governance role for the state as co-coordinator of a diverse range of providers had evolved into a centralising state control, rooted in the new public management's emphasis on contracts and incentives. Such a regime was seen to undermine or weaken the 'soft' employee relations agenda. It contributed to the intensification of work and a stifling of the innovative, flexible and dynamic working practices originally envisaged as a feature of network forms of service delivery. There were other employee relations tensions associated with the model: the government continued to support national collective bargaining and agreements such as Agenda for Change in the NHS and Single Status in local government, supporting joined-up service provision, while continuing to pursue individual and team-related performance pay, a residue of the NPM era. Similarly NPM's emphasis on worker sensitivity to the consumer did not always sit easily alongside the worker's role in enforcing reciprocal citizenship behaviours on the part of the user. This was apparent, for example, in Jobcentre Plus, where the Personal Adviser supported job search but could be called upon to withdraw benefits in the absence of user commitment to the process.

The relationship between New Labour's upstream model of public service provision and employee relations becomes clearer in returning to the three main narratives presented at the outset of the book: the model employer, work experience and legitimate institutions and actors. We now turn to these narratives.

Narratives

The model employer

The model employer approach comprises two features or strains. The first is a values-driven, prescriptive strain, focusing on the role of the state as an exemplar of preferred practice which, as a matter of public policy, the government is keen to see adopted more widely across the economy. The second is a more reactive and pragmatic strain, concentrating on the take-up of 'good practice' from beyond the public services; for example, under the Thatcher government we saw that there was reliance upon the private sector for 'good practice' in managing public services employees. In short the former saw the state as proactive in giving the lead to others in how staff should be managed; the latter viewed the state a reactive in following 'best practice' from other sectors. New Labour sought to re-establish the governments' model employer status, drawing upon, but slightly re-configuring both of these strains.

New Labour presented its model employer status in classic Third Way terms. Certainly it was not seeking to revert to a traditional approach associated with producer-driven public services bureaucracies, and heavily reliant on collective institutions. It was, however, keen to move beyond the

Conservatives' denigration of 'self-seeking' public servants, in the cause of unfettered 'customer sovereignty', which had undermined staff morale and service standards. A new approach required a much more constructive and mutually supportive relationship with the public services workforce, not as an end in itself, but as a means to improved public service. The 'good practice' strain was manifest in government attempts to root high-quality user-centred services in a caring approach to the individual employee: staff were likely to be better motivated and equipped to treat users well if they in turn were well supported. This encouraged a continuing government 'flirtation' with certain individualistic private sector human resource practices, and their promotion in the public services: for instance, the emphasis placed by the private sectors on staff engagement as a means of promoting worker job satisfaction and improvement in service quality (MacLeod and Clarke 2009) and the continued interest shown in outsourcing and in 'lean production' techniques.

New Labour was not, however, infatuated by such practices, often combining them with a residual collectivism. It continued to extol the virtues of performance pay, whilst supporting national agreements which guaranteed regular across-the-board pay increases and ensured that in pay terms public servants fared relatively well over the period. Indeed it is a striking feature of the period that collective bargaining embraced aspects of the employment relationship, particularly associated with work and employment relations, which in the private sector might have remained subject to managerial prerogative: for instance the Workload Agreement in primary and secondary education and the Knowledge and Skills Framework as part of Agenda for Change in the NHS.

This 'good practice' dimension ran alongside a 'model' or an 'exemplar' employer dimension which connected with a series of public policy principles and values. This exemplar dimension was manifest in attempts to ensure that employee relations in the sector were appropriate to a modernised public service, an aspiration which in some respects placed public services ahead of the private sector. Although 'modernisation' has been presented as a contentious and problematic rhetorical device (Newman 2001), the government sought to address a number of employee relations practices viewed as incompatible with a 'modernised' public service: pay discrimination, tackled by Agenda for Change in the NHS and the single-status agreement in local government; other inequalities at the workplace, combated by broadening and strengthening the equalities agenda; work–life imbalance, addressed by attempts to extend and support working time flexibilities.

More striking, New Labour was seen to pursue this values-driven, model employer dimension in novel and distinctive ways. Whilst the prescriptive aspect of the model employer approach had traditionally been embedded in the industrial relations domain, with public policy support for collectivism, under New Labour it resided more within the employment and work relations domains. In part this reflected the influence of high-profile instances of public service failure, the most noteworthy being the murders of Victoria Climbé and Stephen Lawrence. The former gave impetus and meaning to integrative forms of working, especially in children's services. The latter prompted the government to place equalities duties on public service organisations related to race, gender and disability. These duties converted what had formerly been a reactive, narrowly conceived procedural issue, mainly focusing on the equal treatment of staff, into a broader, performance management and culture-change issue, linking the treatment and capabilities of the workforce to the delivery of public services in diverse communities.

Work experience

The work experience narrative draws upon a research tradition in employee relations which looks beyond espoused policies and practices to their enactment and impact upon employees' quality of working life. It is a narrative which has particularly important implications for any final account of developments in employee relations under New Labour and their attempt to reform the public services. While the model employer agenda was partly aspirational, the work experience agenda is focused on implementation and the effects of change on the workforce.

It was suggested at the outset that an interest in work experience within the employee relations literature had often been taken forward by exploring the balance between degradation and enrichment in work organisation and employment conditions. A strong labour process research stream had initially focused on work organisation, linking degradation to management's control strategy of de-skilling (Braverman 1974). A focus on work organisation remains an important site for the exploration of the employee experience, although de-skilling has increasingly been seen as one amongst a number of management control strategies (Thompson and Smith 2010). Some of these other control strategies are not as clearly or readily related to the degradation of work, although changes in work organisation other than de-skilling, such as work intensification, might be seen as an additional source of such degradation. More broadly, the balance between degradation and enrichment has been sought beyond work organisation in a range of other workforce policies with a detrimental effect on the employees' social, economic and psychological well-being. We have suggested that many of these policies lie within the employment relations domain, for example, in how public servants have fared in pay terms; in how tightly their performance has been managed; in whether their employment has become more or less secure and sensitive to the assumed search for work–life balance.

The evidence base on work experience under New Labour has been variable, leading to some differences of view on employee outcomes. This becomes clearer by exploring three themes on work experience which emerged in the preceding chapters: the first relates to the impact of New Labour's public services performance management regime; the second covers consequences for professional and support roles; and the third covers outcomes for workers in different parts of the public services.

Performance management

One of the recurrent findings in the respective chapters has been the adverse workforce consequences of a tight and prescriptive organisational and individual performance management regime, based on regular audit and underpinned by the demonstrable achievement of targets. It has been suggested that this regime often drove out or undermined some of the 'softer', more enriching features associated with New Labour's employee relations agenda, and came to dominate worker views of the period. Any attempt to assess the impact of the performance management regime on work experience must, however, acknowledge the different aspects of this regime and their variable effect.

A distinction can be made between service standards regulation and workforce regulation. The former was based upon a general performance management regime, seeking to regulate public service efficiency and effectiveness. The latter was a more refined and specialist performance management approach, addressing aspects of employee relations.

The performance management regime associated with service standards regulation impacted on work experience in a number of ways. First, there was an element of de-skilling, with the target and audit regime establishing more routine work practices, reducing the scope for workplace discretion and innovation. This was particularly marked in the case of the public service professional, with suggestions that this central control undermined the benefits from the government's more supportive approach to this group of workers.

Second, there was a perceived proliferation of paperwork and bureaucracy associated with the performance management regime. Again the professional was especially adversely affected, attention being drawn to registered nurses and social workers pulled away from the provision of front-line care to maintain and service performance management systems. However the consequences were more pervasive, contributing to the general intensification of work, a major cause of staff turnover, and encouraging the displacement of energy to ensure the achievement of targets.

Third, this regime placed pressure on employees in their relations with users. Whilst the performance measures and targets were clearly designed to strengthen employee accountability to the user, and provide the foundation for informed user choice, they exposed workers to 'consumerist' demands, the aggressive assertion of user rights. Performance targets were perceived by workers as readily deployed by service users as a convenient 'stick' with which to 'beat' them. For example, in the NHS, a patient complaints service was established within the context of a range well-publicised targets: a maximum four hour waiting time in A&E and a maximum of 18 weeks from hospital referral to treatment.

Workforce regulation, the more focused employee relations performance management regime, has been linked to a distinctive and more progressive model employer approach. The outcomes-driven equalities and work–life balance programme in health, local government and the civil service, taken forward on the basis of targets and standards, had contributed to improvements in work experience for women and minority groups. However, this use of targets created a risk of distorting the employee relations agenda, with public service organisations narrowly concentrating on measured outcomes, for example absenteeism, employee turnover, agency spend, completion of employee appraisals. Arguably more important, but less easily measured consequences were given less, if any, attention; for example, in the NHS there was arguably a concentration on the number of appraisals completed rather than on their quality.

Professionals and support staff

For both public service professionals and support workers the impact of employee relations policy and practice was seen as contradictory, often combining elements of degradation and enrichment. In the case of the professions, we suggested the government followed a 'tough love' agenda. A raft of 'soft' policies, designed to enrich work experience were enacted – workforce re-modelling, protection of job titles, graduate status and improved earnings opportunities. This was combined, however, with a series of measures which risked the degradation of work: traditional occupational jurisdictions were challenged; flexibility sought; precarious or temporary forms of employment were increased; and power relations with the service user re-ordered. This approach sparked a crisis of identity across the main public service professions: nurses became fearful of diluting claims to the holistic provision of patient care as they moved away from the bedside (Doherty 2009; RCN 2009); teachers were concerned about relinquishing certain whole class responsibilities; and social workers baulked at compromising their non-elitist values as new barriers into their profession were erected (Lymbery 2001).

Similarly, changes in workforce structure and management impacted on support workers in ambiguous ways. The increasing importance attached by New Labour policy makers to support roles, traditionally peripheral to direct service provision, and often undertaken by women and those at the margins of the labour market, opened up a range of opportunities for post holders. Routinely these workers became more central to service delivery, with scope to extend their roles and take on more technical and varied tasks. This provided a chance for in-role career development by acquiring accredited qualifications, and in some cases for training to become a registered professional. However, as these roles developed the issue of fair reward emerged. Pay levels and rises were not always commensurate with new tasks and responsibilities (Kessler et al. 2010), giving rise to claims of exploitation and support workers as a source of cheap labour (Bach et al. *forthcoming*; Thornley 2000). Indeed, attention was drawn to the ongoing precariousness of employment in some of these roles, reflected in such practices as term-time only working for teaching assistants.

Sub-sector differences

The material presented has revealed some striking similarities in the process of workforce reform across the different parts of the public services, which might be expected to have a standard influence on work experience. There was evidence of copying and shared learning across the different sub-sectors. For example, workforce re-modelling in primary and secondary education was explicitly used as a template for a similar exercise in social care and mental health. Pay reforms in the different part of the sector often revolved around the creation of common pay spines, whilst there was a shared emphasis on social partnership. There was also evidence of a forced convergence, most apparent in relation to the statutory equality duties placed on all public service organisations. At the same time, there were important residual differences in work experience across the various parts of the sector. Traditionally local government comprising (quasi)independent municipal employers has been seen as the most likely to resist or depart from government employee relations policy, with the civil service, directly employed by government, and the centrally funded NHS, more likely to fall in line.

Under New Labour there was evidence to suggest that in some respects these patterns of sub sector variation held. The NHS, supported and underpinned by the authority and influence of the Department of Health, and its range of sponsored bodies, proved better able to co-ordinate the development and roll out of employee relations initiatives, than local government with fewer, weaker integrative institutions. In pay terms, for example, attention was drawn to striking differences between local government and the health service in the implementation of similarly complex national pay and grading agreements. Independent local authority employers made much slower progress on the implementation of single status, than the NHS driven by the Department of Health to introduce Agenda for Change. Similarly the new work roles developed under the auspices of the Department of Health Modernisation Agency were more effectively supported and taken up than those emerging from the local authority sponsored New Type of Worker initiative in social care. Moreover, the weight placed by the National Institute for Innovation and Improvement on 'lean production' ensured that this approach was taken forward with greater alacrity in health than local government. Indeed, the civil service, particularly with the DWP project, also appeared to be ahead of local government in development of such 'production' methods.

There were, however, equally strong grounds for suggesting that some of the most far-reaching and profound changes in employee relations under New Labour were centred on local government. This was not so much a matter of choice, but reflected the fact that key, centrally driven New Labour initiatives disproportionally fell on this sub-sector. For example, one of the most significant public service programmes of the period, Every Child Matters, mainly affected local government's two key service areas: education and children's social care. Certainly there were major change initiatives in other parts of the public services, with important implications for employee relations. The reconfiguration of government departments, with the merger of the revenue service and custom and excise, and of civil service executive agencies, with the emergence of Jobcentre Plus, prompted significant changes in work organisation. The NHS was subject to change with the development of foundation trusts and new operational systems feeding through to affect the employment relationship. Nonetheless, the Every Child Matters prompted perhaps the most profound and sustained change in public services employee relations: the breaking down of service silos; the consequent emphasis on multi-disciplinary, team working; the need for distinctive, generic workforce capabilities stimulating a new workforce training and development agenda; a re-modelling of the workforce and the establishment of new boundary spanning work roles.

Actors and the institutional infrastructure

For much of the twentieth century, the main dynamic for the management of the public services workforce lay within the industrial relations domain. Under public service bureaucracies, often relying on the authority of the professions, the scope or discretion for inclusive discussion and negotiation on ways of working and the treatment of the individual employee was limited. These aspects of employment were heavily codified in procedures or subject to unilateral management or professional control. The residual areas for joint regulation were pay and other terms and conditions of employment, handled by a limited number of actors – the unions, management, government and independent experts – interacting in joint negotiating councils or Review Bodies. It has been suggested that this machinery proved fairly resilient to attacks by Conservative governments in the 1980s and 1990s. But these were attacks not so much designed to create the space for a new and alternative infrastructure, but to more generally de-institutionalise public service employee relations.

In contrast, New Labour emerged as an active institution builder and sponsor of wider stakeholder involvement in employee relations. New Labour developed integrative, regulatory institutions to balance the diversity of the network governance model of service delivery. How deliberative or planned New Labour's approach was in this respect is open to some debate. Our upstream–downstream framework, suggested that a new public service delivery mechanism generated the need for new institutions and forms of engagement: these were pursued by the government with a noteworthy determination, consistency and coherence. At the same time, New Labour's reflexivity was highlighted, its iterative response to the experience of reform and shifting electoral needs. For example, a deepening of the choice and voice agenda over this period of government led to a progressive strengthening of service users' involvement in aspects of employee relations and the continued publication of performance and league tables; while 'wicked problems' such as the persistence of mental health problems and low educational attainment amongst particular social groups encouraged the development of new work roles.

The involvement of new actors in employee relations and the (re-)development of complementary institutions were significantly, although not exclusively, related to the emergence of work relations as the key domain of workforce management under New Labour. These actors and institutions assumed a number of forms. The first set was linked to the development of a stronger performance management system, and might be labelled standards regulatory bodies. A range of such bodies enforced conformance to general standards, structuring and framing workplace activities: the Audit Commission, National Audit Office, Ofsted, the Health Commission, the Commission for Social Care Inspection, and the Mental Health Act Commission, as well as the Care Quality Commission subsuming most of the responsibilities of the latter three bodies in 2009. The second set more specifically regulated aspects of employee relations with quality services requiring public assurance on staff capability and the minimisation of risk associated with employee performance: these might be termed workforce regulatory bodies. A range of such bodies, largely covering the professions, developed and safeguarded standards on entry, training, conduct and continuing professional development. The government was prepared to create new bodies to fulfil these functions in education and social care, while re-organising others, especially in health, to accommodate new and developing allied professional roles. This response should not, however, obscure government ambiguity on workforce regulation, especially related to the non-professional workforce in education, social care and the health services: government procrastination about extending regulation to these groups reflected public policy concerns about the trade-off between low cost, workforce flexibility and high but resource-intensive labour force standards.

A third set of institutions and actors was centred on workforce development. The upstream re-organisation of services delivery was seen to require workforce re-structuring and capacity, in the form of new skills and capabilities. The government established or sponsored a host of new bodies designed to support these needs: Skills for Care and Skills for Health, the NHS Modernisation Agency, the Children's Workforce Development Council, the TDA in education, the Care Service Improvement Partnership, and the Centre for Workforce Intelligence in Health and Social Care.

The most important public services employee relations actor to emerge under New Labour was the service user. The users' role was seen to assume different forms. There was a broadly based or universal citizenship role, linked to the creation of stronger communities, with New Labour seeking to establish an infrastructure to engage the public more fully in the development of services. However, the government also sought more direct user involvement in employee relations, often amongst discrete user or client groups: children-in-need and their families, the elderly, those with physical, mental health and learning disabilities. This increased involvement was founded on attempts to re-orient user-professional relations, placing greater weight on partnership, on the co-design and the co-production of services. It was often connected to the personalisation of services, pursued across the sector, but assuming particular prominence in local government, in the form of direct payments and individual budgets in adult social care. Such user engagement created a number of new and more refined hybrid actors in employee relations: the service user-employer, the service user-worker and the service user-trainer.

In summary, New Labour's ambitious attempt to reform the public services was matched by an equally ambitious drive to re-shape the management of the sector's workforce: the government was aware of the link between the two, and shaped its employee relations programme accordingly. This programme was sensitive to a layered or hybrid model of public service provision rooted in the dualities of network governance and new public management. Relying on social markets comprising a diverse range of partner providers to deliver user choice, voice and control, the government recognised the importance of workforce capacity combining expediency and assertiveness in the context of a 'model employer' approach, as a means of delivering it. Moreover the government appreciated that workforce capacity necessitated the renewal and creation of employee relations institutions across the industrial, employment and work relations domains and the involvement of a new and wider range of actors. As a consequence it came to play a key co-ordinating and supportive role in the promotion of these developments.

However, if the dualities of the upstream layered model were the basis for a planned and constructive link with downstream employee relations, they were also the source of certain tensions, which in the same way fed through to employee relations with unintended and debilitating consequences. New Labour hardened a coordinator role, compatible with network governance, into a controlling activity based upon performance targets and re-connecting with the incentives and contracts of the new public management. This impacted with particular force on work experience. Targeted change-intensified work and limited workplace discretion and innovation. It rendered New Labour's public service modernisation programme vulnerable to modification, a space which the Conservative-led coalition were keen to fill on their election in May, 2010.

Employee relations under the Conservative-led coalition: continuity or departure?

This concluding section explores public service employee relations in the context of the Conservative-led coalition (CLC), which succeeded the New Labour government. It provides an opportunity to assess both New Labour's employee relations legacy in the sector and the likely future direction of workforce management as the CLC seeks to reform the public services. While in power for only a year at the time of writing, the CLC has made a virtue of speedy and 'radical' reform of the public services. However, exploring the impact of this reform on employee relations is complicated by the fact that it is being taken forward against the backdrop of a raft of deficit reduction measures which include immediate and deep cuts in public expenditure. This not only creates some uncertainty in unpacking the reasons for CLC reform of the public service, but in policy terms it renders the delivery of further change in the sector highly problematic.

The discussion in this section draws upon our analytical framework to consider the CLC model of public service delivery, moving on to assess whether and how it relates to the management of the sector's workforce. How do the CLC plans for public service reform connect to New Labour's hybrid model of service delivery? How is the CLC's preferred approach to public service provision likely to shape the nature of employee relations in the sector? How sustainable are the employee relations developed by New Labour likely to be given this direction of travel? Are public services employee relations more likely to be effected by the much tighter expend-iture regime than by any shift in the approach to service delivery? The sec-tion argues that the CLC model of public service provision again combines elements of the NPM and network governance in a new and distinctive way, once more with downstream implications for employee relations. It is a model founded upon strong consumer or user rights, most effectively met through markets, but allies this with a localism leading to the withdrawal of the state as a co-ordinating and performance managing force. It is an approach already contributing to an unravelling of New Labour's employee relations agenda.

Critiques of past government

The CLC's approach to public service reform is nested, but plays a prominent part, in a broader social and political vision, captured by the notion of the Big Society. It would be a mistake to dismiss this notion as founded upon an empty and vacuous rhetoric. It emerges from, and often appears explicitly to be informed by, an emergent critique of New Labour, and to some extent the preceding Thatcher and Major governments. While framed in different ways by various commentators and with some important substantive differences, it is a critique underpinned by a similar set of arguments and generating a distinctive, prescriptive agenda.

In essence it is a twofold critique. The first part questions the role of government and the nature of state action. This is most forcefully put by Blond (2010) for whom the New Labour and the Thatcherite projects, despite, or perhaps because of, their shared emphasis on markets, resulted in a strong centralising and authoritarian state. It is a view which allows Blond to crudely juxtapose Big Government with Big Society; the latter an antidote to the former, and characterised as a civic space relatively free from this top-down state control. This analysis chooses to side-step or collapse the state-market distinction, Big Government becoming the sole source of past failures. In so doing, it challenges New Labour's Third Way supposedly transcending state and markets. Jordan (2010), focusing more specifically on the New Labour period, similarly points to the Labour government's continued reliance on contracts and incentives as the policy instruments of choice. In a more nuanced analysis, distinguishing between governments of different political complexions, Bevir (2005) suggests that New Labour was over reliant on, and naïve in placing too much faith in, the power of formal institutions to change behaviour.

The second, closely related, element of the critique suggests that the New Labour (and the Thatcherite) approach to government was founded upon a profound misconception of what drives individual citizen action and how societies function. This previous approach was seen as based on the assumption of individual utility maximisation, in other words on action informed by a mechanistic economic rationality. Despite claims to have moved beyond markets, New Labour's continued use of contracts and incentives, not least reflected in the continued reliance on markets and the maintenance of a targets-based performance regime, was still based upon these assumptions. Blond (2010) and Jordan (2010) draw upon an eclectic mix of philosophical and theoretical sources to suggest that individuals are deeply embedded in self-organising communities, bound together by shared cultural values and traditions. These community members are driven and energised by collective norm rather individual economic rationality. Bevir (2005) comes at these issues from a different direction. However, in suggesting that an interpretative rather than an institutional analytical lens provides a much greater sensitivity to the contested, contingent and fluid nature of stakeholder engagement with public policy and practice, he arrives at not dissimilar conclusions.

This element of the critique has prescriptive implications, Blond argues that governments should at most 'nudge' (Thaler and Sunstein 2008) rather than dictate from on high; that change and innovation are best achieved in a bottom-up rather than top-down way; and that collective civic actors and traditions should be stimulated, supported and enhanced.

The big society and public service provision

This prescriptive agenda both reflects and informs the Big Society model as presented to the electorate by the Cameron Conservatives (Conservative Party 2010) and then to the public as a framing device for the CLC's policy programme (Cameron 2011). Public service reform was not only central to taking forward this agenda but in an important sense also its engine. In setting out its vision of the Big Society, the Conservative Party (2010) presented this reform as a key area for action, along with empowered communities and culture change to support local groups, and it has continued to hold a central place in the CLC policy agenda (Cabinet Office 2010b; Cameron 2011). Certainly care is needed in overstating the coalition government's ability to retain the coherence and the integrity of its public service reform agenda. This is the first peace time coalition for almost a century, and some uncertainty remains as to whether it will be able to preserve the consensus necessary to deliver on its reform programme. By definition, coalition governments are founded upon a more diverse range of interests than single party government, providing those contesting public policy with greater oppositional leverage: for example, question marks have already been raised about how the government will respond to a vote at the Liberal Democratic spring, 2011, conference opposing aspects of the coalition's NHS reform programme (*Guardian* 2011). At the time of writing, however, a fairly clear picture has emerged of the CLC approach to public services delivery.

In a number of respects the CLC approach to public service provision has explicitly been presented in terms of continuity with the New Labour approach, but with important differences, which reflect its critique of the Big State. Indeed addressing the three dualities of public service provision outlined earlier, but driven by a new set of principles and values, has allowed the CLC to commandeer the previous government's language of 'modernisation'. David Cameron (2011) has asserted: 'I want one of the great achievement of this government to be the complete modernisation of our public services'.

Of the three dualities, the *consumer-citizen* has survived most, indeed largely, intact. New Labour's emphasis on consumer choice, voice and control has been retained, and so essentially has the users' status as citizens with reciprocal obligations. This notion of the consumer as citizen is compatible with the professed values of the Big Society but the CLC has implicitly built on critiques of New Labour as understating the importance of localism (Jordan 2010; Blond 2010) to differentiate itself and accentuate the role of the community volunteer. There are grounds for arguing that these critiques have overlooked the weight placed by New Labour on community (Shaw

2007), a closer examination of the respective approaches suggesting that the differences between New Labour and CLC governments exist in terms of how rather than whether citizenship is fostered.

The *partners-markets* duality has been subject to a more significant re-configuration. Certainly, the CLC has continued, indeed deepened, New Labour's faith in markets as the main guarantor of consumer choice, voice and control. This has been reflected particularly in the NHS where all services have been opened-up to competition and the new regulatory body for health has explicitly been tasked with promoting competition. Moreover, concerns have been raised that in establishing a 'right to provide', the government will be exposing previously protected NHS and other public services to private sector providers, deepening competitive forces (Toynbee 2011). Furthermore, the CLC has continued New Labour's break-up of service provision in the cause of market-creation and as a means of enhancing user choice. Considerable impetus has been given to the establishment of independent providers. NHS trusts have been given a deadline to achieve foundation status. Schools have been encouraged to become academies or 'free'; indeed local authorities are now under a statutory obligation to establish new schools only on the basis of one of these two models.

More distinctive has been the CLC approach to partnership in service delivery, more specifically, how different types of provider have been viewed. Under New Labour public services delivery was founded upon considerable diversity, a mixed economy of public, private and independent providers. This was presented as a pragmatic and contingent policy position: provider types varied in their strengths and weaknesses, with selection made on grounds of their efficiency and effectiveness within the context of particular service needs and circumstances. In contrast, the Big Society model privileges independent or voluntary sector providers, perhaps diluting partner diversity. Indeed, the voluntary sector has become something akin to the CLC's Third Way: 'The time has come for us to think of the voluntary sector as the first sector ... the first place we should look for answers that neither the state not the market can provide' (Conservative Party 2008: 4).

This attachment to the voluntary sector derives from the organisational forms to be found within this part of the economy: mutuals, co-operative, social enterprise and charities. Such organisations have become the new exemplars, the likes of John Lewis and the Nationwide Building Society constantly being quoted as the new source of 'good practice' (Craig et al. 2009). Indeed, the support for such forms has been informed by a preference for small, local and flexible independent providers, more accountable and connected to the community, rather than the larger, established national voluntary sector organisations. If the Conservatives of the Thatcher years elevated and praised 'all things private sector', the Conservatives of the Cameron years praise 'all things voluntary sector'. It is an approach supported by a commissioning process heavily weighted in favour of the voluntary sector. The government is 'promoting independent provision in key public services' through this process (Cabinet Office 2010c: 6), not least reflected in the title of the Cabinet Office (ibid) paper on commissioning, 'Modernising Commissioning: Increasing the role of charities, social enterprises, mutuals and co-operatives in public services delivery'.

The *co-ordination–targets duality* has been subject to the most profound change. In establishing a political space which attacks Big Government, the CLC has withdrawn as an active co-ordinating agent. This withdrawal has been apparent not only at national level but at lower levels as well. Despite the CLC apparent commitment to localism, it has sought to remove or weaken local co-ordinating institutions. For instance, as part of the NHS reform programme, strategic health authorities, traditionally with a planning and integrative role, have been abolished. The funding provided to local education authorities has been severely cutback, the money being dispensed directly to schools who may or may not buy back LEA services, while in broader terms, local area agreements linking service providers will no longer be required. This suggests that if network governance is to arise at these local levels, it is likely to assume a highly disorganised or diffuse form.

More striking has been the erosion of the targets-based performance management regime. As the government's framework for social care explains:

We can no longer rely on top-down programmes or performance management ... the balance of power is shifting dramatically – away from the centre and towards councils managing their own future, and empowered local communities holding them to account.

It is an approach which has already seen central government calling on the Quality Care Commission to cutback on its inspection of care homes. The Audit Commission, the guardian of the performance management regime, particularly in local government, is being wound up. As Eric Pickles, Secretary of State for Communities and Local Government has stressed: 'National targets mean that councils are constantly working on things which matter to Whitehall, regardless of whether local residents give two hoots about them.' (Speech 13 Oct. 2010, Hammersmith and Fulham Town Hall, London). This is echoed in the NHS White Paper where the government notes: 'We will start by discarding what blocks progress in the NHS Today: the overwhelming importance attached to certain top down targets.' (Department of Health 2010a). Indeed a revision to the operating framework for the NHS in England (Department of Health 2010b: 7) has abolished the 18 week waiting time target, and other targets such as the ambulance response time are also likely to be withdrawn or downgraded.

In summary, the CLC's model of public services provision, rooted in notions of the Big Society, assumes a new layered form, re-calibrating our three dualities, and therefore combining elements of network governance and new public management in a distinctive way. NPM's commitment to consumer choice, voice and control pursued through markets has been extended and deepened, and married to a network governance emphasis on a range of local actors combining in the provision of public services, on the assumption of engrained community cohesiveness. However, the state's role as an active agent is severely reduced, with centripetal and integrative forces dissipated: the light-touch central co-ordination of network governance and the national performance targets of the NPM are being scaled back. The contrast between this approach and the New Labour model is set out in Figure 7.2.

It is a model of public service provision which betrays tensions, different to those highlighted as characterising New Labour's approach, but with

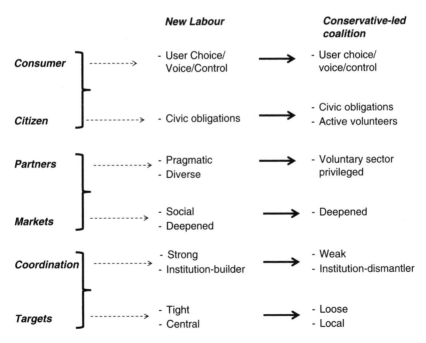

Figure 7.2 Comparing Models of Public Service Delivery

a similar potential to subvert intentions, and corrode political credibility. Whilst apparently shunning a model rooted in economic rationality, contracts and incentives, the new government will find it difficult to escape a commissioning process founded upon such principles and practices. Indeed, the government appears to accept the need for locally determined performance targets, and more tellingly seems wedded to extending a payment by results approach, linking service provider returns to specified outcomes. Moreover, although the government appears to be championing small, local voluntary sector providers, with some suspicion of 'big' independent and indeed private sector organisations, it remains difficult to envisage the former competing on a sustained basis with the latter. Other concerns have been raised: questionable assumptions on the prevalence and enthusiasm of local activists; partly related, the potential for uneven service provision across social groups and regions; and a possible weakening of transparency and political accountable at the national level.

Present economic circumstances, and in particular, the public expenditure cuts implemented and planned as part of the CLC's deficit reduction package arguably present an even more profound challenge to this model. Public expenditure cuts are not necessarily intrinsic to the CLC's Big Society model of public service provision, but the timing of cuts has major implications for its take-up and sustainability. For example, the capacity of independent sector organisations, central to the Big Society vision, to deliver public services has been severely weakened by reduced funding not least from local authority sources.

In line with this book's central argument, it is suggested that CLC's layered model of public service provision, and its associated tensions, has downstream consequences for employee relations. These have already begun to emerge and are explored by returning to our three employee relations narratives: the model employer; work experience and institutional infrastructure.

Downstream employee relations narratives

Model employer

A model employer approach would seem to sit rather ambiguously with the CLC's approach to public services provision. In substantive terms, it might be argued that the traditional collectivism of the immediate post-1945 decades, accords with some of the Big Society principles. For example there are strong grounds for suggesting that trade unions represent a form of collective voluntary organisation deeply embedded in the community and with a strong (industrial) citizenship role. ResPublica, the home of many Big Society ideas, has noted:

> The Conservatives are right to point out that the experience of unchecked trade union power has had serious drawbacks…. However a commitment to giving meaningful power to any organisation – be it a union, a church, a guild, a bank or an environmental group – to effectively challenge or defend the status quo on behalf of its voluntary members means accepting less control for the central state and a diversity of (often conflicting) interests gaining influence. The Big Society will need to include organised workers too. (http://www.respublica.org.uk/blog/2010/04/where-do-trade-unions-fit-big-society)

This might be seen as the platform for a renewed government model employer approach in the public services based on collective principles. The CLC's silence on this issue has, however, been deafening, even though the point has been echoed by Paul Noon, the general secretary of the public sector union, Prospect:

> If the Prime Minister is serious when he talks about encouraging volunteering and involvement in social action, then he must work with trade unions, not against them. (Evening Standard, 2 June 2010, Unions seek Big Society Inclusion)

Indeed, one of the few government signals on this issue has been to weaken collective bargaining machinery, with the abolition of the School Support Staff Negotiating Body. Trade unions might be community-based organisations, but clearly they are 'the wrong' sort of community-based organisation.

More profoundly, the role of the state as model employer in procedural terms, whether as exemplar or follower of good practice, is called into question both by the possible withering away of publicly owned and run service providers, and by an aversion to central prescription in the context of rampart localism. As foundation trusts and school academies increase, and independent and private sector providers proliferate, the directly employed public service workforce reduces and the scope for the state to set an example or follow good practice declines. Moreover, the determined pursuit of a particular approach to employee relations would appear at odds with the CLC's hostility towards central diktat. It was stressed that New Labour sought to develop its equalities agenda through the use of various targets: it remains open to debate whether such an approach will be taken on by the CLC government.

This weakening of the prescriptive model employer approach under the CLC has already been confirmed by the hands-off role adopted by the government to the treatment of staff during the commissioning process. New Labour was prepared to leverage the commissioning process to ensure conformance to certain employment standards. The CLC has explicitly ruled this option out, certainly in relation to any newly established mutuals: 'The Government will not seek to dictate what is best for employees and for the users of services' (Cabinet Office 2011b: 11). More generally, it has also undertaken to review the provisions of TUPE, seen as 'potential barrier' to the greater involvement of civil society organisation in the delivery of public services. (Cabinet Office 2010b), while also scrapping the Two-Tier Workforce Code, formerly providing some protection to outsourced workers.

If there is any residual notion of the model employer approach, it perhaps resides in a preferred organisational form for the delivery of public services. The government is encouraging public services employees particularly in community health and social care to establish themselves as independent service providers. For example:

> The Government's vision for adult social care will reflect the Coalition's programme of commitments to expand the work of mutuals, co-operatives and social enterprises to increase user and staff control. (HM Government 2010: 7)

As providers they are urged to set themselves up as a co-operative or a social enterprise. This has been supported by the government in various ways. At the time of writing a Localism Bill gives local government employees (and civil society organisations) the right to challenge local authorities 'where they believe they could provide services differently or better', while every government department will put in place 'a right to provide' for public sector workers to take over the running of services, a right which extends to civil servants directly employed by departments (Cabinet Office 2010b: 10–11). .

Work experience

The CLC has taken up New Labour's rhetoric on the importance of valuing the public service workforce. Rather than a return to the Thatcherite hostility towards the 'producer', the new Conservative-led coalition government has continued to acknowledge that an agenda based on consumer choice, voice and control depends on worker capability, commitment and motivation. David Cameron has linked praise for public servants with his own family experiences and extolled the virtues of the public service ethos: 'There was insufficient respect for the ethos of public services – and public service' (Cameron 2011). The crude vilification of its own employees, characterising the Thatcher years, has largely vanished, although David Cameron could not resist an attack on 'faceless rulemaking central government bureaucrats, stifling enterprise' in a speech to the Conservative spring conference 2011, causing considerably disquiet amongst senior civil servants (*Financial Times* 2011). More tangibly, the organisational forms underpinning the Big Society model might be seen to hold out the promise of a more enriching working life. After all they are predicated on more direct employee engagement and forms of governance which arguably provide the worker with a greater stake in the organisation and lend work more personal meaning.

At the same time, this praise for the public services workforce has been segmented, as we have already seen being lavished on some groups more than others. Professionals, in particular, are seen as an exemplar and pivotal group within the Big Society, the collective altruism of the public service ethos driving out memories of the more narrow-minded, self-seeking search for occupational closure. Under the CLC, the public service professional emerges once more as the 'knight', banishing the 'knave', so influential in previous public choice and New Right thinking. The new 'knave' becomes the senior public service manager – the local authority or NHS chief executive – whose 'high and inflated pay' has been used to justify the establishment of a Commission chaired by Will Hutton, exploring 'fair pay in the sector' and tighter council scrutiny of and control over chief executive pay in local government.

The renewed trust in the professional is manifest in different ways. As the preface to the government white paper on the NHS stressed: 'We will empower health professions. Doctors and nurses must be able to use their professional judgment about what is right for patients' (2010: 1). It is a view which has been used to justify weakening of performance measures and targets, presented as constraining professional innovation and discretion. This trust in professionals can be seen to underpin a number of reforms: in the NHS, the transferring of service commissioning from PCTs to consortia of GPs; in education, a weakening of LEAs as schools acquire more direct control of resources and an enhancement of teacher discretion in the management of pupil behaviour (DE 2010). Set against the new-found power and authority of the professional, countervailing influences emerge as weak and abstract. Cameron (2011) notes: 'In return for this freedom from central control, professions will have someone new to answer to – people.'

The credibility of a positive and enriching work experience for the public servant has, however, been compromised by a range of factors and developments. First, the government's faith in the professions has not prevented the government from challenging professional discretion, evident in education, with central government attempts to re-structure the national curriculum. Indeed, the faith placed by the government in professionals has not so far always been reciprocated, the BMA, for example, lining up to oppose aspects of the government's NHS reform programme. Second, there is ongoing scope for government as service commissioner to tighten the pressure on terms and conditions of employment. Pressure on unit labour costs is likely to arise, for example, in the health service, where the government has been considering moves away from fixed tariffs for given medical procedures to a system allowing price competition. Third, upstream organisational changes in public provision are creating major uncertainties for workers. Under Transforming Community Services, those provider activities formerly performed by PCTs are being transferred, mainly to acute trusts, but with considerable scope for rationalisation. Moreover, in instituting a consultation exercise on the abolition of the social care duties of local authorities, the government is similarly questioning the provision of certain services.

Fourth, closely related and most significant has been an attack on public service jobs and terms and conditions, particularly within the context of public expenditure cuts. How convincing is the praise heaped on the public services given an estimated 300,000 public sector job losses? How credible is this praise in the light of recommendations from John Hutton's report on reform public sector pension which call for the removal of a final salary scheme, an extension of working life and an increase employee contributions (Treasury 2011 Independent Public Service Pension Commission: Final Report). Indeed, indicative of concerns about work experience under the CLC has been a national co-ordinated campaign to oppose public expenditure cuts and their employee relations consequences.

Institutional infrastructure

To date, the most tangible employee relations consequences of the CLC model of public service provision have been a weakening of *institutional infrastructure* established by New Labour. It will be recalled that as an active agent, particularly in relation to the co-ordination-targets duality, New Labour played a role in integrating public service provision with downstream employee relation consequences. A stratum of state-sponsored, intermediate institutions was established or further encouraged as a means of supporting upstream decisions on public service delivery, for example workforce regulatory bodies to further the service quality agenda; workforce training and development units to nurture capabilities within the context of new work roles and ways of working.

As noted, of the three dualities this one has been subject to most significant change. The new government's withdrawal as a strong integrative force in public service provision has been taken forward into the employee relations agenda with the erosion of its institutional infrastructure. In its first year, the CLC has announced the abolition of the GTC, the GSCC, the TDA and CWDC, while at the same time reducing the funding available to Skills for Care and Skills for Health. The demise of these institutions does not necessarily mean that support activities will cease. Functional equivalents might well be found, for instance, the regulation of social workers will be taken over by the Health Professions Council; the TDA activities have been subsumed within the Department of Education, and it has been suggested that the workforce planning functions of the SHA will be taken over by new local 'skills networks' (Department of Health 2010). However, the bodies abolished by the CLC were devoted to the development of prescriptive, central support which runs against the grain of the Big Society and at the very least the level of dedicated time and expertise devoted to the tasks they performed is likely to reduce.

In conclusion, there can be little doubt that in fostering organisational fragmentation and extending the use of markets in pursuit of user choice, voice and control, New Labour opened the door to a deepening and strengthening of these trends by the CLC. However, in the shadow of the Victoria Climbé and Stephen Lawrence tragedies, New Labour remained heavily committed to the development of integrated public services and to an equality of access to them. While public service providers were often suffocated by a target-based performance management regime, New Labour was prepared to mobilise the state as an active agent in the pursuit of these aims, with consequences for employee relations. New Labour invested in the employee capacity needed to deliver services, and sought to preserve and build those workforce institutions, mainly at a national level, required to sustain them. As the CLC retreats from this active role, already reflected in the unravelling of New Labour's institutional infrastructure of public service employee relations, we await the next Victoria Climbés and Stephen Lawrences.

References

Aaron, B., Nijita, J. and Stern, J. (eds) (1988) *Public Sector Bargaining*, Washington: Bureau of National Affairs.

Achur, J. (2010) *Trade Union Membership 2009*, London: Department for Business Innovation and Skills (BIS).

Ackroyd, S., Hughes, J. and Soothill, K. (1989) 'Public Sector Services and Their Management', *Journal of Management Studies*, 26(6): 603–619.

Alford, J. (2009) *Engaging Public Sector Clients*, Basingstoke: Palgrave Macmillan.

Allen, G. (2001) *The Private Finance Initiative*, Research Paper 01/117, London: House of Commons Library.

Allen, I. (2001) *Stress among Ward Sisters and Charge Nurses*, London: Policy Studies Institute.

Audit Commission (2002) *Recruitment and Retention: A Public Service Workforce for the Twenty-first Century*, London: Audit Commission.

Audit Commission (2003) *PFI in Schools*, London: Audit Commission.

Bach, S. (1989) *Too High a Price to Pay?* Warwick Papers in Industrial Relations, 25, Coventry: IRRU.

Bach, S. (2004) *Employment Relations in the NHS: The Management of Reforms*, London: Routledge.

Bach, S. (2007) 'Going Global? The Regulation of Nurse Migration to the UK', *British Journal of Industrial Relations*, 45(2): 383–403.

Bach, S. and Winchester, D. (1994) 'Opting Out of Pay Devolution? Prospects for Local Pay Bargaining in UK Public Services', *British Journal of Industrial Relations*, 32(2): 263–282.

Bach, S. and Della Rocca, G. (2000) 'The Management Strategies of Public Service Employers in Europe', *Industrial Relations Journal*, 31(2): 82–96.

Bach, S. and Givan, R. (2004) 'Public Service Unionism in a Restructured Public Sector: Challenges and Prospects', in Kelly, J. and Willman, P. (eds) *Union Organization and Activity*, London: Routledge.

Bach, S. and Givan, R. (2005) 'Union Responses to Public-Private Partnerships in the National Health Service', in Fernie, S. and Metcalf, D. (eds)*British Unions: Resurgence or Demise*, London: Routledge.

Bach, S. and Givan, R (2010) 'Regulating Employment Conditions in a Hospital Network: The Case of the Private Finance Initiative', *Human Resource Management Journal*, 20(4): 424–439.

Bach, S., Givan, R. and Forth J. (2009) 'The Public Sector in Transition', in Brown, W., Bryson, A., Forth, J. and Whitfield, K. (eds) *A Quarter Century of Change,* Cambridge: CUP.

Bach, S. and Kessler, I. (2007) 'HRM and the New Public Management', in Boxall, P., Purcell, J. and Wright, P. (eds) *The Oxford Handbook of Human Resource Management,* Oxford: OUP.

Bach, S. Kessler, I. and Heron, P. (2007) 'The Consequences of Assistant Roles in the Public Services', *Human Relations,* 60(9): 1267–1293.

Bach, S. Kessler, I and Heron, P. (forthcoming 2012) 'Nursing a Grievance? The Role of Health Care Assistants in a Modernised NHS', *Gender, Work and Organisation.*

Bacon, N. and Samuel, P. (2009) 'Partnership Agreement Adoption and Survival in the British Private and Public Sectors', *Work, Employment and Society,* 23(2): 231–248.

Bacon, N. and Samuel, P. (2010), 'The Contents of Partnership Agreements in Britain1990–2007', *Work, Employment and Society,* 24(3): 430–448.

Bacon, R. and Eltis, W. (1976) *Britain's Economic Problem: Too Few Producers,* London: Macmillan.

Bain, P. and Taylor, P. (2007) 'A "Third Way"? Industrial Relations Under New Labour', in Mooney, G. and Law, A. (eds) *New Labour/Hard Labour? Restructuring and Resistance Inside the Welfare Industry,* Bristol: Policy Press.

Ball, S. (2007) *Education Plc. Understanding Private Sector Participation in Private Education,* London: Routledge.

Ball, J. and Pike, G. (2006) *Temporary Working: Results from an on-Line Survey of Bank And Agency Nurses,* London: RCN.

Barber, M. (2008) *Instruction to Deliver: Fighting to Transform Britain's Public Services,* London: Methuen.

Barnes, J. (2010) 'From Evidence Base to Practice – Implementation of the Nurse-Family Partnership Programme in England', *Journal of Children's Services,* 5(4): 4–17.

Batstone, E., Ferner, A., Terry, M. (1984) *Consent and Efficiency: Labour Relations and Management Strategy in State Enterprises,* Oxford: Blackwell.

Beattie, R. and Waterhouse, J. (2009) *HRM in Public Services Organizations,* London: Routledge.

Beaumont, P. (1992) *Public Sector Industrial Relations,* London: Routledge.

Bellemare, G. (2000) 'End Users: Actors in Industrial Relations System', *British Journal of Industrial Relations,* 38: 383–406.

Beresford, P. and Hasler, F, (2009) *Transforming Social Care,* Centre for Citizen Participation, London: Brunel University Press.

Bevan, G. and Hood, C. (2006) 'What's Measured is What Matters: Targets in the English Public Health Care System', *Public Administration,* 84(3): 517–538.

Bevir, M. (2005) *New Labour: A Critique,* London: Routledge.

Bhatia, N. and drew, J. (2006) 'Applying Lean Production to the Public Sector', *McKinsey Quarterly,* June, pp. 5–7.

Blair, T. (2002) *The Courage of Our Convictions: Why Reform of the Public Services Is the Route to Social Justice,* London: Fabian Society.

Blair, T. (2004) Speech at the *Guardian*'s public services summit, January.

Blair, T. (2010) *A Journey,* Hutchinson: London.

Blatchford, P. Bassett, P., Brown, P., Martin, C., Russell, A. and Webster, R (2009) *The Deployment and Impact of Support Staff project,* Research Brief 148, London: Department for Children, Schools and Families.

Blond, P. (2010) *Red Tory,* London: Faber and Faber.

Booth, C. (2007) *Determining Pay in the Police Service: The Second Part of a Review of Police Service Pay Arrangements,* London: Home Office.

Bordogna, L. (2008) 'Moral Hazard, Transaction Costs and the Reform of Public Service Employment Relations', *European Journal of Industrial Relations,* 14(4): 381–400.

Boston, J., Martin, J. Pallott, J. and Walsh, P. (1996) *Public Management: The New Zealand Model,* Auckland: OUP.

Bouvaird. T. and Löffler, E. (2009) *Public Management and Governance,* Routledge: Abingdon.

Boyne, G. (2002) 'Public and Private Management: What's the Difference?', *Journal of Management Studies,* 39(1): 101–121.

Bozio, A. and Johnson, P. (2008) 'Public Sector Pay and Pensions', in Chote, R., Emmerson, C., Miles, D. and Shaw, J. (eds) *The IFS Green Budget: January 2008,* London: Institute for Fiscal Studies.

Bozio, A. and Disney, R. (2011) 'Public Sector Pay and Pensions', in Brewer, M., Emerson, C. and Miller, H. (eds) *The IFS Green Budget: February 2011,* London: Institute for Fiscal Studies.

Branfield, F. and Beresford, P. (2006) *Making User Involvement Work,* York: Joseph Rowntree Foundation.

Braverman, H. (1974) *Labor, Monopoly Capital: The Degradation of Work in the Twentieth Century,* New York: Monthly Review Press.

BMA (2004a) *Career Barriers in Medicine: The Doctors' Experience,* London: BMA.

BMA (2004b) *New Roles for Psychiatrists,* London: BMA.

Bryson, A., Nowak, P., Roper, C. and Smith, P. (2010) *Resilient Unions: Strategies for Growth,* London: Unions 21.

Buchan, J. and Evans, D. (2007) *Realising the Benefits? Assessing the Implementation of Agenda for Change,* London: King's Fund.

Buchan, J., Seccombe, I. and Smith, G. (1998) *Nurses Work: An Analysis of the UK Nursing Labour Market,* Aldershot: Ashgate.

Burgess, S., Propper, C., Ratto, M. and Tominey, E. (2004) *Evaluation of the Introduction of the Makinson Incentive Scheme in Jobcentre Plus: Final Report,* http://www.bristol. ac.uk/cmpo/events/2005/markinson/jobcentre.pdf

Burgess, S. Propper, C., Ratto, M. and Tominey, E. (2005) *Evaluation of the Introduction of the Makinson Incentive Scheme in the Child Support Agency,* available at: http://www. bristol.ac.uk/cmpo/events/2005/markinson/childsupport.pdf

Business, Enterprise and Regulatory Reform Committee (2008) *Jobs for the Girls: Two Years On,* London: House of Commons.

Byron, R. (2010) 'Discrimination, Complexity and the Public/Private Sector Question', *Work and Occupation,* 37: 435–475.

Cabinet Office (1998) *Next Steps Report 1997,* Cm 3889, London: HMSO.

Cabinet Office (1999) *Modernising Government,* Cm 4310, London: The Stationery Office.

Cabinet Office (2000) *Partnership Working in the Civil Service,* available at: www.civ-ilservice.gov.uk/Assets/CO-CCSU_tcm6-2713.doc

Cabinet Office (2004) *Trade Union and Employee Involvement in Public Service Reform,* London: Cabinet Office.

Cabinet Office (2005a) *Delivering a Diverse Civil Service: A 10 Point Plan,* London: Cabinet Office.

Cabinet Office (2005b) *Transformational Government,* London: Cabinet Office.

Cabinet Office (2006) *The UK Government's Approach to Public Service Reform,* London: Cabinet Office.

Cabinet Office (2007) *Performance Management Guidance 2007/08 for Permanent Secretaries and the Senior Civil Service,* London: Cabinet Office.

Cabinet Office (2008a) *Excellence and Fairness: Achieving World Class Public Services,* London: Cabinet Office.

Cabinet Office (2008b) *Promoting Equality, Valuing Diversity: A Strategy for the Civil Service,* London: Cabinet Office.

Cabinet Office and Council of Civil Service Unions (2008) *Protocol for Handling Surplus Staff Situations,* London: Cabinet Office.

Cabinet Office (2009) http://www.civilservice.gov.uk/about/improving/engagement/people-survey-results.aspx

Cabinet Office (2010a) The Civil Service People Survey, available at: http://data.gov.uk/dataset/civil-service-people-survey-2010

Cabinet Office (2010b) *Building the Big Society,* May, London: Cabinet Office.

Cabinet Office (2010c) Modernising Commissioning, London: Cabinet Office.

Caines, E. (1993) 'The impact of trusts in the management of the NHS', in Peck, E. and Spurgeon, P. (eds) *NHS Trusts in Practice,* Harlow: Longman.

Cameron, C. Jasper, A., Kleipeodszus, S. Petrie, P. and Wigfall, V. (2010) *Implementing the DCSF Pilot Programme: The Work of the First Year,* Social Pedagogy Briefing paper ll, London: Thomas Coram Research Unit.

Cameron, D. (2011) Speech on the public services, January.

Care Quality Commission (2010a) 'The Adult social care market and the quality of services', *Technical Report,* Nov. London: Care Quality Commission.

Care Quality Commission (2010b) *Supporting Briefing Note: Issues Highlighted By the 2009 NHS Staff Survey in England,* London: Care Quality Commission.

Carey, M. (2009) 'Happy Shopper? The Problem with Service User and Carer Participation', *British Journal of Social Work,* 39: 179–188.

Carr, S. (2004) *Has Service User Participation Made a Difference to Social Care Services?* London: SCIE.

Carter, B. (2006) 'Trade Union Organizing and Renewal: a Response to de Turberville', *Work, Employment and Society,* 20(2): 415–426.

Casey, T. (ed.) (2009) *The Blair Legacy,* Basingstoke: Palgrave.

Certification Officer (2010) *Annual Report of the Certification Officer 2009–2010,* London: The Certification Office.

Chapman, J. (2007) 'Living in the Machine: New Labour and Public Services', in Hassan, G. (ed.) *After Blair: Politics After the New Labour Decade,* London: Lawrence and Wishart.

COI (2010) *Frontline Care: The Future of Nursing and Midwifery in England,* Report of the Prime Minister's Commission on the Future of Nursing and Midwifery, London: COI.

Charlwood A. and Forth, J. (2009) 'Employee Representation', in Brown, W., Bryson, A., Forth, J. and Whitfield, K. (eds) *The Evolution of the Modern Workplace,* Cambridge: CUP.

Chief Nursing Officer (2004) 'Keynote Address', CNO Conference 14 January.

Children's Workforce Development Council (2010) *Common Core of Skills and Knowledge,* Leeds: CDWC.

Christensen, T. and Laegreid, P. (2007) *Transcending New Public Management: The Transformation of Public Sector Reforms,* Aldershot: Ashgate.

Christensen, T., Lie, A. and Laegreid, P. (2007) Still Fragmented Government or Reassertion of the Centre? In Christensen, T and Laegreid, P. (eds). *Transcending New Public Management*, Aldershot: Ashgate.

Clarke, J. and Newman, J. (1997) *The Managerial State: Power, Politics and Ideology in the Remaking of Social Welfare*, London: Sage.

Clarke, J., Newman, J. Smith, J., Vidler, E. and Westmarland, L. (2007) *Creating Citizen-Consumers*, London: Sage.

Coates, D. (2001) 'Capitalist Models and Social Democracy: the Case of New Labour', *British Journal of Politics and International Relations*, 3(3): 284–307.

Colgan, F. Wright, T, Creegan, C. and McKearney, A. (2009) 'Equality and Diversity in the Public Services: Moving Forward on Lesbian, Gay and Bisexual Equality?' *Human Resource Management Journal*, 19(3): 280–301.

Community Interest Company (2010) *Expert Patients Programme: Self Care Reduces Costs and Improves Health – The Evidence*, London: Community Interest Company.

Confederation of British Industry (2006) *For What it's Worth. Managing Public Sector Reward 2008–2011*, London: CBI.

Conley, H. (2006) 'Modernisation Or Casualisation? Numerical Flexibility in Public Services', *Capital and Class*, 30(1): 31–57.

Conservative Party (2008) *A Stronger Society: Voluntary Action in the 21st Century*, Policy Green paper No.5, London: Conservative Party.

Conservative Party (2010) *Big Society, Not Big Government*, March, London: Conservative Party.

Colling, T. (1999) 'Tendering and Outsourcing Working in the Contract State?', in Corby, S. and White, G. (eds) *Employee Relations in the Public Services*, London: Routledge.

Cooper, C., Anscombe, J. Avenall, J. McLean, F. and Morris, J. (2006) *A National Evaluation of Community Support Officers*, Home Office Research Study 297, London: Home Office.

Corby, S. (2007) 'Equality and Diversity', in Dibben, P., James, P. and Roper, I. (eds) *Modernising Work in Public Services*, Basingstoke: Palgrave.

Coyle-Shapiro, J. Morrow, P. and Kessler, I. (2006) 'Serving Two Organizations: Exploring the Employment Relationship of Contracted Employees', *Human Resource Management*, 45(4): 561–583.

Cottam, H. and Leadbeater, C, (2004) *Red paper 01, Health: Co-creating services*, London: Design Council.

Cox, A. (2007) *Re-visiting the NVQ Debate: 'Bad' Qualifications, Expansive Learning Environments and Prospects for Upskilling Workers.* SKOPE Research Paper No 71, SKOPE: Cardiff University.

Craig, J. Horne, M. and Mongon, D. (2009) *The Engagement Ethic: The Potential of Cooperative and Mutual Governance for Public Services*, London: Innovation Unit, Think Place.

Creegan, C., Colgan, F., Charlesworth, R. and Robinson, G. (2003) 'Race Equality Policies at Work: Employee Perceptions of the 'Implementation Gap in a UK Local Authority', *Work, Employment and Society*, 17(4): 617–640.

Cunningham, R. (2000) 'From Great Expectation to Hard Times? Managing Equal Opportunities Under New Public Management', *Public Administration*, 78(3): 699–714.

Cutler, T. and Waine, B. (2001) 'Performance Management – the Key to Higher Standards in Schools?', *Public Money and Management*, 21(2): 69–72.

Danford, A., Richardson, M., and Upchurch, M. (2002) '"New Unionism", Organising and Partnership', *Capital and Class*, 76: 1–27.

Darlington, R. (2010) 'The State of Union Reps' Organization in Britain today', *Capital and Class*, 34(1): 126–135.

Department for Children, Schools and Families (2008) *2020 Children and Young's Workforce Strategy*, London: Department for Children, Schools and Families.

Department for Children, Schools and Families (2009) *Social Work Task Force Interim Report*, London: Department for Children, Schools and Families.

Department of Education (2010) *The Importance of Teaching*, London: Department of Education.

Department for Education and Skills (1998) *Teachers Meeting the Challenge of Change*, London: Department for Education and Skill.

Department for Education and Skills (2001) 'Professionalism and Trust', Speech by Estelle Morris to the Social Market Foundation, November, London: Department for Education and Skills.

Department for Education and Skills (2002a) *Time for Standards*: Reforming the School Workforce, London: Department for Education and Skills.

Department for Education and Skills (2002b) Developing the Role of School Support Staff, London: Department for Education and Skills.

Department for Education and Skills (2003) *Every Child Matters*, London: Department for Education and Skills.

Department for Education and Skills (2005) *Youth Matters*, London: Department for Education and Skills.

Department of the Environment, Transport and the Regions (1999) *Local Government Act 1999: Part 1 Best Value, Circular 10/99*, London: Department of the Environment, Transport and the Regions.

Department of Health (1997) *The New NHS: Modern Dependable, Cmnd 3807*, London: HMSO.

Department of Health (1998) *Working Together: Securing a Quality Workforce for the NHS*, London: HMSO.

Department of Health (1999a) *Agenda for Change: Modernising the NHS Pay System*, London: The Stationery Office.

Department of Health (1999b) *Report of the NHS Taskforce on Staff Involvement*, London: The Stationary Office.

Department of Health (2000a) *Improving Working Lives Standard*, London: Department of Health.

Department of Health (2000b) *Looking beyond Label: Widening the Employment Opportunities for Disabled People in the NHS*, London: Department of Health.

Department of Health (2000c) *Vital Connection – An Equalities Framework for the NHS*, London: Department of Health.

Department of Health (2000d) *The NHS Plan: A Plan for Investment, A Plan for Reform*, London: Department of Health.

Department of Health (2001a) *NHS Plan Essence of Care Plan*, 2001, Leeds: NHS Estates.

Department of Health (2001b) *Mental Health Policy Guidelines*, London: Department of Health.

Department of Health (2001c) *Mental Health NSF Workforce Planning, Education and Training Underpinning Programme-Main Report*, London: Department of Health.

Department of Health (2001d) *Working Together, Learning Together: A Framework for Lifelong Learning in the NHS*, London: Department of Health.

Department of Health (2002) *Delivering the NHS Plan: Next Steps on Investment, Next Steps on Reform,* London: Department of Health.

Department of Health (2003a) *Modernising Medical Careers,* London: Department of Health.

Department of Health (2003b) *Fast Forwarding Primary Care Mental Health: Gateway Workers,* London: Department of Health.

Department of Health (2003c) *Promoting the Status of Social Work,* London: Department of Health.

Department of Health (2004a) *Agenda for Change: Final Agreement,* London: Department of Health.

Department of Health (2004b) *Patient and Public Involvement in Health,* London: Department of Health.

Department of Health (2004c) *The Ten Essential Shared Capabilities: A Framework for the Whole of the Mental Health Workforce,* London: Department of Health.

Department of Health (2004d) *NHS Improvement Plan: Putting People at the Heart of Public Services,* London: Department of Health.

Department of Health (2005a) *A National Framework to Support Local Workforce Strategy Development: A Guide for HR Directors in the NHS and Social Care,* London: Department of Health.

Department of Health (2005b) *Modernising Medical Careers: Next Steps,* London: Department of Health.

Department of Health (2005c) *New Ways of Working for Psychiatrists: Enhancing Person Centred Services through New Ways of Working in a Multi Disciplinary and a Multi Agency Context,* London: Department of Health.

Department of Health (2005d) *Delivering Race Equality in Mental Health Care,* London: Department of Health.

Department of Health (2005e) *Creating a Patient led NHS,* London: Department of Health.

Department of Health (2006a) *Modernising Nursing Careers: Setting the Direction,* London: Department of Health.

Department of Health (2006b) *Our Health, Our Care, Our Say: A New Direction for Community Services,* London: Department of Health.

Department of Health (2007a) *Hospital Organisation, Specialty Mix and MSRA,* London: Department of Health.

Department of Health (2007b) *Single Equalities Scheme, 2007–10,* London: Department of Health.

Department of Health (2007c) *Facing the Future: A Review of the Role of Health Visitors,* London: Department of Health.

Department of Health (2007d) *Putting People First: A Shared Vision to Transform Adult Social Care,* London: Department of Health.

Department of Health (2007e) *Support Time and Recovery Workers: Final Handbook,* London: Department of Health.

Department of Health. 2008a. *What Matters to Staff in the NHS,* available at: http://www.dh.gov.uk/en/Publicationsandstatistics/Publications/DH_085536

Department of Health (2008b) *Common Core Principles to Support Self Care: A Guide to Support Implementation,* London: Department of Health.

Department of Health (2009a) *Building a Safe, Confident Future: Final Report of the Social Work Task Force,* London: Department of Health.

Department of Health (2009b) *Expert Patient Programme*, London: Department of Health.

Department of Health (2010a) *Developing the Healthcare Workforce*, London: Department of Health.

Department of Health (2010b) *Revision to NHS Operating Framework, 2010–11*, London: Department of Health.

Department for Work and Pensions (2009) *Flexible Working: Working for Families, Working for Business*, Report by the Family Friendly Work Hours Task force, London: Department for Work and Pensions.

Department for Work and Pensions (2010*) Flexibility for the Future: The Government's Response to the Recommendations of the Family Friendly Working Hours Taskforce*, London: Department for Work and Pensions.

Department of Trade and Industry (1998) *Fairness at Work*, Cm 3968, London: HMSO.

Dickens, L. (1999) 'Beyond the Business Case: A Three prolonged Approach to Equality Action', *Human Resource Management Journal*, 9(1): 9–19.

Dickens, L. and Hall, M. (2010) 'The Changing Legal Framework of Employment Relations', in Colling, T. and Terry, M. (eds) *Industrial Relations: Theory and Practice, 3rd Edition*, Chichester: John Wiley.

Dix, S. and Forth, J. (2009) 'Equality and Diversity at Work', in Brown, W., Bryson, A., Forth, J. and Whitfield, K. (eds) *The Evolution of the Modern Workplace*, Cambridge: CUP.

Dix, G., Sisson, K. and Forth, J. (2009) 'Conflict at Work: The Changing Pattern of Disputes', in Brown, W., Bryson, A., Forth, J. and Whitfield, K. (eds) *The Evolution of the Modern Workplace*, Cambridge: CUP.

Doherty, C. (2009) 'A Qualitative Study of Health Service Reform on Nurses' Working Lives,' *International Journal of Nursing Studies*, 46(8): 1134–1142.

Downs, A. (1967) *Inside Bureaucracy*, Boston: Little, Brown.

Dunlop, J. (1958) *Industrial Relations Systems*, New York: Holt.

Eborall, C., Fenton, W. and Woodrow (2010) *The State of the Adult Social Care Workforce in England*, Leeds: Skills for Care.

Eliassen, K. and Sitter, N. (2008) *Understanding Public Management*, London: Sage.

Entwistle, T., Martin, S.J. and Enticott, G. (2005) 'Leadership and Service Improvement: Dual Elites or Dynamic Dependency', *Local Government Studies*, 31(5): 541–554.

Equality and Human Rights Commission (2009) *Public Sector Equality Duties*, Manchester: Equality and Human Rights Commission.

Escott, K. and Whitfield, D. (1995) *The Gender Impact of CCT*, Manchester: EOC.

Esping-Andersen, G (1990) *The Three Worlds of Welfare Capitalism*.Cambridge: Polity Press

Evans, D. and Forbes, T. (2009) 'Partnerships in Health and Social Care: England and Scotland compared', *Public Policy and Administration*, 24(1): 67–83.

Fairbrother, P. (1996) 'Workplace Trade Unionism in the State Sector', in Ackers, P. Smith, C. and Smith, P. (eds) *The New Workplace and Trade Unionism*, London: Routledge.

Fairbrother, P. (2000) *Trade Unions at the Crossroads*, London: Thomson Learning.

Farnham, D, Horton, S. and White, G. (2003) 'Organisational Change and Staff Participation and Involvement in Britain's public services', *International Journal of Public Sector Management*, 16(6): 434–445.

Ferlie, E., Ashburner, L., Fitzgerald L. and Pettigrew, A. (1996). *The New Public Management in Action*, Oxford: OUP.

Ferner, A. (1988) *Government, Managers and Industrial Relations*, Oxford: Blackwell.

Flanagan, R. (2008) *Independent Review of Policing by Sir Ronnie Flanagan –Final Report, available at:* http://police.homeoffice.gov.uk/publications/police-reform/Review_of_policing_final_report/

Foreign and Commonwealth Office (2002) *Work Life Balance Mangers' Guide*, London: Foreign and Commonwealth Office.

Foster, C. (2008) 'Defra: Implementing a Flexible Working Programme', *Equal Opportunities Review*, 181: 5–13.

Francis, R. (2010) *Independent Inquiry into Care Provided by Mid Staffordshire NHS Foundation Trust*, Vol. 2, London: Department of Health.

Fredman, S. and Morris, G. (1989) *The State as Employer: Labour Law in the Public Services*, London: Mansell.

Garrett, G. (2000) 'Capital Mobility, Exchange Rates and Fiscal Policy in the Global Economy', *Review of International Political Economy*, 7(1): 153–170.

Gash, T. (2008) *The New Bill: Modernising the Police Workforce*, London: Institute for Public Policy Research.

Gash, T., Hallsworth, M., Ismail, S. and Paun, A. (2008) *Performance Art: Enabling Better Management of Public Services*, London: Institute for Government.

Gershon, P. (2004) *Releasing Resources to the Frontline: Independent Review of Public Sector Efficiency*, London: The Treasury.

Giddens, A. (2000) *The Third Way and Its Critics*, Cambridge: Polity.

Gill-McLure, W. and Seifert, R. (2008) 'Degrading the Labourer: the Reform of Local Government Manual Work', *Capital and Class*, 94(1): 1–30.

Glendinning, C. and Challis, D. (2008) *Evaluation of Individual Budgets Pilot Programme*, York: University of York.

Gospel, H. (1992) *Markets, Firms and the Management of Labour in Modern Britain*, Cambridge: CUP.

Greene, A-M. and Kirton, G. (2008) *Diversity Management Meets Downsizing: The Case of a Government Department*, Paper at BUIRA Conference.

Griffiths, R. (1983) *NHS Management Inquiry: Report*, London: Department of Health and Social Security.

Grimshaw, D., Vincent, S. and Willmott, H. (2002). 'Going Privately: Partnership and outsourcing in UK Public services, *Public Administration*, 80(3): 475–502.

Grimshaw, D. and Hebson, E., (2005) 'Public-Private Contracting: Performance, Power and Change', in Marchington, M., Grimshaw, D., Rubery, J. and Wilmott, H. (eds) *Fragmenting Work*, Oxford: OUP.

Grimshaw, D. Rubery, G., Marchington, M. (2010) 'Managing People across Hospital Networks in the UK', *Human Resource Management Journal*, 20(4): 407–423.

Grimshaw, D. and Carroll, M. (2008) 'Improving the Position of Low-Wage Workers Through New Coordinating Institutions: The Case of Public Hospitals', in Lloyd, C., Mason, G. and Mayhew, K. (eds) *Low Wage Work in the United Kingdom*, New York: Russell Sage Foundation.

Gunter, H and Forrester, G. (2009) 'School Leadership and Education Policy-Making in England', *Policy Studies*, 30(5): 495–511.

Hale, D. (2010) 'Labour Disputes in 2009', *Economic and Labour Market Review*, 4(6): 47–59.

Hall, M. (2008) 'Landmark Court Ruling on Equal Pay Bargaining', available at: http://www.eurofound.europa.eu/eiro/2008/08/articles/uk0808029i.htm

Hall, D. and Hall, S. (2007) *The Family Nurse Partnership: Developing an Instrument for Identification, Assessment and Recruitment of Clients*, Research Report: DCSF:RWW022, London: Department for Children, Schools and Families.

Hammersley-Fletcher, D. and Adnett. P (2009) 'Empowerment or Prescription? Workforce Remodelling at the National and School Level', *Education Management Administration and Leadership*, 37(2): 180–197.

Hansard (2001), 17 October, quoted in Unison, Feb, 2008, Tackling the Two Tier Workforce.

Harker, L. and Oppenheim, C. (2010) *Will New Labour Leave a Legacy?* London: IPPR.

Harris, J. (1998) 'Scientific Management, Bureau-Professionalism, New Managerialism: The Labour Process of State Social Work', *British Journal of Social Work*, 28(6): 839–862.

Harrison, S. (2002) 'New Labour, Modernisation and the Medical Labour Process', *Journal of Social Policy*, 31: 465–485.

Hay, C. (1999) *The Political Economy of New Labour: Labouring Under False Pretences*, Manchester: Manchester University Press.

Hayward, B. Fong, B. and Thornton, A. (2007) *The Third Work Life Balance Employer Survey*, London: Dept. of Business, Enterprise and Regulatory Reform.

Healthcare Commission (2004) *2003 NHS staff survey.*

Health and Social Care Information Centre (2010) *NHS Health and Community Health Services Medical and Dental Staff in England 1999–2009.*

Healthcare Commission (2007) *National NHS Staff Survey 2007.*

Health Committee (2007) *Workforce Planning: Fourth Report of Session 2006-07*, London: The Stationary Office.

Heery, E. (2003) 'Trade Unions and Industrial Relations', in Ackers, P. and Wilkinson, A. (eds) *Understanding Work and Employment: Industrial Relations in Transition*, Oxford: OUP.

Heery, E., Kelly, J. and Waddington, J. (2003) 'Union Revitalization in Britain', *European Journal of Industrial Relations*, 9(1): 79–97.

Heery, E. (2005) *Trade Unionism Under New Labour*. The Shirley Lerner Memorial Lecture 2005, Manchester: Manchester Industrial Relations Society.

Heery, E. (2006) 'Union Workers, Union Work: A Profile of Paid Union Officers in the United Kingdom', *British Journal of Industrial Relations*, 44(3): 445–471.

Heery, E. and Simms, M. (2008) 'Constraints on Union Organizing in the United Kingdom', *Industrial Relations Journal*, 39(1): 24–42.

Hickey, R., Kuruvilla, S. and Lakhani, T. (2010) 'No Panacea for Success: Member Activism, Organizing and Union Renewal', *British Journal of Industrial Relations*, 48(1): 53–83.

Hicks, S. and Lindsey, C. (2005) 'Public Sector Employment', *Labour Market Trends*, April, 139–147.

Hicks, S., Walling, A., Heap, D. and Livesay, D. (2005) *Public Sector Employment Trends*, London: ONS.

Hills, J. and Stewart, K. (eds) (2005) *A More Equal Society*, Bristol: Policy Press.

Hirschman, A. (1970) *Exit, Voice and Loyalty*, Cambridge, MA: Harvard University Press.

H.M. Government (2005) *Children's Workforce Strategy*, London: HM Government.

H.M. Government (2007) *Children's Workforce Strategy: Update* – Spring, London: HM Government.

H.M. Government (2010) *Building a Stronger Civil Society*, London: Cabinet Office.

Hood, C. (1991) 'A Public Management for all Seasons?', *Public Administration*, 69(1): 3–19.

Hood, C. (2005) 'Public Management: The Word, the Movement, the Science', in Ferlie, E. Lynne, L. and Pollitt, C. (eds) *Oxford Handbook of Public Management*, Oxford: OUP.

Hooker, H., Neathey, F., Casebourne, J. and Munro, M. (2007) *The Third Work Life Balance Employee Survey*, Report, London: Department of Trade and Industry.

Hoque, K. and Noon, M. (2004) 'Equal Opportunities Policy and Practice in Britain: Evaluating the Empty Shell Hypothesis', *Work, Employment and Society*, 18(3): 481–506.

House of Commons Health Committee (2006) *Independent Sector Treatment Centres, Volumne 1 HC934-1*, available at: http://www.publications.parliament.uk/pa/cm200506/cmselect/cmhealth/934/934i.pdf

House of Commons Public Administration Select Committee (2008) *User Involvement in Public Services*, Sixth Report of Session 2007–2008, London: House of Commons.

Howell, C. (2004) 'Is There a Third Way for Industrial Relations?', *British Journal of Industrial Relations*, 42(1): 1–23.

Howson, J. and Spigade, A. (2010) *The State of the Labour Market for Senior Staff in Schools in England and Wales*, available at: http://www.naht.org.uk/welcome/resources/key-topics/leadership/unfilled-posts-leave-profession-on-knife-edge/

Hutchings, M., Seeds, K., Coleman, N., Harding, C., Mansaray, A., Maylor, U., Minty, S. and Pickering, E. (2009) *Aspects of School Workforce Remodelling: Strategies Used and Impact on Workload and Standards*, London: Department for Children, Schools and Families.

Hutt, R. and Buchan, J. (2005) *Trends in London's NHS Workforce*, London: King's Fund.

I&Dea (2007) *The Equality Standard for Local Government*, Oct. London: I&Dea.

Hyman, R. (1987) 'Strategy or Structure?', *Work, Employment and Society*, 1(1): 24–55.

Ibbs, R. (1988) *Improving Management In Government: The Next Steps*, London: HMSO.

Incomes Data Services (2000) 'Equal Pay', *IDS Pay Report*, No. 805: 10–13.

Incomes Data Services (2006) 'Understanding Reward', *IDS Pay Report*, No. 957: 14–15.

Incomes Data Services. (2007) 'Pay in the Civil Service', *IDS Pay Report*, No. 972: 12–20.

Incomes Data Services (2008a) 'Local Government Pay Benchmarking Survey', *IDS Pay Report*, No. 995: 7–17.

Incomes Data Services (2008b) 'Strike at Birmingham City Council over pay and grading', *IDS Pay Report*, No. 995: 5.

Incomes Data Services (2010) 'Pitfalls of comparing private and public sector earnings', *IDS Pay Report*, 1042: 12–13.

Industrial Relations Services (1999) 'Working towards Common HR Goals: The State of Play in 75 Trusts', *Health Service Report*, 24: 4–13.

Industrial Relations Services (2008) 'Case Study: Total Reward at Kent County Council', *IRS Employment Review*, 911: 1–7.

IFF Research (2008) *Employment Aspects and Workforce Implications of Direct Payments*, London: IFF Research

Institute of Fiscal Studies (2008) *The IFS Green Budget 2008*, available at: http://www.ifs.org.uk/publications/4112

Institute of Fiscal Studies (2010) *IFS Green Budget 2010*, available at: http://www.ifs.org.uk/publications/4112.

Institute of Fiscal Studies (2011) *IFS Green Budget 2011,* available at: http://www.ifs.org.uk/publications/4112.

Institute for Government (2009) *The State of the Service: A Review of Whitehall's Performance and Prospects for Improvement,* London: Institute for Government.

IPA (Involvement and Participation Association) (2008)*NHS Social Partnership Forum Review – Final Report,* London: IPA.

IPA (2010) *Ensuring High Quality Public Services: Recognizing the Role of the Workforce in the Future of Outsourcing,* London: IPA.

Ironside, M. and Seifert, R (1995) *Industrial Relations in Schools.* London: Routledge.

Jas, P. (2004) I*nterim Management in Local Authorities Recovering from poor Performance,* London: Office of the Deputy Prime Minister.

Jenkins, S. (2007) *Thatcher and Sons: A Revolution in Three Acts,* London: Penguin.

Jewson, N. and Mason, D. (1986) 'The Theory and Practice of Equal Opportunities Policies: Liberal and Radical Approaches', *Sociological Review,* 34(2).

Jethwa, K. (2007) 'The Effects of Crisis Resolution and Home Treatment on Patient Admissions', *The Psychiatrist,* 31: 170–172.

John, P. and Johnson, M. (2008) 'Is There Still a Public Service Ethos', in Park, A. et al. (eds) *British Social Attitudes: The 24*th *Report,* London: Sage.

Johns, N. and Jordan, B. (2007) 'New Labour, Trust, Equality of opportunity and Diversity', *Social and Public Policy,* 1: 1.

Jordan, B. (2010) *Why the Third Way Failed,* Bristol: Policy Press.

Julius, D. (2008). *Public Services Industry Review.* London: BERR, available at: http://www.berr.gov.uk/files/file46965.pdf.

Karger, H. (1986) 'The De-Skilling of Social Work: An Examination of the Impact of the Industrial Model of Production on the Delivery of Social Services', *Journal of Sociology and Social Welfare,* 31(1): 115–129.

Keep, E., Lloyd, C. and Payne, J. (2010) 'Skills Policy and the Displacement of Industrial Relations: The Elephant in the Corner?' in Colling, T. and Terry, M. (eds) *Industrial Relations: Theory and Practice, 3rd Edition,* Chichester: Wiley.

Kelly, J. (2006) 'Central Regulation of English Local Authorities: An Example of Meta-Governance?', *Public Administration,* 84(3): 603–621.

Kelly, G., Mulgan, G. and Muers, S. (2002) *Creating Public Value: An Analytical Framework for Public Service Reform,* London: Cabinet Office.

Kersley, B., Alpin, C., Forth, J., Bryson, A., Bewley, H., Dix, G. and Oxenbridge, S. (2006) *Inside the Workplace: Findings from the 2004 Employment Relations Survey,* London: Routledge.

Kessler, I. (1993) 'Pay Determination in the British Civil Service Since 1979', *Public Administration,* 71(3): 31–18.

Kessler, I. (2003) *Recruitment and Retention of Senior Mangers in Local Government,* London: SOLACE.

Kessler, I. (2005) 'Consulting and Informing Employees in the Public Sector', in Storey, J. (ed.) *Adding Value through Information and Consultation,* Basingstoke: Palgrave Macmillan.

Kessler, I. and Purcell, J. (1996) 'Developments in Public Sector Industrial Relations: A Strategic Choice Model', *International Journal of Human Resource Management,* 7(1): 206–229.

Kessler, I. Coyle-Shapiro, J. and Purcell, J. (1999) 'Outsourcing and the Employee Perspective', *Human Resource Management Journal,* 9(2): 5–19.

Kessler, I. and Heron, P. (2001) 'Steward Organisation in a Professional Union: The Case of the Royal College of Nursing', *British Journal of Industrial Relations*, 39(3): 367–382.

Kessler, I. and Dickens, L. (2008) 'Dispute Resolution and the Modernization of the Public Services in Britain: The Case of the Local Government Pay Commission', *Journal of Industrial Relations*, 50(4): 612–629.

Kessler, I. and Bach, S. (2011) 'The Citizen-Consumer as Industrial Relations Actor in Social Care', *British Journal of Industrial Relation*, 49(1): 80–102.

Kessler, I, Bach, S. and Heron, P. (2007) 'Comparing Assistants Roles in Education and Social Care', *International Journal of Human Resource Management*, 18(9): 1648–1666.

Kessler, I., Heron, P. and Gagnon, S. (2006). 'The Fragmentation of Pay Determination in the British Civil Service: a Union Member Perspective', *Personnel Review*, 35(1): 6–28.

Kessler, I. Heron, P. and Dopson, S. (2010) *The Nature and Consequences of Healthcare Assistants: Final Report*, Southampton: SDO.

King's Fund (2010) *A High-Performing NHS? A Review of Progress 1997–2010*. Thorlby, R. and Maybin, J. (eds) London: King's Fund.

Kirkpatrick, I. and Hoque, K. (2006) 'A Retreat from Permanent Employment? Accounting for the Rise of Professional Agency Work in UK Public Services', *Work, Employment and Society*, 20(4): 649–666.

Kirkpatrick, I. Hoque, A. De Ruyter and Lonsdale, C. (2009) *Professional Agency Working: Implications for Management*, Policy Report No. 3 Centre for Employment Relations Innovation and Change, Leeds: Leeds University.

Kirkpatrick, I., Ackroyd, S. and Walker, R. (2005) *The New Managerialism and Public Service Professionals*, Basingstoke: Palgrave.

Kochan, T. (1974) 'A Theory of Multilateral Bargaining in City Governments', *Industrial and Labor Relations Review*, 27(4): 325–342.

Korczynski, M. (2001) *Human Resource Management in Service Work*, Basingstoke: Palgrave.

Labour Party (1996) *New Labour, New Life for Britain*, London: Labour Party.

Labour Party (1997) *New Labour: Because Britain Deserves Better*, London: The Labour Party.

Laffin, M. (2008) 'Local Government Modernisation in England: a Critical Review of the LGMA Evaluation Studies', *Local Government Studies*, 34(1): 109–125.

Lambley, C. and Chamberlain, J. (2009) *A Partnership Approach to Mystery Shopping*. Walsall: VT Research.

Laming, D. (2003) *The Victoria Climbé Inquiry, Report*, London: Department of Health.

Laming, D. (2009) The *Protection of Children in England: A Progress Report*, London: HMSO.

Langlands, A. (2005) *Gateways to the Professions Report*, London: DfES.

Lawson, N. (2007). *Machines, Markets and Morals*, London: Compass, available at: http://clients.squareeye.com/uploads/compass/documents/MachinesMarketsandMorals.pdf

Le Grand, J. (2003) *Motivation, Agency and Public Policy*, Oxford: OUP.

Le Grand, J. (2007) *The Other Invisible Hand: Delivering Public Services through Choice And Competition*, Princeton: Princeton University Press.

Levenson, R. Dewar, S. and Shepherd, S. (2008) *Understanding Doctors: Harnessing Professionalism*, London: King's Fund.

Levinson, H. (1972) *Collective Bargaining by British Local Authority Employees*. Michigan: University of Michigan.

Lewis, C. (2002) *Taking the Lid Off Term Time Working in Education*, London: Unison.

Leys, C. (2001) *Market Driven Politics: Neoliberal Democracy and the Public Interest*, London: Verso.

Light, P. (1999) *The True Size of Government*, Washington: Brookings Institute.

Local Government Group (2010) *Spending Review 2010: Local Government Group Submission*.

Lipsky, M. (1980) *Street Level Bureaucracy: Dilemmas of the Individual in Public Services*, New York: Russell Sage Foundation.

Local Government Association (LGA) (2009) *Local Government Workforce Survey 2009 – England*.

Local Government Association (2009) *Local Government Earnings Survey*, London: LGA.

Local Government Association (2010) *Local Government Workforce Survey: England 2010*, London: LGA.

Lodge, G. (2006) *Is Whitehall fit for Purpose?* London: IPPR.

Lodge, G. and Rogers, B. (2006) *Whitehall's Black Box*, London: IPPR.

Lomas, C. (2009) Nursing Prescribing: The Next Steps, *Nursing Times*, 14 July.

Ludlum, S. (2004) 'New Labour 'Vested Interests' and the Union Link', in Ludlum, S. and Smith, M. (eds) *Governing as New Labour: Policy and Politics Under Blair*, Basingstoke: Palgrave Macmillan.

Lymbery, M., (2001) 'Social Work at the Crossroads', *The British Journal of Social Work*, 31(3): 369–384.

Lynn, L. (2005) 'Public Management: A Concise History of the field', in Ferlie, E., Lynn, L. and Pollitt, C. (eds) *Oxford Handbook of Public Management*, Oxford: OUP.

Lyons, M. (2004) *Well Placed to Deliver? Shaping the Pattern of Government Services*, London: HM Treasury.

MacLeod, D. and Clarke, N. (2009) *Engaging for Success: Enhancing Performance through Employee Engagement*, London: BIS.

Makinson, J. (2000) *Incentives for Change: Rewarding Performance in National Government*, London: Treasury.

Malhorta, G. (2006) *Grow Your Own*, London: King's Fund.

Mandelson, P. (2010) *The Third Man*, London: Harper Press.

Marchington, M., Grimshaw, D. Rubery, J. and Wilmott, H. (2005) *Fragmenting Work: Blurring Organizational Boundaries and Disordering Hierarchies*, Oxford: OUP.

Marchington, M., Rubery, J. and Cooke, F-L. (2005) 'Prospects for Worker Voice Across Organizational Boundaries', in Marchington, M., Grimshaw, D., Rubery, J. and Wilmott, H. (eds) *Fragmenting Work: Blurring Organizational Boundaries and Disordering Hierarchies*, Oxford: OUP.

Marquand, D. (2004) *Decline of the Public: The Hollowing Out of Citizenship*, Cambridge: Polity.

Marsden, D. (2004) 'The Role of Performance-Related Pay in Renegotiating the "Effort Bargain": The Case of the British Public Sector', *Industrial and Labor Relations Review*, 57(3): 350–370.

Marsden, D. and Richardson, R. (1994) 'Performance Pay: The Effects of Merit Pay on Motivation in the Public Services', *British Journal of Industrial Relations*, 32(2): 377–399.

Martin, R. (2003) 'Politics and Industrial Relations', in Ackers, P. and Wilkinson, A. (eds) *Understanding Work and Employment*, Oxford: OUP.

Martin, S. (2010) 'Regulation', in Ashworth, R., Boyne, G. and Entwhistle T. (eds) *Public Service Improvement: Theories and Evidence*, Oxford: OUP.

Martin, D. (2010) 'The Removal of Workplace Partnership in the UK Civil Service: A Trade Union Perspective', *Industrial Relations Journal*, 41(3): 218–232.

MartinezLucio, M. and Stuart, M. (2002) 'Assessing Partnership: The Prospects for, and Challenges of, Modernisation', *Employee Relations*, 24(3): 252–261.

Martinez Lucio, M. and Stuart, M.(2007) 'Sustaining New Industrial Relations in the Public Sector: The Politics of Trust and Cooperation in the context of Organisational Dementia and Disarticulation', in Dibben, P., James, P. and Roper, I. (eds) *Modernising Work in Public Services*, Basingstoke: Palgrave Macmillan.

Mathews, D. (2010) 'The Changing Face of Public Sector Employment 1997–2009', *Economic and Labour Market Reviews*, 4(7): 28–35.

May, D. and Smith, L. (2003) 'Evaluation of the New Ward Housekeeper Role In UK NHS Trusts', *Facilities*, 21(7/8): 168–174.

McKenna, H., Hasson, F. and Keeney, S. (2004) 'Patient Safety of Care: the Role of HCAs', *Journal of Nursing Management*, 12(4): 52–59.

Mcafferty, T. and Mooney, G. (2007) 'Working "for" Welfare in the Grip of the "Iron" Chancellor: Modernization and Resistance in the Department for Work and Pensions', in Mooney, G. and Law, A. (eds) *New Labour/Hard Labour? Restructuring and Resistance Inside the Welfare Industry*, Bristol: Policy Press.

McGivern, G. and Ferlie, E. (2007) 'Playing Tick-box Games: Interrelating Defences in Professional Appraisal, *Human Relations*, 60(9): 1361–1385.

McIlroy, J. (1999) 'New Labour, New Unions, New Left', *Capital and Class*, 71: 11–45.

Mercer, M. Buchan, J. and Chubb, C. (2010) *Flexible Nursing*, Report for NHS Professionals, Brighton: IES.

Merson, M. (2000) 'Teachers and the Myth of Modernisation', *British Journal of Educational Studies*, 48: 155–169.

Millar, A. (2006) 'English NHS Trusts Fail in Their Duties Under Race Relation Rules', *Personnel Today*, 18 August.

Mintzberg, H. (1979) *The Structuring of Organizations: A synthesis of the Research*, Englewood Cliffs: Prentice Hall.

Mooney, G. and Law, A. (2007) *New Labour/Hard Labour? Restructuring and Resistance Inside the Welfare Industry*, Bristol: Policy Press.

Morrell, G., Tennant, R., Kotecha, M., Newmark, T. and O'Connor, W. (2010) *Factors Contributing to the Referral and Non-Referral of Incompetence Cases to the GTC*, London: General Teaching Council.

Mulgan, G. (2009) *The Art of Public Strategy Mobilizing Power and Knowledge for the Public Good*, Oxford: OUP.

Munro, A. (2002) 'Working Together – Involving Staff', *Employee Relations*, 24(3): 277–289.

Murray, A. (2003) *A New Labour Nightmare: The Return of the Awkward Squad*, London: Verso.

NASUWT (2010) *Current Working Conditions and Experience of Supply Teachers*, London: NASUWT.

National Audit Office (2004) *Delivering Public Services to a Diverse Society*, December, London: National Audit Office.

National Audit Office (2006a) *Improving Poorly Performing Schools in England*, London: National Audit Office.

National Audit Office (2006b) *Improving the Use of Temporary Nursing Staff in NHS Acute and Foundation Trusts*, London: National Audit Office.

National Audit Office (2006c) *Sure Start Children's Centres*, London: National Audit Office.

National Audit Office (2007) *Pay Modernisation: A New Contract for NHS Consultants in England*, London: National Audit Office.

National Audit Office (2008) *NHS Pay Modernisation: New Contracts for General Practice Services in England, HC 307*, London: National Audit Office.

National Audit Office (2009) *Pay Modernisation in England: Agenda for Change*, London: National Audit Office.

NBPI (1969) *The Pay and Conditions of Manual Workers in Local Authorities, the NHS, Gas and Water Supply*, Report No. 29, London: HMSO.

NHS Employers (2006) *Agenda for Change: From Pay Reform to System Improvement: Briefing*, June 2006.

NHS Employers (2009) *Managing Diversity: Making it core business*, London: NHS Employers.

NHS Executive (2000) Vital *Connection: An Equalities Framework for the NHS*, Leeds: NHS Executive.

NHS Executive (2000) *Positively Diverse Report, Leeds*: NHS Executive.

NHS Information Centre (2010). NHS *Hospitals and Community Health Series, Non medical workforce census*, England, Sept. 2009, London: NHS Information Centre.

NHS Employers (2008) *Contract proposals for specialty doctors and associate specialists*, available at: www.nhsemployers.org/sas

National Institute for Innovation and Improvement (201) *The Productive Ward: Releasing Time to Care: Learning and Impact Review*, Warwick: NIII.

NJC for Local Government Services (2010) *Working Party on Recruitment, Retention and Career Progression of Social Workers, Interim Report and Recommendations*.

NUT (2010) *Supply Teachers: Pay, Conditions and Working Time*, London: NUT.

Needham, C. (2007) *The Reform of Public Services Under New Labour: Narratives of Consumerism*, Basingstoke: Palgrave Macmillan.

Needham, C. (2010) 'Debate: Personalised Public Services – a New State/Citizen Contract?', *Public Money and Management*, 30(3): 136–138.

Newman, J. (2001) *Modernising Governance: New Labour Policy and Society*, London: Sage.

Newman, J. Gendenning, C. and Hughes, M. (2008) 'Beyond Modernisation? Social Care and the Transformation of Welfare Governance', *Journal of Social Policy*, 37(4): 531–557.

Newman, J. and Clarke, J. (2009) *Publics, Politics and Power: Remaking the Public in Public Services*, London: Sage.

Niskanen, W. (1971) *Bureaucracy and Representative Government*, Chicago: Aldine Atherton.

Normington, D. (2008) *Senior Civil Service Workforce and Reward Strategy: Report of the Steering Group to the Cabinet Secretary*, London: Cabinet Office.

Nurses and Midwives Council (2008) *The Code: Standards of Conduct, Performance and Ethics for Nurses and Midwives*, London: NMC.

Nursing Times.Net 7 Oct. 2008.

OECD (2008) *Public-Private Partnerships: in Pursuit of Risk Sharing and Value-for-Money*, Paris: OECD.

O'Donnell, G. (2006) 'The Modern Civil Service', Speech, 27 January, St. Albans, Hertfordshire.

O'Donnell, G. (2004) *Financing Britain's Future: Review of the Revenue* Departments, London: HM Treasury.

Ofsted (2007) *Reforming and Developing the School Workforce,* London : Ofsted.

ORC International (2009) *DWP Survey 2009,* available at:http://www.dwp.gov.uk/docs/dwp-survey-results-2009.pdf

Osborne, S. (2010) 'Introduction: The (New) Public Governance: A Suitable Case for Treatment?', in Osborne, S. (ed.) *The New Public Governance,* London: Routledge.

Osborne, D. and Gaebler, T. (1992) *Reinventing Government: How the Entrepreneurial Spirit is Transforming the Public Sector,* Reading, MA; Addison-Wesley.

Ozga, J. (1995) 'Deskilling a Profession: Professionalism, Deprofessionalization and the New Managerialism', in Busher, H. and Saran, R. (eds) *Managing Teachers as Professionals in Schools,* London: Kogan Page.

Paton, C. (2006) *New Labour's State of Health: Political Economy, Public Policy and the NHS,* Aldershot: Ashgate.

Paton, C. (2007) 'Visible hand or invisible fist? The New Market and Choice in the English NHS', *Health Economics, Policy and Law,* 2: 317–325.

Parker, S. (2001) 'Blair Promised More Radical Reform of Public Services', *Society Guardian,* 16 May.

Pearson, N. (1994) 'Employment in the Public and Private Sectors', *Economic Trends,* 483 (January), 92–98.

Perkins, S. and White G. (2010) 'Modernising Pay in the UK Public Services: Trends and Implications', *Human Resource Management Journal,* 20(3): 244–257.

Pope, C. (2010) *Local Government Chronicle,* 19 August.

Peters, T. and Waterman, R. (1982) *In Search of Excellence,* London: Profile Books.

Pollitt, C. and Bouckaert, G. (2004) *Public Management Reform: A Comparative Analysis, 2nd Edition,* Oxford: OUP.

Pollitt C., van Thiel S. and Homburg V. (eds) (2007) *New Public Management in Europe: Applications and Alternatives,* New York: Palgrave Macmillan.

Pollock, A. (2004) *NHS plc: The Privatisation of Our Healthcare ,* London: Verso.

Power, M. (2001) *The Audit Society: Rituals of Verification,* Oxford: OUP.

Propper, C., Sutton, M., Whitnall, C. and Windmeijer, F. (2007) *Did 'Targets and Terror' Reduce Waiting Times In England for Hospital Care,* CMPO Working Paper Series No. 07/179, Bristol: University of Bristol.

PricewaterhouseCoopers, (2007) *Developing the Local Government Services Market: Working Paper on Shared Services,* Dept of Communities and Local Government: London.

Prime Minister and Minister of the Cabinet Office (1999) *Modernising Government,* London: Prime Minister and Minister of the Cabinet Office.

Public Accounts Committee (2009) *NHS Pay Modernisation in England: Agenda for Change,* Twenty-Ninth Report of Session 2008–2009, HC 310, London: The Stationery Office.

Public Administration Select Committee (2003) *On Target? Government by Measurement,* Fifth Report of Session 2002–2003, HC 62-I. London: House of Commons.

Public Administration Select Committee (2010) *Outsiders and Insiders: External Appointments to the Senior Civil Service,* HC241, available at: http://www.publications.parliament.uk/pa/cm200910/cmselect/cmpubadm/241/241.pdf

Public and Commercial Services Union (PCS) (2010) *National Organising Strategy 2010,* London: PCS.

Radnor, Z. and Boaden, R. (2008) 'Lean in Public Services- Panacea or Paradox?' *Public Money and Management,* February, 3–7.

Rawnsley, A. (2010) *The End of the Party: The Rise and Fall of New Labour,* London: Viking.

Review Body on Senior Salaries (2010) *Thirty-Second Report on Senior Salaries 2010, Cm.7804.*

Rewards and Incentives Group (2009) *Model Performance Management Policy for Schools,* London: RIG.

Richardson, M. Tailby. S., Danford, A., Stewart, P. and Upchurch, M.(2005) 'Best Value and Workplace Partnership in Local Government, *Personnel Review,* 34(6): 713–728.

Richardson, R. and Thompson, M. (1999) *The Impact of People Management Practices on Business Performance: A Literature Review,* London: CIPD.

Rhodes, R. (1988) *Beyond Westminster and Whitehall,* London: Unwin Hyman.

Rhodes, R (1997) *Understanding Governance: Policy Networks, Governance, Reflexivity and Accountability,* Buckingham: Open University Press.

Rhodes, R. (2007) 'Understanding Governance – Ten Years On', *Organization Studies,* 28(8): 1243–1264.

Roper, I., James, P. and Higgins, P. (2005) 'Workforce Partnership and Public Service Provision: The Case of the "Best Value" Performance Regime in British Local Government', *Work, Employment and Society,* 19(3): 639–649.

Rosenthal, P. and Peccei, R. (2007) 'The Work you Want, the Help you Need: Constructing the Customer in Jobcentre Plus', *Organization,* 14(3): 201–223.

Royal College of Nursing (2005) *Maxi Nurses. Advanced and Specialist Nursing Roles,* London: RCN

Royal College of Nursing (2009) *Breaking Down Barriers, Driving Up Standards: The Role of the Ward Sister and Charge Nurse,* London: RCN.

Royal College of Surgeons in England (2010) *Locum Doctors Costs In NHS Trusts in England: Report,* London: Royal College of Surgeons.

Saks, M. and Allsop, J. (2007) Social Policy, Professional Regulation and Health Support Work in the UK, *Social Policy and Society,* 6(2): 165–177.

Samuel, P. and Bacon, N. (2010) 'The Contents of Partnership Agreements in Britain 1990–2007', *Work, Employment and Society,* 24(3): 430–448.

Schoenborn, A. (2010) http://respublica.org.uk/blog/2010/04/where-do-unions-fit-big-society.

Seifert, R. (1992) *Industrial Relations in the NHS,* London: Chapman and Hall.

Seifert, R, and Sibley, T. (2005) *United They Stood: The Story of the UK Firefighters' Dispute, 2002–4,* Cambridge: CUP.

Select Committee on Work and Pensions, (2007) *Seventh Report,* London: House of Commons.

Sewotka, M. (2007) *The Future of Public Services Under Labour,* University of Hertfordshire Business School, Working Paper 3.

Shaw, E (2008) 'New Labour and the Unions: The Death of Tigmoo?', in Beech, M. and Lee, S. (eds) *Ten Years of New Labour,* Basingstoke: Palgrave Macmillan

Shaw, E. (2007) *Losing Labour's Soul: New Labour and the Blair Government 1997–2007,* London: Routledge.

Skills for Health (2007) *The Competence and Curriculum Framework for Emergency Practitioners,* Bristol: Skills for Health.

Smith, G. and Seccombe, I. (1998) *Changing Times: A Survey of Registered Nurses in 1998, Report 351,* Brighton: Institute for Employment Studies.

Smith, P. and Morton, G. (2001) 'New Labour's Reform of Britain's Employment Law: The Devil Is Not Only in the Detail But in the Values and Policy Too', *British Journal of Industrial Relations,* 39: 119–138.

Smithers, A. and Robinson, P. (2007) *School Headship: Present and Future.* Centre for Education and Employment Research: University of Buckingham, available via NUT website.

Spilsbury, K. and Studdard, L. (2009) 'Mapping the Introduction of Assistant Practitioner roles in Acute NHS Trusts in England', *Journal of Nursing Management,* 17(5): 615–626.

Stevens, S. (2004) 'Reform Strategies for the English NHS', *Health Affairs,* 23(3): 37–44.

Stevenson, H. (2007) 'Re-structuring Teachers' Work and Trade Union Responses in England', *American Educational Research Journal,* 44(2): 224–251.

Stevenson, H. and Carter, B. (2009) 'Teachers and the State: Forming and Re-forming 'Partnership', *Journal of Educational Administration and History,* 41(4): 311–326.

Strain, J., Hutnik, N., Gregory, J. and Bowers, G. (2006)*Graduate Primary Care Mental Health Workers: The Process of Introducing the Role in PCTs,* Surrey: Higher Education Academy.

Stuart, M and Martinez Lucio, M. (2000) 'Renewing the Model Employer', *Journal of Management in Medicine,* 14(5/6): 310–326.

Stuart, M. and Martinez Lucio, M. (2008) 'The New Benchmarking and Advisory State: The Role of the British Advisory, Conciliation and Arbitration Service in Facilitating Labour-Management Consultation in Public Sector Transformation', *Journal of Industrial Relations,* 50(5): 736–751.

Suff, P. (2008) 'Case Study: Rotherham Metropolitan Borough Council', *IRS Employment Review,* 897: 1–6. XpertHR.

Tailby, S., Richardson, M., Stewart, P., Danford, A. and Upchurch, M. (2004). 'Partnership at Work and Worker Participation: An NHS Case Study', *Industrial Relations Journal,* 35(5): 403–418.

Tailby, S. and Winchester, D. (2005) 'Management and Trade Unions: Partnership at Work?', in Bach, S. (ed.) *Managing Human Resources, 4th Edition,* Oxford: Blackwell.

Tattersall, A.(2010) *Power in Coalition: Strategies for Strong Unions and Social Change,* Ithaca: ILR Press.

Taylor, R. (2001) 'Employment Relations Policy', in Seldon, A. (ed.) *The Blair Effect: The Blair Government 1997–2001,* London: Little, Brown and Company.

Terry. M. and Smith, J. (2003) *Evolution of the Partnership at Work Fund,* Department of Trade and Industry, Employment Relations Research Series, No.17. London: DTI.

Thaler, R. and Sunstein, C. (2008) *Nudge,* London: Penguin.

Thelen, K (2004) *How Institutions Evolve: The Political Economy of Skills in Germany, Britain, the United States and Japan,* Cambridge, MA: CUP.

Thomson, A. and Beaumont, P. (1978) *Public sector Bargaining: A Study in Relative Gain.* Farnborough: Saxon Hall.

Thompson, P. and Smith, C (2010) Working Life: Renewing Labour Process Analysis, Basingstoke: Palgrave.

Thornley, C. (2000) 'A Question of Competence? Re-Evaluating the Roles of the Nursing Auxiliary and Health Care Assistant in the NHS', *Journal of Clinical Nursing,* 9: 451–458.

Timmins, N. (2010) 'The Unions are Back in Town', *British Medical Journal*, 340(5): 342–343.

Tooke, J. (2008) *Aspiring to Excellence, Final Report of the Independent Inquiry on Modernising Medical Careers*, London: MMC.

Toynbee, P. and Walker, D. (2010) *The Verdict: Did Labour Change Britain?* London: Granta.

Trade Union Congress (2001) *Partners for Progress: Winning at Work*, London: Trades Union Congress.

de Turberville, S. (2004) 'Does the 'Organizing Model' Represent a Credible Union Renewal Strategy', *Work, Employment and Society*, 18(4): 775–794.

HM Treasury (2007) *Civil Service Pay Guidance 2007-08*, London: The Stationery Office.

Tyson, A., Brewis, R. and Crosby, N. (2010) A Report on In Control's Third Phase, 2008–2009, London: In Control.

Unison (2008a) *Driven by Dogma? Outsourcing in the Health Services*, London: Unison.

Unison (2008b) Tackling the Two Tier Workforce: Problems and Issue, Feb, London: Unison.

Unison (2010) *Who Cares Who Pays?* London: Unison.

Unison (undated) *Work Life Balance Campaign*, London: Unison.

Unite-Amicus (2005) *Unite-Amicus Guide to the Warwick Agreement – National Policy Forum 2005.*

Varney, D. (2006) *Service Transformation: A Better Service for Citizens and Business, a Better Deal for the Taxpayer*, London: HM Treasury.

Vincent-Jones, P. (1999) 'Competition and Contracting in the Transition from CCT to Best Value: Towards a More Reflexive Regulation', *Public Administration*, 77(2): 273–291.

Visser, F. and Williams, L. (2006) *Work-Life Balance: Rhetoric versus Reality?* London: Work Foundation.

Waddington, J. and Kerr, A. (2009) 'Transforming a Trade Union? An Assessment of the Introduction of an Organizing Campaign', *British Journal of Industrial Relations*, 47(1): 27–54.

Walsh, J. (2007) 'Equality and Diversity in the British Workplace: The 2004 Workplace Employment Relations Survey', *Industrial Relations Journal*, 38(4): 303–319.

Wanless, D., Appleby, J., Harrison, A. and Patel, D. (2007) *Our Future Health Secured? A Review of NHS Funding and Performance*, London: King's Fund.

West, P. (1997) *Understanding the NHS Reforms: The Creation of Incentives*. Buckingham: Open University Press.

White, G. (1996) 'Public Sector Pay Bargaining: Comparability, Decentralization and Control', *Public Administration*, 74(1): 89–112.

White, G. (2004) 'Back to the Future? Pay Modernization in the UK Public Services', *Employment Relations Record*, 4(1): 41–54.

Whitfield, D. (2006) *New Labour's Attack on Public Services*, Nottingham: Spokesman.

Willman, P., Gomez, R. and Bryson, A. (2009) 'Voice at the Workplace Where Do We Find It, Why Is It There and Where Is It Going?', in Brown, W., Bryson, A., Forth, J. and Whitfield, K. (eds) *The Evolution of the Modern Workplace*, Cambridge: CUP.

Wills, J. (2009) 'Subcontracted Labor and Its Challenge to Labor', *Labor Studies Journal*, 34(4): 441–460.

Wills, J. and Simms, M. (2004) 'Building Reciprocal Community Unionism in the UK, *Capital and Class*, 82: 59–83.

Winchester, D. (1983) Industrial Relations in the Public Sector', in Bain, G. (ed.) *Industrial Relations in Britain*, Oxford: Blackwell.

Wind-Cowie, M. and Oliff-Cooper, J. with Bratlett, J. (2009) *Leading from the Front*, London: Demos.

Wise, S. (2007) 'Wanted the Next Generation of Nurse and Midwifery Managers', *International Journal of Public Sector Management*, 20(6): 473–483.

Wolf, A. (2010) *More Than We Bargained for: the Social and Economic Costs Of National Wage Bargaining*, London: CentreForum.

Woodland, S., Simmonds, N., Thornby, M., Fitzgerald, R. and McGee, A. (2003) *The Second Work Life Balance Survey: Results from the Employers Survey*, London: Department of Trade and Industry.

Woods, D. (2009) 'Civil Service Advised to Be More Imaginative in Job Design and Advertising to Widen Talent Pool', *Human Resource Magazine*, 28 April.

Work Foundation (2004) *Trade Union and Employee Involvement in Public Service Reform*, London: Office of Public Services Reform.

Worrall, L., Mather, K. and Seifert, R. (2010) 'Solving the Labour Problem Among Professional Workers In the UK Public Sector: Organisation Change and Performance Management', *Public Organisation Review*, 10: 117–137.

Yeandle, S. and Stiell, B. (2007) 'Issues in the Development of the Direct Payments Scheme for Older People in England', in Ungerson, C. and Yeandle, S. (eds) *Cash for Care in Developed Welfare States*, Basingstoke: Palgrave Macmillan.

Index

work relations and, 99–100
Enderby case, 55
engagement, 128
environmental services, 20
equality, 73–4, 85–90, 95–8, 161
equal opportunities, 73, 74, 85–90
    in civil service, 90–1
    in local governments, 94–5
    in NHS, 92–3
equal pay, 22, 55–6, 70, 86
Essence of Care Plan, 107
ethnic minorities, 22, 89, 90–5
European Union, 8, 31, 102
Every Child Matters initiative, 2, 102,
        108–9, 126, 160, 161, 168
Excellent Teachers (ETs), 71
executive agencies, 8, 12, 18

fairness, in service delivery, 74, 96
fair pay, 49, 58
family-friendly reforms, 22, 76–9
Family Friendly Working Hours Task
        Force, 76
Family-Nurse Partnership (FNP), 108
financial incentives, 31, 37, 48
flexibility, 73–85, 95–8
    lifestyle, 73–4
    outside contractors, 82–5
    temporary workers, 79–82
    working time, 75–9
Flexible Working Regulations, 75
foundation trusts, 39, 61, 126, 159, 179
fragmentation, 31–2, 35, 44, 146, 183
front-line staff, 62–4

gateway workers, 106
Gender Duty, 89
Gender Equality Duty, 67
gender inequality, 36, 55–6, 73, 86
general government paybill, 47
General Social Care Council, 118
General Teaching Council, 118
global economic crisis, 5
globalisation, 33, 157
governance, 21, 28
    actors and, 30–2
    definitions of, 29
    network, 28–32, 40, 43–5, 128, 150,
        161–2, 169, 176

head teachers, 21, 36, 50, 53, 65, 149
Health and Social Care Act, 112, 114
healthcare
    see also National Health Service (NHS)
    mental healthcare, 104, 106, 108, 109,
        124
    new roles in, 106
    reforms, 39–41
    self-care, 114–15
    work relations in, 124
healthcare assistants, 103, 105–6, 118, 126
Health Commission, 170
hierarchy, 6–7
hospital-acquired infections, 107
hospitals, 40–1
hospital waiting times, 1, 39, 51–2
human resource management, 2, 16, 22

Improving Work Life Standard, 77, 92
incentives, 7–9, 13, 30, 31, 37, 45, 48, 54, 58,
        63, 162, 173
Inclusion Movement, 113
Independent Living Movement, 113
Independent Sector Treatment Centre
        (ISTC), 39
indirect involvement, 133–4
individual budgets, 114, 126
individual choice, 42
individual performance related pay (IPRP),
        12
industrial relations, 9–12, 22–4, 127–52
    see also trade unions
    modernisation and, 144–51
    New Labour and, 129–33
    partnership at work, 139–44
    staff participation, 130–3
    trends in, 133–8
inequality, 74
infrastructure
    institutional. *see* institutional
        infrastructure
    supportive, 115–19
inspection regimes, 50
institutional collectivism, 100
institutional infrastructure, 14–15, 22–3,
        154–6, 169–71, 182–3
institutions, 30–2, 36
instrinsic rewards, of public sector work, 13
integration, 108–9

performance management, 8, 9, 13–14, 22, 27, 30, 32, 35–6, 42, 48–54, 165–6, 169–70
  performance appraisal, 52–4
  targets and, 49–50, 51–2, 176–7
performance-related pay (PRP), 48, 61–2, 163
personal assistants, 115, 119
personalised services, 23, 113–14, 115, 119
policy development, 31, 38–9
policy making, 35
political accountability, 20
politicians, 15
Priestly Commission report, 14–15
Primary Care Trusts, 20
Primary Care Trusts (PCTs), 40
principal-agent theory, 29–30
private contractors, 4
Private Finance Initiatives (PFI), 82, 150
private sector, 27
  expertise, 38
  management practices, 16
  outsourcing to, 82–5
  pay, 58–9
  provision of services by, 34
privatisation, 38, 39
producer capture, 7, 101–2, 157
professional authority, 13–14
professional bureaucracy, 6
professionals, 13–14, 44, 125, 166–7
  degradation of, 13–14, 125, 166–7
  regulation of, 117–18
  trust in, 181–2
  work relations and, 101–4
public administration, 6
Public and Commercial Services (PCS) union, 66, 67, 78, 111, 144, 147–8
public choice theory, 29–30
public expenditure cuts, 178, 182
public management, 3–4, 16
  see also New Public Management (NPM)
  definition of, 6
  emergence of, 7
  origins of field, 6
  vs. private management, 16
public management perspective, 6–9
public policy, 130–3, 155
Public-Private Partnerships (PPPs), 31, 82
public sector pay, 58–62

public sector paybill, 47
Public Service Agreements (PSAs), 35–6, 51
public service expenditures, 27
public services
  demand for, 3
  employee relations and, 3
  failures in, 1, 14, 102, 126
  fragmentation of, 8, 30, 31, 44
  importance of employee relations in, 2
  as interactive, 15
  privatisation of, 27
  provision of, 4, 7, 11, 34, 99–100, 156–7, 174–83
  sub-sectors, 17–21
Public Services Forum (PSF), 132
public services reform, 3–5
  under Conservative-led coalition, 171–83
  by Conservatives, 25–8
  employee relations and, 45, 156–62
  modernisation agenda, 5, 21–4, 34–43
  by New Labour, 1–3, 27–8, 32–43, 153–62
  sub-sector differences in, 167–8
public service workforce
  attack on, 180–2
  composition of, 58–9, 61, 76
  decline in, 3–4
  earnings of, 58–62
  front-line staff, 62–4
  growth in, 47
  increase in, 5
  management of, 3–4
  praise for, 180–1
  relationship with, 36
  restructuring of, 23
  self-interest of, 30
  by sub-sector, 19
pupil choice, 41
Putting People First, 114, 123

Qualified Teacher Status, 118
Quality Care Commission, 176

Race Relations Act, 89, 93
Reagan government, 7
recruitment, 58–62, 63, 71, 130, 132
regulation, 34, 117
  workforce, 117–19, 122–3, 166, 170
regulatory bodies, 15

Re-modelling the School Workforce, 70
retention, 58–63, 71, 130, 132
reward management, 54–66
  contribution-based pay, 64–6
  maintaining front-line staff, 62–4
  pay reform, 54–8
  recruiting and retaining staff, 58–62
Rewards and Incentives Group (RIG), 70
risk, 117
role development, 103
roles, 116
  new, 104–7
  recast, 105–6
  support, 105–6, 118
Royal College of Nursing, 149

School Improvement Partner, 53
schools, 20
  see also education; teachers
  academy, 37, 41, 159, 175
  academy schools, 179
  community engagement and, 107
  pay determination in, 70–1
  performance appraisal in, 52–3
  reforms, 20–1
  specialist, 37
  spending on, 27
  standards for, 41
School Teachers' Review Body (STRB),
    70–1
sector skills agreement, 117, 123
self-care, 115
self-interest, 30
semi-autonomous agencies, 8, 66, 159
senior civil service (SCS), 38, 90
senior managers, 65–6
service delivery, 132–3, 155
  bureaucratic model of, 99–100
  comparison of models of, 177
  under Conservative governments,
    156–7
  under Conservative-led coalition, 171–83
  to diverse communities, 89
  fairness in, 74, 96
  flexible approach to, 103–4
  under New Labour, 157–62
  partnership in, 175
  producer capture of, 101–2
  user-driven services, 113–15

service improvement, 132
service quality, 45
service users, 22–3, 31, 170–1
  as employer, 115
  empowerment of, 40
  as partners, 115
  partnership with, 104
  risk of, 117
  as workers, 114–15
  work relations and, 111–15, 125–6
shadow state, 4
Shipman, Harold, 102
Single Equality Schemes (SES), 89
single-status agreement, 55, 162
skills, 117, 170
Skills Escalator, 117
Skills for Care New Type of Worker
    (NToW) programme, 106, 126
social care, 17, 20
  reforms, 42
  user-driven services and, 113
  work relations in, 120–1, 123
social inclusion, 41
social market, 26–7, 34
Social Partnership Forum, 141
social workers, 20, 41, 42, 101, 103
  regulation of, 118
  role of, 116
  temporary work and, 81–2
staff
  see also public service workforce; workers
  front-line, 62–4
  recruiting and retaining, 58–64, 71
  reductions, 67
  support, 166–7
staff involvement, 133–8
staff management, 2
staff morale, 132
staff opinion surveys, 134–8
staff participation, 130–3
stakeholder engagement, 32, 130–3
stakeholders, 34
  see also service users
standards, 37, 41
state
  as employer, 14, 36, 179
  hollowing out of, 31–2
  interventionist, 33–4
  role of, 9, 26, 173, 179